EU-Turkey relations have a long historic trajectory. Turkey is in future likely to remain, despite political tensions, an important country for the EU in economic, political and geostrategic terms. On the one hand, recent developments affecting the EU have motivated the Heads of State or Government to rediscover Turkey's relevance as ‚key strategic partner'. On the other hand, prospects of Turkey's accession to the EU have reached an all-time low in the light of Turkey distancing itself from the political accession criterion as well as the multiple internal crises the EU has been confronted with. This renders EU-Turkey relations a highly topical issue for academic research.

The Centre for Turkey and European Union Studies (CETEUS) aims at providing a framework for publications dealing with Turkey, the European Union as well as EU/German-Turkish relations regarding multiple thematic dimensions as well as geographic contexts including the neighbourhood and the global scene.

Turkey and European Union Studies

edited by

Funda Tekin
Ebru Turhan
Wolfgang Wessels

Volume 4

Funda Tekin | Anke Schönlau [Eds.]

The EU-German-Turkish Triangle

Narratives, Perceptions and Discourse
of a Unique Relationship

Nomos

The Deutsche Nationalbibliothek lists this publication in the
Deutsche Nationalbibliografie; detailed bibliographic data
are available on the Internet at http://dnb.d-nb.de

ISBN   978-3-8487-8054-9 (Print)
            978-3-7489-2441-8 (ePDF)

British Library Cataloguing-in-Publication Data
A catalogue record for this book is available from the British Library.

ISBN   978-3-8487-8054-9 (Print)
            978-3-7489-2441-8 (ePDF)

Library of Congress Cataloging-in-Publication Data
Tekin, Funda | Schönlau, Anke
The EU-German-Turkish Triangle
Narratives, Perceptions and Discourse of a Unique Relationship
Funda Tekin | Anke Schönlau (Eds.)
216 pp.
Includes index.
ISBN   978-3-8487-8054-9 (Print)
            978-3-7489-2441-8 (ePDF)

1st Edition 2022
© The Authors
Published by
Nomos Verlagsgesellschaft mbH & Co. KG
Waldseestraße 3–5 | 76530 Baden-Baden
www.nomos.de

Production of the printed version:
Nomos Verlagsgesellschaft mbH & Co. KG
Waldseestraße 3–5 | 76530 Baden-Baden

ISBN   978-3-8487-8054-9 (Print)
ISBN   978-3-7489-2441-8 (ePDF)
DOI   https://doi.org/10.5771/9783748924418

Onlineversion
Nomos eLibrary

List of Abbreviations

AAPD	Acts on the Foreign Policy of the Federal Republic of Germany
AKP	Justice and Development Party
CATI	Computer Aided Telephone Interview
CDU/ CSU	Christian Democratic Union/Christian Social Union
EC	European Communities
EEC	European Economic Community
EEZ	Exclusive Economic Zone
EP	European Parliament
EU	European Union
FDP	Liberal Democratic Party
FEUTURE	The Future of EU-Turkey Relations: Mapping Dynamics and Testing Scenarios
GMF	The German Marshall Fund of the United States
IMF	International Monetary Fund
ISIS	Islamic State of Iraq and Syria
NATO	North Atlantic Treaty Organisation
OSCE	Organisation for Security and Co-operation in Europe
SPD	Social Democratic Party
TEU	Treaty on European Union
TFEU	Treaty on the Functioning of the European Union
TTS	Transatlantic Trends Survey
UK	United Kingdom
USA	United States of America
USSR	Union of Soviet Socialist Republics

List of Figures

Table of Contents

Table of Contents

The EU-German-Turkish Triangle: A Conceptual Framework for Narratives, Perceptions and Discourse of a Unique Relationship

Funda Tekin, Anke Schönlau

1. Introduction

"Turkey has been moving further away from the European Union (EU)".[1] This narrative has been driving relations between the EU and Turkey for the past years. Yet, considering the complexity and interdependencies that determine these relations, such an assessment falls short of providing a full picture of this relationship. Ever since the Association (Ankara) Agreement of 1963, which aimed at establishing a Customs Union (Article 4) and referred to examining Turkey's possible accession to the Community[2] (Article 28), relations have grown deeper and become subject to multifaceted institutionalisation and formalisation.

Today, in general terms three frameworks structure the overall relationship. Firstly, the Association Agreement frames EU relations with Turkey, which is seen as a key partner in economy and trade. The Customs Union was successfully established in 1995. Secondly, in 1999 Turkey became a candidate country for accession to the EU, with accession negotiations starting in October 2005. However, this second framework of Turkey as a candidate for accession began to weaken almost from the outset, with negotiations starting to stagnate almost immediately following initiation, eventually culminating in a complete standstill with the Council's conclusions of June 2018, which consider "no further chapters [...] for opening or closing".[3] Thirdly and finally, the EU engages with Turkey as a strategic

---

1 Council of the European Union. Enlargement and Stabilisation and Association Process. Council Conclusions. ELARG 41,10555/18. Brussels, 26.06.2018, p.13, https://www.consilium.europa.eu/media/35863/st10555-en18.pdf [20.07.2022].

2 The Accession Agreement was signed between Turkey and the European Economic Communities. The European Union was established only by the Maastricht Treaty in 1993.

3 Council of the European Union. Enlargement and Stabilisation and Association Process, p. 13.

partner in multiple areas of mutual interest such as security, migration, counter-terrorism and energy. Institutionally, this third framework is structured most prominently by so-called 'High Level Dialogues'. Hence, the relationship between the EU and Turkey can be classified as 'unique' in the sense that it ranges from a rules-based integration perspective and association to purely interest-based transactional cooperation.

That being said, EU-Turkey relations have grown increasingly conflictual over the past years reaching an all-time low in 2020[4] for various reasons, ranging from the process of de-democratisation in Turkey, together with rising nationalism and populism on both sides to bilateral conflicts between Turkey and individual EU Member States such as Germany and the Netherlands in 2017 as well as Greece, Cyprus and France in the Eastern Mediterranean region during 2020. Yet, significantly such developments have not brought about a complete breakdown in relations. What we see instead is the EU considering targeted measures including sanctions against Turkey[5] and launching "a positive political agenda [...] provided constructive efforts to stop illegal activities vis-à-vis Greece and Cyprus are sustained"[6] by Turkey, at the same time. Accordingly, the concept of "conflictual cooperation" best characterises the current state of EU-Turkey relations in which conflictual dynamics within certain dimensions such as politics and security are contained by demands and interests for cooperation in others such as the economy, trade, migration and energy.[7]

---

4 Cf. European Commission. Turkey 2021 Report. Commission Staff Working Document. SWD (2021) 290final/2. Strasbourg, 19.10.2021, p. 2, https://ec.europa.eu/n eighbourhood-enlargement/system/files/2021-10/Turkey%202021%20report.PDF [20.07.2022].

5 Cf. Council of the European Union. Outcome of the Council Meeting. Foreign Affairs. 3720th Council meeting, 13066/19. Luxembourg, 14.10.2019, https://www .consilium.europa.eu/media/41182/st13066-en19.pdf [20.07.2022]; European Council. Press release. European Council conclusions on external relations, 1 October 2020. Brussels, 01.10.2020, https://www.consilium.europa.eu/en/press/press-releas es/2020/10/01/european-council-conclusions-on-external-relations-1-october-2020/ [20.07.2022].

6 European Council. Conclusions. Special meeting of the European Council, 1 and 2 October 2020, EUCO 13/20. Brussels, 02.10.2020, p. 8, https://www.consilium.euro pa.eu/media/45910/021020-euco-final-conclusions.pdf [20.07.2022].

7 For a complete elaboration of this concept cf. Saatçioğlu, Beken/ Tekin, Funda (Eds). Turkey and the European Union. Key Dynamics and Future Scenarios. Turkey and European Union Studies. Vol. 3. Baden-Baden, 2021.

Among EU Member States, relations between the EU and Turkey are more relevant to some than others[8] depending on: the size of a country's Turkish diaspora, the largest of which is in Germany; security interests in counter-terrorism, which is the case in France and Belgium; economic ties that are particularly strong with Germany and Bulgaria; as well as the degree of impact created by refugees from Syria and the middle east, most prominently the case in Greece currently, but previously crucially relevant for Germany in 2015.[9] Considering such structural factors, bilateral relations between Germany and Turkey are particularly close: Germany is Turkey's most important trading partner and source of Foreign Direct Investment, thus constituting a fundamental pillar of the Turkish economy. In 2020, bilateral trade volume amounted to EUR 36.6 million, with an estimated 7,400 German companies as well as Turkish companies with German partnerships being active in Turkey. Germany is the third largest importer of Turkish goods after Russia and China. Social and cultural ties are equally relevant with almost 3 million people of Turkish background living in Germany. Germany is thus home to the greatest share of an estimated 5.5 million people with Turkish roots living in Western European countries, followed by the Netherlands with just under 400,000 people. Those strong structural factors are one reason why Germany's Turkey policy has so far been able to exert influence over EU-Turkey relations.[10] Furthermore, motivated by the comparable size of Germany and its experienced leadership during the Merkel-era, Turkey's political elite tends to perceive the German government as a key access point to Brussels and any decisions taken there. This partial misconception was even enhanced somewhat when former German Chancellor, Angela Merkel, took "refuge in leadership" during the EU's negotiations for EU-Turkey statements on migration in November 2015 and March 2016, with Turkey's leaders apparently increasingly understanding Germany as representing the EU vis-à-vis Turkey at a political level.[11]

---

8 Cf. FEUTURE EU 28 Country Reports. H2020 project. The Future of EU-Turkey Relations: Mapping Dynamics and Testing Scenarios. Cologne, March 2017, www.feuture.eu [15.06.2022].

9 For more details cf. Aydıntaşbaş, Aslı. The discreet charm of hypocrisy. An EU-Turkey power audit. European Council on Foreign Relations. March 2018.

10 Paul, Amanda/ Smith, Juliane. Turkey's relations with Germany and the EU: Breaking the vicious circle. Policy Brief. European Policy Centre. Brussels, October 2017.

11 Reiners, Wulf/ Tekin, Funda. Taking Refuge in Leadership? Facilitators and Constraints of Germany's Influence in EU Migration Policy and EU-Turkey Affairs

The German General Election in September 2021 brought about a change in government from the 'grand coalition' of Christian Democrats (CDU/CSU) and the Social Democratic Party (SPD), that had governed the country for eight years, to a so-called 'traffic lights coalition' of the SPD (red), the Alliance 90/The Greens (The Greens) and the Liberal Party (FDP) (yellow). This triggered a debate on what the new traffic lights shining on EU-Turkey relations would entail for the future.[12] The main question in this context is whether or not we can expect a change in Germany's Turkey policy and with this also a change in Germany's stance towards EU-Turkey relations. Considering the structural factors explained above, no fundamental change in Germany's political interests should be expected.[13] Yet, the Greens' influence can be expected to make a difference when it comes to narratives in policy-making, following their take-over of the Federal Foreign Office and the Federal Ministry of Economics and Climate as well as the head of the European Affairs Committee in the German Bundestag. They have introduced the climate issue as a cross-cutting element in the German government linking climate dossiers to the Ministries of Economics and Foreign Affairs. More importantly, the Greens' foreign policy approach is generally strongly values-based. They were the only party whose manifesto in the electoral campaign referred to the possibility of re- activating the EU's accession procedure with Turkey.[14] They formulated this prospect as a lever for motivating Turkey to return to democracy and the rule of law, as this was the condition for bringing accession back on the table.

To provide a solid assessment of EU-Turkey relations and its future prospects, this volume focuses on the triangular relationship between the block and Turkey on the one hand, coupled with bilateral relations between Germany and Turkey on the other hand. Informed by historical institutionalism, it builds on the assumption that a fundamental restruc-

---

During the Refugee Crisis (2015–2016). In: *German Politics*, 2019, Vol. 29, No. 1, pp. 115–130.

12 Referring to the colours of the three political parties that form the new government, it is referred to as 'traffic-light coalition'; Tekin, Funda/ Toygür, Ilke. A traffic-light shining for Europe. Prospects after Germany's general elections. Berlin Perspective No. 9. Berlin, October 2021.

13 Tekin, Funda. EU-Turkey Relations and general elections in Germany – Headwinds for Turkey? In: Policy Brief Series. Berlin Bosphorus Initiative, April 2021.

14 The Alliance 90/The Greens. Deutschland. Alles ist drin. Bundestagswahlprogramm 2021. June 2021, pp. 230–231.

turing of EU-Turkey relations requires "critical junctures"[15] that entail a 'paradigm shift'. The term 'critical juncture' refers to a significant turning point in path-dependent institutional relations,[16] whilst a 'paradigm shift' constitutes a fundamental change in the dominant narratives detailing how EU-Turkish relations are perceived and described by political actors. There is a comprehensive and substantial body of literature tracing EU-Turkey relations in institutional and policy terms.[17] Literature on narratives, though, is rather scarce. Our volume, therefore, contributes to filling this research gap by deconstructing the political discourse on EU-Turkey relations, in order to identify, analyse and assess the main perceptions and narratives not only in Germany and Turkey, but also at EU level in Brussels. We build on a contextualised definition of political discourse by considering texts and speeches of political actors, their recipients as well as the contexts to which those texts and speeches relate.[18] Consequently, we identify narratives on EU-Turkey relations by analysing (political) statements made by politicians, political institutions and stakeholders relevant for the relationship as well as public opinion in Turkey.

Narratives are understood as 'mental maps' that can provide an analytical grid for assessing the state of EU-Turkey relations. This can help structuring the analysis of the relationship that, in reality, represents a 'moving target' witnessing repeated fundamental changes in its scope and pace. This volume assembles a number of analytical contributions that within the framework of a research project on the triangle of EU/German-Turkish relations[19] aimed to answer the general questions of whether and at what point in time a paradigm shift can be identified; if so, what are the driving

---

15 Cf. Capoccia, Giovanni/ Kelemen, Daniel R. The Study of Critical Junctures: Theory, Narrative, and Counterfactuals in Historical Institutionalism. In: *World Politics*, 2007, Vol. 59, No. 3, pp. 341–369; Pierson, Paul. The path to European integration. In: *Comparative Political Studies*, April 1996, Vol. 29, No. 2, pp. 123–163.

16 Ibid.

17 E.g. Schröder, Mirja/ Tekin, Funda. Institutional Triangle EU-Turkey-Germany: Change and Continuity. In: Ebru Turhan (Ed.). German-Turkish Relations Revisited. The European Dimension, Domestic and Foreign Politics and Transnational Dynamics. Turkey and European Union Studies. Vol. 2. Baden-Baden, 2019, pp. 31–58.

18 Cf. van Dijk, Teun. What is Political Discourse Analysis? In: *Belgian Journal of Linguistics*, 1997, Vol. 11, No. 1, pp. 11–52.

19 „Blickwechsel in EU/German-Turkish Relations Beyond Conflicts – Towards a Unique Partnership for a Contemporary Turkey?" (TRIANGLE), funded by the Stiftung Mercator from 01.01.2017 to 31.12.2020.

factors of such a shift; and do narratives of EU-Turkey relations change over time or are old patterns simply reborn or revisited. Consequently, the general research question of this volume is what impact narratives have on this relationship between the EU, Turkey and Germany including its institutional set-up.

In what follows we will briefly outline the research gap that this volume addresses and elaborate the concept of narratives together with its relevance for political science. Additionally, this chapter sets out the basic parameters that make an analysis of narratives on EU-Turkey relations relevant and conceptualises three different scenarios for future trajectories, depending on the scope of a narrative-induced paradigm shift. We conclude with an overview on how the individual chapters of this volume contribute to answering the general research question.

2. *A Narrative Approach – A New Perspective in Analysis of EU-Turkey Relations*

There is a very broad body of literature on relations between the EU and Turkey that is as rich and multifaceted as the relationship itself. This varied range of work includes: analysis of the institutional relationship including aspects of the EU's enlargement and alternative forms of differentiated integration or association; Europeanisation or de-Europeanisation in Turkey; geostrategic aspects of EU-Turkey relations in the realms of trade, migration, security and energy; as well as identity related issues.[20] Recently, the European Commission funded one of the largest research projects explicitly dealing with "The Future of EU-Turkey Relations: Map-

---

20 Cf. among others Adyın-Düzgit, Senem/ Kaliber, Alper. Encounters with Europe in an Era of Domestic and International Turmoil: Is Turkey a De-Europeanising Candidate Country? In: *South European Society and Politics*, 2016, Vol. 21(1), pp. 1–14; Müftüler-Baç, Meltem. Turkey's future with the European Union: an alternative model of differentiated integration. In: *Turkish Studies*, 2017, Vol. 18, No. 3, pp. 416–438; Nas, Çiğdem/ Özer, Yonca. Turkey and the European Union. Processes of Europeanisation. 2012, Routledge; Reiners, Wulf/ Turhan, Ebru (Eds.). EU-Turkey Relations – Theories, Institutions and Policies. Palgrave Macmillan, 2020; Saatçioğlu, Beken. The European Union's refugee crisis and rising functionalism in EU-Turkey relations. In: *Turkish Studies*, 2020, Vol. 21, No. 2, pp. 169–187; Schimmelfennig, Frank et.al. Enlargement and the integration capacity of the EU. Interim Scientific Results. Maximizing the Integration Capacity of the European Union, No. 1, May 2015.

ping Dynamics and Testing Scenarios" (FEUTURE).[21] Although not as comprehensive or extensive, there is also a body of literature dealing with the bilateral relationship between Germany and Turkey. It analyses and assesses the European dimension of that relationship, the German-Turkish dialogue from the perspective of foreign and domestic politics, as well as the transnational space such as issues of election campaigning, media and education.[22]

However, regrettably there is very little literature dealing with narratives covering EU-Turkey relations outside of the main reference source which is rooted within FEUTURE's research. Hanna-Lisa Hauge, Ebru Ece Özbey, Atila Eralp and Wolfgang Wessels have compiled a comprehensive dataset on narratives from EU institutions and Turkey since the 1960s. Within a comparative approach both across time and geographical borders they have arrived at three main conclusions. Firstly, narratives are different in nature, meaning that Turkish and European narratives vary considerably. The former all share the same goal of full membership, albeit subject to changing plots and different lines of argumentation. Another work by Gözde Yılmaz, though, traces a change from EU-phoria to EU-phobia in Turkish narratives on EU-Turkey relations.[23] By contrast, EU narratives differ both in terms of their plot and the *finalité* of EU-Turkey relations. Secondly, it is clear that since the 1960s there has not only been a gradual increase in the number of narratives concerning Turkey and the EU, but the various debates have also become more divergent. Thirdly, narratives confirm that conflictual rhetoric is a recurring pattern and not new to debates on EU-Turkey relations, albeit over recent years the level of escalation on both sides has increased considerably.[24]

Narratives make up one significant factor that helps us periodise the EU-Turkey relationship. Wolfgang Wessels, for example, traces shifts in

---

21 FEUTURE was funded by the European Commission under the Horizon 2020 programme and ran from 1 April 2016 to 31 March 2019; its publications can be accessed here: www.feuture.eu.

22 For a concise overview cf. Turhan, Ebru (Ed.). German-Turkish Relations Revisited. The European Dimension, Domestic and Foreign Politics and Transnational Dynamics. Baden-Baden, 2019.

23 Yılmaz, Gözde. From EU-phoria to EU-phobia? Changing Turkish Narratives in EU-Turkey Relations. In: *Baltic Journal of European Studies*, June 2019, Vol. 9, No. 1.

24 Ebru Ece Özbey et.al. Narratives of a Contested Relationship: Unravelling the Debates in EU-Turkey Relations. In: Beken Saatçioğlu/ Funda Tekin (Eds.). Turkey and the European Union. Key Dynamics and Future Scenarios. Turkey and European Union Studies. Vol. 3. Baden-Baden, 2021, pp. 31–56.

narratives since the beginning of European integration by referring to important milestones of that process, the EU's enlargement and EU-Turkey relations themselves.[25] Furthermore, narratives can shed light on the relevance of the three key institutional frames of EU-Turkey relations outlined above, namely accession, association and transactional cooperation, by identifying Turkey as an accession country, a key partner or a strategic partner for the EU respectively.[26] When negotiating the EU-Turkey statement on migration in November 2015 the then-German Chancellor, Angela Merkel, referred to Turkey as both an "accession candidate" and a "strategic partner" in the very same press conference,[27] perfectly reflecting the duality and ambiguity of a rules-based framework and the transactional character of this relationship. EU institutions in Brussels have also continued to produce various parallel narratives. The European Parliament's (EP) narrative on EU-Turkey relations is clearly linked to Turkey being an accession candidate. Its resolutions, statements and decisions, therefore, have a very strong focus on the accession criteria – particularly in regard to democracy, the rule of law and human rights issues. In 2016, the EP recommended "freezing of the accession negotiations"[28] for the first time. Thereafter, the tone has gradually hardened with the EP starting to call for the "suspension of accession negotiations" whilst emphasising that human rights and the rule of law must remain central within EU-Turkey relations. However, these issues are almost entirely absent from the European Council's conclusions. Since 2015 only two conclusions have contained references to the rule of law, with the latest mentioning this issue merely

---

25 Wessels, Wolfgang. Narratives Matter: In search of a partnership strategy, IPC-Mercator Policy Brief, April 2020; Suratlı, Harun/ Wessels, Wolfgang. The EU's Attitude towards Turkey – Shift of Narratives with Limited Actions? An Analysis of the Leaders' Narratives. VIADUCT Policy Paper. Issue No 5. Cologne, December 2020.

26 Wessels, Wolfgang/ Suratlı, Harun. How to understand the EU's Policy towards Turkey? A dual track strategy without effective results? An Analysis of the Leaders' Narratives. Policy Brief. Track – Teaching and Researching the European Council. Cologne, May 2021.

27 Merkel, Angela. Pressekonferenz von Bundeskanzlerin Merkel beim EU-Türkei-Gipfel am 29. November 2015. Brussels, 29.11.2015, https://www.bundesregierun g.de/Content/DE/Mitschrift/Pressekonferenzen/2015/11/2015-11-30-merkel-bruess el.html [30.03.2016].

28 European Parliament. EU-Turkey relations. European Parliament Resolution of 24 November 2016 on EU-Turkey relations, (2016/2993(RSP), 24.11.2016, https:// www.europarl.europa.eu/doceo/document/TA-8-2016-0450_EN.pdf [20.07.2022].

as a "concern".[29] The European Council's narrative is strongly driven by geostrategic considerations. On the one hand, this dual narrative-approach mirrors the relationship's multidimensionality and complexity. It also allows for a balanced approach vis-à-vis Turkey in which each institution is attributed a clear role – the EP being the values-watchdog versus the European Council and the Council being the interest-based actor open for package deals in areas of mutual interest. On the other hand, those two different approaches undermine a comprehensive and coherent strategy being adopted by the EU for framing EU-Turkey relations in the future.[30] This has contributed to postulating a new EU narrative of Turkey as the "distant and increasingly hostile neighbour".[31] Regarding the 'moving target' nature of EU-Turkey relations, Russia's invasion into Ukraine has actually changed geopolitical considerations, including those on Turkey's geostrategic relevance. Hence, without in-depth analysis it is difficult to assess whether or not this new narrative already constitutes a paradigm shift in EU-Turkey relations. By contrast, one analysis postulates that the EU is oscillating between various narratives with inclusively interlinked elements and a trend towards "a limited partnership with partial forms of cooperation [...] [instead of] a master narrative for a fundamental, global and stable relationship in form of an upgraded partnership".[32]

To date, German narratives on EU-Turkey relations or German-Turkish relations respectively have been subject to very little analysis. Poststructuralist works identify different visions of Europe that are created in debates on Turkey's accession to the EU among German politicians.[33] Others have chosen an identity-related approach, analysing German discourse according to the concept of 'othering' and hence the question of whether or

---

29 Cf. European Council. Press release. European Council conclusions, 17–18 March 2016. 143/16. Brussels, 18.03.2016, https://www.consilium.europa.eu/en/press/p ress-releases/2016/03/18/european-council-conclusions/ [20.07.2022]; European Council. European Council meeting (24 and 25 June 2021) – Conclusions. EUCO 7/21. Brussels, 25.06.2021, https://www.consilium.europa.eu/media/50763/2425-0 6-21-euco-conclusions-en.pdf [20.07.2022].
30 Cf. also Toygür et.al. Turkey's foreign policy and its consequences for the EU. In-depth analysis requested by the AFET committee, European Parliament, 2022.
31 Suratlı/ Wessels, The EU's Attitude towards Turkey, 2020, p. 3.
32 Suratlı/ Wessels, How to understand the EU's Policy towards Turkey, 2021, p. 2.
33 Cf. Aydın-Düzgit, Senem. A Poststructuralist Approach to EU-Turkey Relations: Foreign Policy and Discourse Analysis in the Case of Germany. In: *Uluslararası İlişkiler*, 2011, Vol. 8, No. 29, pp. 49–70.

not Turkey belonged to Europe.[34] For the sake of completeness, it should be noted that there is also work on the issue of 'othering' in France[35] and, vice-versa, in Turkey towards Europe.[36] Specifically in the early years of the European integration process after the end of the second world war narratives on the bilateral relationship between Germany and Turkey were more prominent than on relations between Europe and Turkey. Multilateral institutions were still in the making and therefore including narratives of German-Turkish relations in historical narrative analysis can facilitate our understanding of the matter.

We identify two main factors impacting the development of German narratives on EU-Turkey relations. Firstly, to some extent German narratives relate to milestones in EU-Turkey relations and the European integration process. The massive movements of refugees in 2015 when Angela Merkel underlined Turkey's dual character as accession country and key strategic partner is one example; another is the United Kingdom's (UK) exit of the EU, the so-called Brexit, when the Minister of Foreign Affairs at the time, Sigmar Gabriel, considered the new relationship between the EU and the UK as a potential blueprint for EU-Turkey relations.[37] Developments in bilateral relations between Germany and Turkey, though, might have even greater relevance. The years 2016 and 2017 mark a period in which those relations were heavily strained by diplomatic tensions over various issues: a resolution by the German Bundestag which declared that the killings of Armenians in the Ottoman Empire during 1915 should be regarded as a genocide for which the German Empire as closest ally

---

34 Cf. Erkem, Gul Pinar. Identity Construction of Europe by Othering: A Case Study of Turkey and the EU Relations from a Cultural Perspective. In: *Europolis. Journal of Political Analysis and Theory*, Vol. 5/2009, pp. 489–509.

35 Cf. Tekin, Beyza Ç. Representations and Othering in Discourse. The construction of Turkey in the EU context. Amsterdam, 2010.

36 Cf. Aydın-Düzgit, Senem. Foreign policy and identity change: Analysing perceptions of Europe among the Turkish public. In: *Politics*, 2018, Vol. 38, No. 1, pp. 19–34.

37 Gabriel, Sigmar. Der Brexit-Vertrag als Modell für die Türkei-Beziehungen. In: Die Zeit, 26.12.2017.

must assume joint responsibility; [38] the so-called 'Böhmermann-affair'; [39] the aftermath of a failed coup-attempt in Turkey, during which German nationals were arrested in Turkey; and finally the question of Turkey's extra-territorial campaigning for the constitutional referendum in 2017. This increased the relationship's politicisation as well as brought about modification in both sides' rhetoric.

Secondly, changes in government can potentially impact German narratives on EU-Turkey relations. Traditionally, the SPD has enjoyed strong support within the Turkish diaspora. Most Turkish citizens initially came to Germany with the so-called *Gastarbeiter* programme in the 1960s and had therefore strong links with trade unions, [40] hence political affinity with the more left-leaning SPD. Links between the Turkish diaspora and the CDU/CSU are less straightforward. It was the CDU/CSU that coined the concept of "privileged partnership" for EU-Turkey relations; [41] furthermore a change from the Christian democratic and liberal democratic government to that of the SPD and Greens in 1998 is said ultimately to have contributed to granting Turkey the status of accession country in 1999 following its previous denial in 1997. [42] Currently, it is too early to tell, whether or not the new German government of SPD, Greens and FDP, that took office in December 2021, will mark yet another shift in Germany's narratives on EU-Turkey relations. The Greens place a strong focus on issues of democracy, rule of law and human rights. During her time in opposition, Annalena Baerbock, who became the Greens' *Spitzenkandidat* in Germany's 2021 general elections, took a highly critical

---

38 Deutscher Bundestag. Erinnerung und Gedenken an den Völkermord an den Armeniern und anderen christlichen Minderheiten in den Jahren 1915 und 1916. Antrag der Fraktionen CDU/CSU, SPD und Bündnis 90/Die Grünen, Drucksache 18/8613, 31.05.2016, https://dip21.bundestag.de/dip21/btd/18/086/1808613.pdf [16.06.2022].

39 The Guardian. The Guardian view on the Jan Böhmermann affair: no joke, 22.04.2016, https://www.theguardian.com/commentisfree/2016/apr/22/the-guardian-view-on-the-jan-bohmermann-affair-no-joke [16.06.2022].

40 Reichhold, Clemens et al. Migrantische Organisationen und Gewerkschaften in den 70er und 80er Jahren. Das Beispiel Frankfurt am Main. In: Hans Böckler Stiftung (Ed). Working Paper Forschungsförderung, No. 208, March 2021, p. 41.

41 Guttenberg, Karl Theodor. Preserving Europe: Offer Turkey a 'privileged partnership' instead. In: New York Times, 15.12.2004.

42 For more details, cf. Schönlau, Anke/ Schröder, Mirja. A Charged Friendship: German Narratives of EU-Turkey Relations in the Pre-accession Phase, 1959–1999. In this volume, p. 57-77.

stance towards Turkey and EU-Turkey relations.[43] The coalition agreement gives evidence of some continuity as well as some changes that might be less evident, albeit still noteworthy. Regarding the wording, the current coalition agreement uses almost the exact wording as the agreement of the previous coalition government by stating that "we will [therefore] not close any chapters or open any new ones in the accession negotiations".[44] It is interesting to note, though, that relations with Turkey are not part of the section dealing with the European Union Policy, but of chapter 7 "Germany's Responsibility to Europe and the World" in the section "bilateral and regional relations". The narrative communicated by the coalition agreement references Turkey as an "important neighbour of the EU and a partner in NATO".[45] Additionally, it applies a constructive approach to the relationship by aiming to "breathe life into the EU-Turkey dialogue agenda and expand exchanges with civil society and youth exchange programmes".[46] It seems as if Germany is still struggling to come up with an alternative narrative for EU-Turkey relations at times when the accession narrative is patently not an option.

In Turkey, changes in government cannot have had an impact on narratives on EU-Turkey relations since the early 2000s. Instead, during the Justice and Development Party's (AKP) long time in office it has been more relevant to analyse and assess which political actor or person made what kind of statements in front of which audience in order to identify narratives and their potential changes. Additionally, we can also view a high degree of politicisation in Turkish debates on various issues of EU-Turkey relations. One constantly repeating narrative in Turkish discourse, for example, links with the EU's Refugee Facility and Turkey's accusation that the EU is not keeping its financial promise of paying a total of EUR 6 billion. Discussing the validity of this statement would exceed the scope of this chapter, but such a narrative breeds on the country's general frustration regarding the stagnating accession procedure.

---

43 Güzeldere, Ekrem Eddy. Germany's New Government Coalition: A Red, Yellow or Green Light for German-Turkish Relations? In: Hellenic Foundation for European and Foreign Policy. Eliamep Policy Paper, No. 90, December 2021.

44 Cf. CDU/ CSU / SPD. Ein neuer Aufbruch für Europa. Eine neue Dynamik für Deutschland. Ein neuer Zusammenhalt für unser Land. Coalition Agreement 2018; SPD/ Alliance 90/The Greens/ FDP. Mehr Fortschritt wagen. Bündnis für Freiheit, Gerechtigkeit und Nachhaltigkeit. Coalition Agreement 2021.

45 SPD/ Alliance 90/The Greens/ FDP. Coalition Agreement 2021, pp. 154–155.

46 Ibid.

One general challenge in EU-Turkey relations in view of EU, German and Turkish narratives is that each side claims the 'moral of the story' for itself expecting other parties to concede and acknowledge officially. This results in a blame-game of 'take-it-or-leave-it'-positions, leading to a vicious spiral of mutual accusations.

Accordingly, this volume puts at centre-stage narrative analysis for assessing EU-Turkey relations. The underlying idea is that such narratives are a "force in themselves" as they describe and analyse policy issues in a certain way.[47] In very broad terms we understand narratives as "stories people tell"[48] that mostly include a "moral of the story"[49] in terms of any normative statement on how the framework and intensity of EU-Turkey relations should be designed. Hence what we aim to understand with the collected contributions in this volume is whether or not we can observe a fundamental change of the story on EU-Turkey relations – and if so, what drives this change and which future scenario can be linked to it. Narratives can hence provide an important link between the analysis of past and current trends that inform an analytical assessment of prospects in EU-Turkey relations. To this end, "we need to identify mindsets as mental maps that use past interpretations of certain historical events as explanations for the unsatisfactory state of present-day political affairs".[50] This can provide the foundation for formulating strategies for achieving a certain future regarding any relationship.

3. Key Elements of the Narrative Analysis on EU-Turkey Relations

Narrative analysis does not feature heavily in political science. Yet, "narratives play a critical role in the construction of political behaviour insofar as they affect our perceptions of political reality".[51] They are either the object of research or the strategy of conducting research in terms of storytelling as a methodology of analysis. In this volume we focus prominently on the former with the aim of tracing collective memories and understandings

---

47 Roe, Emery. Narrative policy analysis: Theory and practice. Durham, 1994, p. 2.
48 Patterson, Molly/ Renwick Monroe, Kirsten. Narrative in political science. In: *Annual Review of Political Science*, 1998, Vol. 1, pp. 315–331.
49 Jones, Michael/ McBeth, Mark. A Narrative Policy Framework: Clear Enough to be Wrong? In: *The Policy Studies Journal*, 2010, Vol 38, No. 2, pp. 329–353.
50 Wessels, Narratives Matter, 2020, p. 2.
51 Patterson/ Renwick Monroe, Narratives in political science, 1998, p. 315.

by political actors regarding the evolution of EU-Turkey relations and in doing so "interpret and understand the political realities around us".[52]

Nevertheless, as editors of this volume, we need to reflect on the fact that our analysis is also subject to a narrative strategy. Narratives can or cannot be used intentionally; they are invented or reproduced by way of human interaction. Since this book is a contribution to an academic debate, it might also contribute to narrative building. An example from the editing process is the notion of "EU-Turkey relations" employed here. Our Turkey-based contributors opted in the early drafts for "Turkey-EU relations", but changed this sequence of words so as to follow the rules that we as (German) editors had pre-defined in order to provide consistency in the use of terminology. The name mentioned first in a relationship is what usually draws our attention – hence, any name mentioned thereafter to some extent moves out of the spotlight.

3.1 Narratives in Political Science Analysis – What Do They Tell Us?

Narratives can broadly be defined as "a story constructed by a specific actor or a group of actors".[53] They provide an "insight on how different people organise, process and interpret information and how they move toward achieving their goals".[54] In this sense narratives have the potential to legitimise political actions and policy activities.[55] In fact, any narrative is a story about "events and actions [that] are drawn together into an organized whole by means of a plot".[56] Put differently, each narrative, which results from different sub-narratives, is a construct of reality consisting of two main elements: goal and plot. Whereas the goal indicates the narrative's intended objective (for example, Turkey's full membership in the EU), the plot is determined by three elements: time (when the narrative unfolds);

---

52 Ibid.
53 Wodak, Ruth. Discourse and European Integration. KFG Working Paper Series. Berlin: Technische Universität Berlin, May 2018.
54 Patterson, Renwick Monroe. Narrative in political science, p. 316.
55 Cf. Tekin, Funda/ Meissner, Vittoria. Political Differentiation as the End of Political Unity? A Narrative Analysis. In: *The International Spectator*, 2022, Vol. 57, No. 1, pp. 72–89; Bouza Garcia, Luis. 2017. The 'New Narrative Project' and the Politicisation of the EU. In: *Journal of Contemporary European Studies*, 2017, Vol. 25 No. 3, pp. 340–53.
56 Polkinghorne, Donald E. Narrative Configuration in Qualitative Analysis. In: *International Journal of Qualitative Studies in Education*, 1995, Vol. 8 No. 1, pp. 5–23, p. 5.

space (where actors constructing the narrative stand geographically and institutionally); and relationality (how actors constructing the narrative are regarded by their audience).[57]

3.2 Four Elements of Analysis

In relevant academic literature, different detailed definitions of narratives and their elements exist.[58] Accordingly, each contribution in this volume provides a concise definition and understanding of 'narratives' as a concept. At the same time, four general analytical elements guide those individual analyses tying them into a joint research frame (see Figure 1).

Figure 1: Analytical Frame of Narrative Analysis in the Triangular Relationship Between the EU, Germany and Turkey

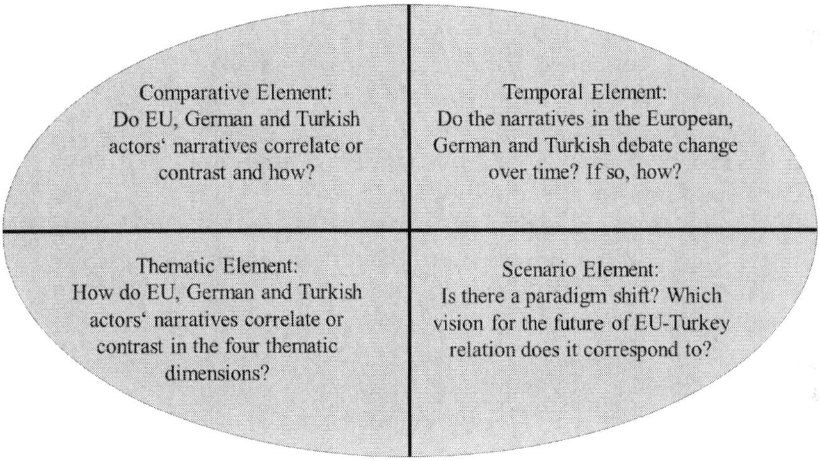

Comparative Element:
Do EU, German and Turkish actors' narratives correlate or contrast and how?

Temporal Element:
Do the narratives in the European, German and Turkish debate change over time? If so, how?

Thematic Element:
How do EU, German and Turkish actors' narratives correlate or contrast in the four thematic dimensions?

Scenario Element:
Is there a paradigm shift? Which vision for the future of EU-Turkey relation does it correspond to?

Source: own compilation.

---

57 Cf. Manners, Ian/Murray, Philomena. The End of a Noble Narrative? European Integration Narratives after the Nobel Peace Prize. In: *Journal of Common Market Studies*, 2016, Vol. 54 No. 1, pp. 185–202, p. 186.

58 Cf. Özbey et.al., Narratives of a Contested Relationship, 2021; Patterson/ Renwick Monroe, Narratives in political science, 1998; Forchtner, Bernhard. Introducing 'Narrative in Critical Discourse Studies'. In: *Critical Discourse Studies*, 2021, Vol. 18, No. 3, pp. 304–313.

Firstly, a comparative element produces stimulating insights and traces how narratives have varied in the EU, Germany and Turkey. Respective analysis contrasts and correlates those individual narratives.

Secondly, the analysis examines how narratives have changed over time, depending also on shifts at the national, regional or global level, such as the consequences of the end of the Cold War and of the bi-polar structure of the international system or most recently the Russian invasion into Ukraine.

Thirdly, narratives are clustered according to the dominant thematic dimensions of their respective plots, because they will vary in line with the viewpoint taken, for instance from political, security, economic or identity perspectives.

The political dimension links strongly with the so-called 'political Copenhagen Criteria' for accession, that is aspects of democracy, the rule of law and the EU's so-called "absorption capacity".[59] It relates to milestones such as: granting the status of candidate country for accession to the EU in 1999; the Gezi Park protests in 2013; the failed coup attempt in Turkey of July 2016; Turkey's 2017 constitutional referendum; and Turkey's resignation from the Istanbul Convention in 2021.

The geostrategic dimension deals with Turkey's geopolitical significance for the European continent and hence defence aspects are key. Plots that determine narratives are driven by regional and international conflicts and *détentes*. Prime examples are: the 1990s' Balkan wars that eventually impacted on Turkey's prospects of becoming a candidate country for accession to the EU; the Arab Spring that started at the end of 2010 and promoted the narrative of Turkey being a role model for the region; or tensions in the Eastern Mediterranean Sea that put EU-Turkey relations on the verge of becoming openly hostile throughout 2020; and finally Russia's invasion of Ukraine that for some marks the return of NATO and Turkey within NATO.[60]

The economic dimension focuses on the importance of trade. While the potential for plots turning conflictual is rather high in the other three

---

59 Soler i Lecha, Eduard/ Tekin, Funda/ Sökmen, Melike. It Takes Two to Tango: Political Changes in Europe and the Impact on Turkey's EU Bid. FEUTURE Online Paper No. 17. Cologne, April 2018.

60 For a discussion cf. Seufert, Günter. Erdoğan's tightrope act: In the conflict with Ukraine, Turkey is cautiously moving toward the West. Point of View, 9 March 2022, Stiftung Wissenschaft und Politik; Toygür, Ilke. Why is there no time for strategic ambiguity this time around on the European continent? Point of view, 2 March 2022, Stiftung Wissenschaft und Politik.

dimensions, economic plots are more likely to highlight the potential for cooperation if not coherence between the two blocs. All components of EU-Turkey economic relations exhibit a high degree of cooperation and minimal conflict. Economic flows of finance as well as goods and services are not only sound but also more or less stable, giving little reason for conflictual plots in narratives on EU-Turkey relations.[61] Yet, the current downward spiral in Turkey's economy with the Turkish Lira having been the most depreciated currency across the emerging markets during December 2021 and a soaring inflation rate of around 50 percent in January 2022[62] might represent a source of tension affecting parts of the relevant constructed storylines. The modernisation of the Customs Union represents one of the key reference points for narratives relating to the economic dimension.[63]

In the societal dimension issues of identity as well as cultural and social ties come into play. Depending on the way in which identities are constructed, narratives can promote either closer or more distant relations between the EU and Turkey. The degree of "otherness" in identity representation is decisive in finding common grounds for cooperation.[64] This has not only created substantial conflict potential but also determined German debate in the early 2000s when the concept of 'privileged partnership' was coined.

Fourthly, our analysis aims to identify shifts in the constructed stories and thereby assess whether continuing and new narratives argue for or against Turkey's EU membership or point to other forms of collaboration. Accordingly, the analysis will reveal which narratives dominate political discourses; it will also highlight whether or not "counter narratives" pose any challenge to them.[65] Three ideal-type scenarios provide the framework for this analysis:

---

61 Cf. Cömert, Hasan. The Financial Flows and the Future of EU-Turkey Relations. FEUTURE Online Paper No. 9. Cologne, November 2017; Mertzanis, Charilaos. Understanding the EU-Turkey Sectoral Trade Flows During 1990–2016: A Trade Gravity Approach, FEUTURE Online Paper No. 8. Cologne, November 2017.

62 The World Bank Group. Turkey Economic Monitor. Sailing Against the Tide. Washington, February 2022, p. ii-iii.

63 Cf. Saatçioğlu/ Tekin (Eds.), Turkey and the European Union, 2021.

64 Aydin-Düzgit, Senem/ Rumelili, Bahar. Contested Identities: Historicising and Deconstructing Representations in EU-Turkey Relations. In: Beken Saatçioğlu, Funda Tekin (Eds.). Turkey and the European Union. Key Dynamics and Future Scenarios. Turkey and European Union Studies. Vol. 3. Baden-Baden, 2021, pp. 57–76.

65 Roe, Emery. Narrative policy analysis: Theory and practice. Durham, 1994, p. 3.

- the '(re-)energised accession process' builds on narratives linking geostrategic, economic, political and identity-related arguments that suggest a return to a conventional accession paradigm in the EU, Germany and Turkey alike.
- the 'Unique Partnership with privileges specific for Turkey' requires narratives linking geostrategic, economic, political and identity-related arguments that constitute a 'paradigm shift' by accepting a partnership with privileges in the EU, Germany and Turkey alike.
- the 'stagnating and increasingly conflictual relations with a difficult neighbour' relates to narratives linking geostrategic, economic, political and identity-related arguments that eventually result in giving up on the empty promise of potential accession in the distant future; the key focus will be on Turkey as an important though increasingly non-reliable and problematic neighbour.

Bearing in mind that scenarios "do not serve as descriptive but rather analytical tools, mapping out variations of oversimplified realities that can serve as terms of reference for scholarly assessment of future relations",[66] the aim of the collected contributions is not necessarily to identify one of those three scenarios as the most likely option for the future of EU-Turkey relations. Instead, the guiding assumption is that narratives will find the truth somewhere in the middle. For example, elements of conflict may have become more dominant within the identity-dimension during recent decades, whereas security considerations were more present during the Cold War period. They re-emerged in recent years with rising conflicts in the region and now form one of the prime concerns in view of the war in Europe. Scenarios help to navigate within the complex context of EU-Turkey relations, structure analysis and identify elements that steer the relationship in a more conflictual or more cooperation-prone future.

3.3 Methodological Considerations

In terms of methodology, contributions in this volume use different sets of data depending on the debate, which is the key object of analysis. Generally, all sources represent documents that are well prepared and aim to

---

66 Tekin, Funda. The Future of EU-Turkey Relations: Exploring the Dynamics and Relevant Scenarios. In: Beken Saatçioğlu, Funda Tekin (Eds.). Turkey and the European Union. Key Dynamics and Future Scenarios. Turkey and European Union Studies. Vol. 3. Baden-Baden, 2021, pp. 11–28.

convey a special message. Research on narratives at EU level operationalises European Council conclusions and statements, resolutions and debates in the European Parliament as well as European Commission statements as data sources. For Germany and Turkey, this analysis focusses on government statements, press conferences and statements by high-ranking political officials, as well as debates in the German Bundestag and the Turkish Grand National Assembly. Occasionally, though, public speeches can include elements of spontaneous adjustments. Full information on whether or not this is the case may not be available, because either the written document or oral file of the delivered speech is lacking. Nevertheless, our analysis pays due heed to the potential for spontaneous adjustments which can display the speakers' feelings and assessment of the situation as they might also convey a special message. For instance, one chapter deals exclusively with narratives promoted by the Turkish Republic President, Recep Tayyip Erdoğan. Considering many different views and perceptions in the Turkish public sphere one chapter refers to public opinion polls to identify public opinion narratives in Turkey across the four thematic dimensions. Building on Forchtner, analysis in this volume perceives narratives as a notion of discourse[67] and hence operationalises the respective methodology mostly using MaxQDA-coding software.

Our aim is to provide a comprehensive analysis and assessment of narratives in Germany, the EU and Turkey on EU-Turkey relations and hence considers data that reaches as far back as 1958. This does not mean, though, that each chapter covers the entire period spanning across more than half a century. Both the chapter on identity representations in narratives and that on German narratives of EU-Turkey relations in the pre-accession phase apply a historical approach and take the early years of the relationship into detailed and structured consideration. The chapter on EU leader's narratives similarly refers to conclusions from the European Council since its inauguration. Yet, initially the European Council paid hardly any attention to Turkey. Empirical evidence starts becoming richer only in the 1990s. All remaining chapters are concerned with an in-depth analysis of narratives since the early 2000s – in other words following Turkey's attainment of accession candidate country status in 1999. Because all chapters reflect situations up to the end of 2021, this volume will not provide a full account of the impact caused by Russia's invasion of Ukraine. Nevertheless, the findings presented by each chapter provide

---

67 Forchtner, Introducing 'Narrative in Critical Discourse Studies', 2021, p. 305.

detailed information on how to assess the effects that war in Europe might have on both narratives and EU-Turkey relations.

4. Findings and Outlook: The Moral of The Story

The contributions in this volume provide for a very good understanding of exactly what perceptions and narratives constitute political discourse within the triangular relationship between the EU, Germany and Turkey. Each chapter takes another angle to analysing and assessing the topic at hand and hence contributes an important piece that completes the jigsaw of narratives on EU-Turkey relations.

4.1 Findings

In the first chapter, *Özbey, Hauge* and *Eralp* revisit the historic roots of narratives both in the EU and Turkey, track their evolution over time. This analysis showcases the identity dimension in EU-Turkey relations. The authors stress that, since 1958, identity perceptions and descriptions have changed. This, in turn, has had different implications on both sides. Whilst mutual acknowledgement of each other's importance on the world stage is a dominant feature, narratives – after a short period of convergence on Turkey's 'Europeanness' in the 1960s and 1970s – increasingly deviate over the following decades. Since the 2000s, Turkey's dominant self-perception of strength does not find any equivalent on the EU side. The authors highlight that a common vision of relations is lacking, which increasingly leads to conflictual narrations. It is argued that a dissolution of this conflictual atmosphere would require the EU to perceive Turkey as European. Their almost reconciliatory conclusion is that narratives in EU-Turkey relations have always been subject to ups and downs and, in view of the identity dimension, they expect this trend to continue in the future.

The analysis by *Schönlau* and *Schröder* supports the previous chapter's findings and takes a closer look at Germany's role in the triangle. This analysis also applies a historical approach by covering the period from 1958 to 1999. The two authors identify the narrative of Turkey as an important geostrategic factor and ally. Furthermore, this is found to be a continuing feature of Turkish-German relations and German narration of Turkey's place in European and international alliances. Perception and narration of cultural incompatibility put a brake on Turkey's EU candidacy bid in 1997, which was largely driven by German concerns. It required a different German government and a different narrative to be put in place, before Turkey was able to receive candidate status in 1999. Though the geopolitical landscape between 1997 and 1999 had not changed much with ongoing war in the Balkans, the narration of Turkey's importance as a geopolitical actor and lesser emphasis on identity-based narratives led to this institutional break-through.

Weise and *Tekin* continue where the analysis of Schönlau and Schröder left off. They investigate German narratives between 2002 and 2018 based on debates in the German *Bundestag* and elaborate on how identity-based narrations compete with geostrategic arguments. The authors discuss the extent to which the change in Germany to a conservative-led government during 2005, which coincided with the opening of Turkey's accession negotiations, impacted German interests and perceptions of Turkey as well as EU-Turkey relations. They identify the Gezi Park protests of 2013 as marking an important turning point in German narratives on EU-Turkey relations when political actors started questioning in fundamental terms whether or not Turkey would be capable of returning to the path of necessary institutional and political reforms. Generally, they observe that political narratives dominate parliamentary discourse. Looking at recent years, the two authors identify an unspoken 'twin-track strategy' among parliamentarians' positions on EU-Turkey relations. On the one hand, they seem to promote continuation of accession negotiations, because they do not want to isolate Turkey. On the other hand, they perceive as essential reconsideration of how institutionalised EU-Turkey relations should be taken forward. Narratives reflect this strategy by less references to 'EU membership' and more to 'Strategic Partnership'.

While the previous chapters examined narratives of political institutions, *Gedikli*, *Bedir* and *Şenyuva* analyse Turkish narrations of the relationship by focusing on speeches and statements by Recep Tayyip Erdoğan, president of the Turkish Republic. Their analysis is driven by an assumption that key narratives in today's Turkey are shaped by the president himself, rather than a group of people or political parties. Their findings give evidence of Erdoğan's narratives being dependent on historical and conjunctural contexts, which are sometimes even contradictory. While a focus on cooperation is characteristic over the first decade of this century, here too the Gezi protests of 2013 mark a turning point, with accusations and conflict beginning to dominate. The authors find that while narratives certainly lead to a conflictual cooperation scenario, Erdoğan's simultaneous use of different narratives enables him to pursue several strategies (conflict or cooperation oriented) at the same time.

Erdoğan's group of counterparts in Brussels, the Heads of States or Governments in the European Council – communicating only at an extreme of diplomatically agreed language – structured the narration of EU-Turkey relations over the years along the lines of Turkey being a potential member, a transactional partner and a problematic neighbour, as *Rau, Ersoy* and *Wessels* analyse in their chapter. They argue that narratives have become increasingly conflictual over recent years, whilst at the same time no far-reaching changes in the institutional set-up for cooperating with Turkey have been made. The authors, therefore, expect an increasingly transactional relationship, rather than a common vision for cooperation.

Finally, *Şenuyuva* and *Çengel's* chapter on public opinion in Turkey completes this analysis of political discourse covering EU-Turkey relations. Their findings seem unexpected at first sight: Germany remains one of Turkish societies' favourite cooperation countries. Furthermore, public perception of Germany's long-term former leader Angela Merkel is extremely positive. This, as the authors argue, reflects intense and good long-term relations as well as comparatively extensive knowledge of Germany. Though Germany is not spared from general Turkish scepticism towards foreign countries, analysis highlights that attitudes towards Germany are not influenced by party political preferences. The authors' conclusion is that Germany should invest more in public diplomacy to increase trust levels.

4.2 Outlook

Throughout the decades, EU-Turkey relations have resembled a roller-coaster ride. This means that there have been ups and downs with several U-turns in the relationship. Since the failed coup attempt in Turkey of July 2016 relations have been on a steep downward ride that almost led to a train crash in 2020 because of the conflict in the Eastern Mediterranean Sea and Turkey's increasingly assertive foreign policy. Yet, we have not reached a critical juncture that would completely derail EU-Turkey relations. Since beginning of 2021 relations have neither drifted further apart nor can we witness any sort of rapprochement. Narratives can contribute to finding an explanation to this state of affairs.

Identity Representations in Narratives on EU-Turkey Relations

Ebru Ece Özbey, Hanna-Lisa Hauge, Atila Eralp

1. Introduction

If the crux of relations[1] between the European Union (EU)[2] and Turkey could be defined in one term, it would be 'seesawing'. As we approach the 60th anniversary of institutional ties being launched with the so-called Ankara Agreement in 1963, both parties are still far from reaching a conclusion on how to (re-)structure their joint path. Given their geographical proximity, close economic relations, common political challenges along with cultural and historical linkages, though, they are tied by the need for some perspective in the not-too-distant future. That said, Turkey's EU membership, the professed end goal that has shaped this relationship for the last six decades, seems to be off the table, perhaps for good. Moreover, the last couple of years appear to have brought about an unprecedented escalation of tension and conflict on both sides, jeopardising whatever once existed in terms of cooperation. The latest controversies over Turkey's interventions in Syria and Libya, the refugee crisis on the land border with Greece together with disputes over maritime borders and gas exploration activities in the eastern Mediterranean are apt examples of this ongoing deterioration within an already strained relationship.

---

1 This study draws strongly on the following publications by its authors and further co-authors working within the EU-funded FEUTURE project: Cf. Hauge, Hanna-Lisa et. al. Narratives of a Contested Relationship: Unravelling the Debates in the EU and Turkey. FEUTURE Online Paper No. 28. Cologne, February 2019; Özbey, Ebru Ece/ Hauge, Hanna-Lisa. Methodological Appendix for FEUTURE Online Paper No. 28 "Narratives of a Contested Relationship: Unravelling the Debates in the EU and Turkey". Cologne, February 2019; Özbey, Ebru Ece et. al. Narratives of a Contested Relationship: Identity Representations in the Narratives on the EU-Turkey Relations. FEUTURE Online Paper No. 32. Cologne, March 2019. All translations by Ebru Ece Özbey unless stated otherwise.

2 Although the institution in question is referred to as the 'European Union' throughout this chapter for ease of reading, it should be noted that it is specified as the 'European Economic Community' from 1957 to 1992 and the 'European Community' from 1992 to 2007.

Against such a background, this chapter looks at an essential, albeit under-researched, aspect of EU-Turkey relations by investigating identity representations in EU and Turkish narratives. At its heart, the very simple argument presented here is that narratives, acts of (political) storytelling, matter. They are critical: in transforming vague descriptions of social reality into meaningful, coherent interpretations; reconstituting the past by organising events in sequential order; contextualising agents' attitudes and behaviour; and unveiling clues about the projected futures.

Narratives are stories that are created and used by individuals, as well as collective units such as groups, parties, and nations, to interpret and intertwine disparate parts of reality. They are "the type of discourse composition that draws together diverse events, happenings, and actions of human lives into thematically unified goal-directed processes".[3] By orchestrating a particular series of actions, which would otherwise be viewed as discrete, "in a particular temporal order for a particular purpose",[4] narrators perform the essential function of producing common-sensical knowledge. Fundamental questions on social objects of inquiry such as 'What happened?', 'Who was involved?', 'How and why did it happen?', or 'Why does it matter?' find answers through narrations, which selectively weave events, characters and backgrounds into a plot with a meaningful continuum.[5]

Insofar as agents affect (directly or indirectly, partially or wholly) the sense-making of other agents by enacting their own stories, narratives hold a persuasive power and an essential role in constructing political behaviour. Such discourses contain explanatory adequacy and re-constitutive ability as analytical prisms through which actors: ponder their power, influence duties, responsibilities and interests; reproduce institutional reality; and interact with others. However, these discursive practices also matter independently in and of their own right. Our research takes up identity representations and narratives in line with this insight. Studying how Turkish and European actors construct and describe certain identities in their self-created 'story-worlds' can shed light on the underlying reasons

---

3 Polkinghorne, Donald E. Narrative Configuration in Qualitative Analysis. In: *International Journal of Qualitative Studies in Education*, 1995, Vol. 8, No. 1, p. 5.

4 Griffin, Larry J. Narrative, Event-Structure Analysis, and Causal Interpretation in Historical Sociology. In: *The American Journal of Sociology*, 1993, Vol: 98, No. 5, p. 1097.

5 Cf. Shenhav, Shaul R. Political Narratives and Political Reality. In: *International Political Science Review/ Revue Internationale de Science Politique*, 2006, Vol. 27, No. 3, p. 251.

for this peculiar status quo within which the parties are and have valuable policy implications in crafting their joint pathway. That said, the salient traits in character descriptions, components of the given interactional roles, categorical properties residing in narrators' minds and the like can constitute a line of research which in itself has a promising future.

Political narratives are rooted in factual, real-life events as opposed to other (i.e., literary) stories that take place in an entirely fictitious time-space. Yet, these narratives are often imbued with fiction and should not be seen as mere reporting of the facts, but instead as "an artful blend of explanation and interpretation".[6] They are products of a particular perspective, the perspective of the narrator(s), and therefore involve critical assessments, moral judgments, taxonomies, and causal connections that cannot be proven or disproven. They do not faithfully represent 'reality', nor have they to be complete, coherent, or consistent with it. In fact, narratives can (intentionally or unintentionally) lack detail, leave some space for the audience's interpretation, or include juxtapositions of seemingly contradictory elements. As long as they resonate with listeners' perceptions and convince them to align with the storytellers, narratives are deemed persuasive and successful.[7]

This chapter starts from an assumption that political narratives emanate from the socio-political and socio-cultural contexts within which story-tellers are embedded. They are the products of historical processes and interactions between agents, drawing strongly on memories from the past. Narrators, when creating their story-worlds, build shared representations from a repertoire of identities (Turkey, EU, United States, Russia, Cyprus, European Parliament and so on); characterise them in specific ways; establish them as members of certain groups (i.e., Eastern, Western, European, Muslim, Christian); and relate them to particular actions and reactions.[8] The traits that are salient in descriptions of these character representations, the clashes or alignments between these traits, their expression or manifestation in behaviour are all essential components of the story arc.

Put differently, identity constructions and perceptions of self and other(s) are important building blocks of narratives. Such constructions are not entirely creative and locally-managed processes, but rather informed

---

6 Griffin, Narrative, Event-Structure Analysis, p. 1099.
7 Cf. Mayer, Frederick. Narrative Politics: Stories and Collective Action. New York, Oxford University Press, 2014.
8 Cf. De Fina, Anna. Group Identity, Narrative and Self-Representations. In: Anna De Fina/ Deborah Schiffrin/ Michael Bamberg (Eds.). Discourse and Identity. Cambridge, Cambridge University Press, 2006, pp. 351–75.

by socially established resources and grounded in particular inventories of identities.[9] Similarly, as the narratives below show, mutual accounts of one another and the relationship itself by agents in Turkey and the EU establish the basis for the reasons of cooperation (or the lack thereof). They encompass expositions of existing settings and drivers of the relationship on different (i.e., national, bilateral, regional, or global) levels. They also propound imagined futures, which in the case of EU-Turkey relations can range from full membership, as the closest form of rapprochement, to total alienation.[10]

This chapter has a strong empirical basis as it draws its conclusions from a comprehensive narrative study conducted within the framework of an EU-funded project, 'The Future of EU-Turkey Relations: Mapping Dynamics and Testing Scenarios' (FEUTURE).[11] While the definition of narrative adopted here is tailored to the specific research design and questions raised by this study, it is at the same time based on the main approaches of narrative analysis, particularly as applied in the field of political science.[12] Accordingly, the term 'narrative' refers to "interpretations by political actors of the evolution, drivers, and actors, as well as the goal (or *finalité*) of the EU-Turkey relations".[13]

The abovementioned study has identified predominant narratives by political actors from both sides of the relationship and inquired about

---

9 Cf. Ibid, pp. 353–354.
10 Cf. Hauge et al., Narratives of a Contested Relationship, p.1.
11 Cf. Ibid; Cf. Özbey et al., Methodological Appendix, p.1.
12 Cf. Czarniawska, Barbara. Narratives in Social Science Research. London, 2004; Fischer, Frank/ Forester, John (Eds.). The Argumentative Turn in Policy Analysis. Durham, 1993; Hyvärinen, Matti. Analyzing Narratives and Story-Telling. In: Pertti Alasuutari, Leonard Bickman, Julia Brannen (Eds.). SAGE Handbook of Social Research Methods. Los Angeles, 2008, pp. 447–460; Jones, Michael/ Shanahan, Elizabeth/ McBeth, Mark (Eds.). The Science of Stories. Applications of the Narrative Policy Framework in Public Policy Analysis. Basingstoke, 2014; Kaplan, Thomas. The Narrative Structure of Policy Analysis. In: *Journal of Policy Analysis and Management*, 1986, Vol. 5, No. 4, pp. 761–778; Kohler Riessman, Catherine (Ed.). Narrative Analysis. Qualitative Research Methods Series. Vol. 30, Newbury Park, 1993; Roe, Emery. Narrative Policy Analysis. Theory and Practice. Durham, 1994; Shenhav, Shaul. Political Narratives and Political Reality. In: *International Political Science Review*, 2006, Vol. 27, No. 3, pp. 245–262. See also for an overview of narrative approaches in political science Patterson, Molly/ Renwick Monroe, Kristen. Narrative in Political Science. In: *Annual Review of Political Science*, 1998, Vol. 1, pp. 315–331; Gadinger, Frank/ Jarzebski, Sebastian/ Yıldız, Taylan. Politische Narrative. Konzepte, Analysen, Forschungspraxis. Wiesbaden, 2014.
13 Hauge et al., Narratives of a Contested Relationship, p. 4.

their development comparatively over time. For this purpose, the authors coded a set of 282 official documents and statements from actors in Turkey and the EU from 1958 to 2017 by means of QDA software.[14] Because narratives do not necessarily emerge as complete stories in the documents analysed, the authors (re)constructed them by classifying individual constitutive elements and organising them into complete stories.[15] The findings of this study allowed the authors to trace the narratives that have shaped the political debate over time and pinpoint the commonalities as well as differences between them. This chapter, while based on the findings of the said study, takes up another aspect of the narratives in detail and focuses on the interplay of identity representations and character descriptions on the two sides of the relationship, again covering the period from 1958 to 2017.

The next section gives a brief historical overview and explains why identity constructions are particularly important when it comes to debates on EU-Turkey relations. The third section revisits Turkish and European narratives identified by the study, considering their relevance over time and elaborating on ways in which actors' accounts of each other are woven into these narratives. The last section concludes by summarising key results and implications both for the present and the future.

2. A Love-Hate Relationship: The Role of Identity in Forming the EU-Turkey Partnership

Academic literature dealing with identity, perceptions and discourse in EU-Turkey relations is already extensive.[16] This chapter aims to contribute

---

14 For Turkey, the data set included: speeches, presentations and statements by Presidents and Prime Ministers, official documents by the Ministries of EU Affairs and Foreign Affairs. For the EU, the data set included: European Parliament resolutions and selected debates, European Council conclusions and statements, European Commission reports and communications, as well as speeches by leaders of EU institutions.

15 Cf. Polkinghorne, Narrative Configuration, p. 15.

16 Cf. Aydın-Düzgit, Senem et al. Turkish and European Identity Constructions in the 1946–1999 Period. FEUTURE Online Paper No. 15. Cologne, March 2018; Aydın-Düzgit, Senem. Constructions of European Identity. Debates and Discourses on Turkey and the EU. Basingstoke, 2012; Çağatay-Tekin, Beyza. Representations and Othering in Discourse: The construction of Turkey in the EU context. Amsterdam and Philadelphia, 2010; Casanova, José. The Long, Difficult, and Tortuous Journey of Turkey into Europe and the Dilemmas of European Civilization. In: *Constellations*, 2006, Vol. 13, No. 2; Eralp, Atila/ Torun, Zerrin.

to ongoing scholarly debate on the numerous ups and downs during the six decades of relations on the basis of collective stories told by different actors in Turkey and Europe. It argues that understanding where current narratives originate and identifying their constituents – particularly representations of identity and mutual perceptions on one another – offers important insights into assimilating the relationship itself.

Official relations between the EU and Turkey started with Turkey's application to the European Economic Community (EEC) in 1959, less than two years after its establishment. Signed in 1963, the so-called Ankara Agreement envisaged Turkey's association and laid out three phases for the establishment of a Customs Union. Yet, from the outset, further hopes were linked to this agreement since, as stated by the Turkish Ministry of Foreign Affairs, it "aimed at securing Turkey's full membership in the EEC through the establishment [...] of a Customs Union, which would serve as an instrument to bring about an integration between the EEC and Turkey".[17] Similarly, EU political figures at the time openly supported

---

Perceptions and Europeanization in Turkey before the EU Candidacy. In: Ali Tekin, Aylin Güney (Eds.). The Europeanization of Turkey. London, 2015, pp. 14–30; Ergin, Melz. Otherness within Turkey, and between Turkey and Europe. In: Paul Gifford, Tessa Hauswedell (Eds.). Europe and Its Others. Essays on Interperception and Identity. Oxford, 2010; Lindgaard, Jakob/ Uygur Wessels, Ayça/ Stockholm Banke, Cecilie Felicia. Turkey in European Identity Politics: Key Drivers and Future Scenarios. FEUTURE Online Paper No. 19. Cologne, 2018; Macmillan, Catherine. Discourse, Identity and the Question of Turkish Accession to the EU. Through the Looking Glass. Farnham, 2013; Müftüler-Baç, Meltem/ Süleymanoğlu-Kürüm, Rahime. Deliberations in the Turkish Parliament: The External Perceptions of European Foreign Policy. In: *Journal of Language and Politics*, 2015, Vol. 14, No. 2, pp. 258–284; Müftüler-Baç, Meltem/ Taşkın, Evrim. Turkey's Accession to the European Union: Does Culture and Identity play a Role? In: *Ankara Review of European Studies*, 2007, Vol. 6, No.2, pp. 31–50; Nas, Çiğdem. Turkish Identity and the Perception of Europe. In: *Avrupa Araştırmaları Dergisi*, 2001, Vol. 9, No. 1, pp. 177–189; Rumelili, Bahar. Negotiating Europe: EU-Turkey Relations from an Identity Perspective. In: *Insight Turkey*, 2008, Vol. 10, No. 1, pp. 97–110; Rumelili, Bahar. Turkey: Identity, Foreign Policy, and Socialization in a Post-Enlargement Europe. In: *Journal of European Integration*, 2011, Vol. 33, No. 2, pp. 235–249; Schneeberger, Agnes. Constructing European Identity through Mediated Difference: A Content Analysis of Turkey's EU Accession Process in the British Press. In: *Journal of Media and Communication*, 2009, Vol.1, pp. 83–102; Wimmel, Andreas. Beyond the Bosphorus? Comparing Public Discourses on Turkey's EU Application in the German, French and British Quality Press. In: *Journal of Language and Politics*, 2009, Vol. 8, No. 2, pp. 223–243.

17 Turkish Ministry of Foreign Affairs. History of EU-Turkey Relations. 12.02.2020, https://www.ab.gov.tr/111en.html [23.10.2020].

Turkey's quest for future membership of the Community. Walter Hallstein, European Commission President when the Ankara Agreement was signed, expressed his hope that "[o]ne day the final step is to be taken: Turkey is to be a full member".[18]

Over time, many of the steps laid out in this agreement, together with some subsequent additions, have been realised, even though a few decades later than had been anticipated in the 1960s. A little over 30 years after the agreement's signature, Turkey eventually completed the progressive establishment of the Customs Union in 1996. Having applied for membership in 1987, Turkey became an accession candidate in 1999 and started accession negotiations in 2005. Hence, from a macro-historical perspective, one could argue that progress has been continual, albeit ponderous.

Conversely, at the same time, there has been a decline in faith and support for Turkey's EU membership both in Turkey[19] and the EU.[20] Data from Standard Eurobarometer surveys for the last two decades, for instance, suggest that the share of Turkish respondents who have a positive image of the EU has been showing a downward trend with fluctuations, which Şenyuva argues, is not arbitrary but responding to the political developments in Turkish-European relations.[21] Currently, the outlook is even gloomier because, as Tocci points out, "[n]ever has Turkey's European aspiration been so vacuous and the EU's distancing so acute".[22]

Overall, in regard to the present state of EU-Turkey relations, it would be safe to claim that despite the continual progress, phases of estrangement have largely superseded phases of rapprochement. But why does this relationship stand at a historic low despite the hard facts that arguably should motivate both parties to align with each other? Economically speaking, Turkey and the EU, linked by a functioning (although problematic) Customs Union, remain crucial trade partners. The mutual concerns and

---

18 Hallstein, Walter. Address by Prof. Dr. Walter Hallstein, President of the Commission of the European Economic Community, on the occasion of the signature of the Association Agreement with Turkey. Ankara, 12.09.1963, http://aei.pitt.edu /14311/1/S77.pdf [23.10.2020].

19 Cf. Şenyuva, Özgehan. Turkish Public Opinion and the EU Membership: between Support and Mistrust. FEUTURE Online Paper No. 26. Cologne, October 2018; Şenyuva, Özgehan/ Çengel, Esra. Turkish Public Perceptions of Germany: Most Popular among the Unpopular. In this volume, p. 161-180.

20 Cf. Lindgaard, Jakob. EU Public Opinion on Turkish EU Membership: Trends and Drivers. FEUTURE Online Paper No. 25. Cologne, October 2018.

21 Cf. Şenyuva/ Çengel, Turkish Public Perceptions of Germany, 2022, p. 161-180.

22 Tocci, Nathalie. Beyond the storm in EU-Turkey relations. FEUTURE Voices No. 4. Cologne, January 2018.

interests of these neighbours in the face of regional and global turmoil are numerous and often pronounced. In geostrategic terms, partnerships and joint actions such as the EU-Turkey Statement and Action Plan (on migration) or the High-Level Energy Dialogue demonstrate the parties' clear intention for closer cooperation on an array of issues.

It is widely recognised that over the past few years the relationship has been particularly challenged due to various domestic developments in Turkey (more specifically, the constitutional changes establishing an executive presidential system, economic difficulties, cross-border operations in Syria and Libya and the crises with Greece over the Mediterranean gas reserves and Cyprus) as well as the EU (namely, the Brexit process, rising populism and radicalism). As expected, these arguably worrisome developments have heated already existing debates, not only on the future of the relationship but also on the fundamental question of whether or not Turkey could be considered an adequate candidate, let alone a European country. Such a discussion on Turkey's 'Europeanness' had already been particularly prevalent around the milestone decisions of 1999 (accession candidacy) and 2005 (start of accession negotiations). More recently, this issue has been addressed more frequently from both cultural and institutional aspects in the statements of certain party leaders, discussions at plenary sessions at national and European parliaments, as well as campaigns for referendums and elections.[23]

Needless to say, the term 'European' here is not interpreted in a strictly geographical sense. Turkey's eligibility to meet the geographic criteria, one could argue, was confirmed some thirty years ago when, unlike Morocco's

---

23 Some examples include the video released by Geert Wilders, a Dutch MEP and the leader of the Party for Freedom (Partij voor de Vrijheid, PVV), which addressed the Turkish citizens and stated "You are no Europeans and you will never be" (Wilders denounced over "Turkey, you are not welcome here". In: NL Times (video). 07.12.2015); The 'Leave' campaign rally, where UK Independence Party (UKIP) leader Nigel Farage warned of a "Turkish-dominated Europe" (Bennett Owen. There Will Be More Cologne-Style Sex Attacks If Turkey Joins The EU, Claims Nigel Farage. In: Huffington Post, 29.04.2016); The debates at the European Parliament on the resolutions of November 2016 (European Parliament. European Parliament resolution of 24 November 2016 on EU-Turkey relations. Resolution. P8_TA (2016)0450), 24.11.2016) and July 2017 (European Parliament. European Parliament resolution of 6 July 2017 on the 2016 Commission Report on Turkey. Resolution. P8_TA (2017)0306), 06.07.2017) which called on the Commission to initiate a temporary freeze on the ongoing accession negotiations with Turkey.

application, Turkey's application was not rejected.[24] Going further, one might argue that the underlying reason for these discussions persisting is that the "criteria [are] subject to political assessment",[25] as one briefing of the European Parliament contends. According to this argumentation, any decision on Turkey's place in the EU ought to be context-bound and rely on certain collective understanding and identity-building processes. It is the agents who exercise the practice of 'interpreting' or 'assessing' this question, ultimately resolving what 'Europeanness' stands for and whether or not Turkey can qualify as such. Through this resolution, all goals and visions for the relationship (be it full membership or something else) are settled both for now and the future, being reflected in how the relationship is narrated.

The ways in which actors perceive, interpret and respond to each other, of course, is not the only determinant for this relationship. One might even argue that it is not a determinant at all, but rather an outcome of concrete political processes and interactions between and around the parties. The position taken in this study lies between these two interpretations, suggesting that identity constructions (in the form of narratives) and the actual set of events are not only closely interlinked but also mutually constitutive of one another. Just as the actual set of events conditions narratives, so do narratives help to contemplate these events, by capturing some act of reality and shedding light on what has happened, which in turn recurrently impacts how the present is considered and parties behave. Narratives can also contain implications for the future, firstly by changing how we comprehend and act in the present and secondly by presenting story-like descriptions of the future.

If the end goal of EU-Turkey relations is achieving cooperation at the highest possible level (if not necessarily Turkey's joining the Union), then it is the condition precedent for parties not only to develop an understanding of each other's perceived realities but also reach agreement on the possible trajectories of action. This would require parties intersubjectively and continually to (re)define themselves in relation to each other while making practical and normative decisions. A complete consensus would not be obligatory, but there would still need to be concurrence over rele-

---

24 In 1987, Morocco lodged an application to become a Member of the Communities, but the application was rejected by the Council "on the grounds that Morocco was not a European State" (Council Decision of 1 October 1987, as cited in European Parliament Briefing No 23 "Legal Questions of Enlargement", www.europarl.europa.eu/enlargement/briefings/ 23a2_en.htm [23.10.2020]).
25 European Parliament, Briefing No 23.

vant problems, demands, dilemmas, conditions and the like in the face of many ambiguities posed by evolving situations.

It is acknowledged here that questions such as those about Turkey's 'Europeanness' are unlikely to be settled once and for all, because first and foremost collective identity constructions themselves have a dynamic nature; they are not static or fixed. Thus, any question of Turkish identity in relation to Europe, and vice versa, is bound to be answered differently by different actors at different times. These constructions are intrinsically bound to space and time. They change and transform in light of "the temporally connected, continuously interacting events of the past".[26] Furthermore, the processes of identity construction do not develop in distinct spheres. The formation of one's own identity is rather closely linked with the perception of a respective 'Other'. Or, as Browning argues, "it is only through emplotting ourselves in constitutive stories differentiating the self from others that we are able to attribute meaning to the social world and to construct a sense of our own identity and interests".[27] Nevertheless, we subscribe to the idea that glancing at these ever-changing, constantly interacting 'storification' processes is a worthwhile endeavour. The form and content of this will become clearer in the next section as it outlines the major narratives identified by the authors in the history of official political debates in Europe and Turkey, analysing their historical foundations with a focus on their underlying identity frames.

3. Identity Perceptions and Representations in Turkish and European Narratives

Here then is an overview of the dominant narratives that have surfaced since the beginning of institutionalised relations in 1959.[28] It summarises the main constituents of five Turkish narratives (*Westernisation, Europeanisation, Eurasianisation, Turkey as 'the Heir', and Turkey as a 'Great Power'*) along with four European narratives (*Membership, Strategic Partner, Distant*

---

26 Hauge et al., Narratives of a Contested Relationship, p. 8.
27 Browning, Christopher S. Constructivism, Narrative and Foreign Policy Analysis. A Case Study of Finland. Bern/ Oxford, 2008, p. 11.
28 See for a more detailed analysis of the narratives as well as the methodological approach the FEUTURE Paper by Hauge et al. 2019, which is complemented by an elaborative appendix.

Neighbour and *Special Case/Candidate*).[29] It puts a focus on encapsulating and comparing the identity representations manifested in these narratives as well as their development over time.

3.1 Narratives in Turkey

One crucial point that should be underlined from the outset is that all five narratives identified on the Turkish side share the same goal, or *finalité*, which is membership. Turkey's accession to the EU appears as a consistent element across all narratives from the initiation of this relationship. However, the story structures (and the character representations) built around this goal are subject to five different rationales.

The *Westernisation* narrative considers Turkey as a crucial part of 'the West', a form of alliance that includes the EU along with some other Western actors. Fuelled by insecurity and anxiety stemming from the bipolarity and nuclear armament at the height of the Cold War, great emphasis is placed on the need for cooperation, primarily with NATO and the United States, but also with Europe-based institutions such as the Council of Europe and the EU. This narrative brings forward Turkey's democratic, secular, liberal side, underlining the country's geopolitical and geostrategic importance. It certainly deems the EU to be an important ally, albeit not necessarily valued above other westerners.

From a security perspective, for instance, former President Celal Bayar refers to NATO as "an especial creation, which was brought into being by nations that are determined to live freely" and asserts that "the role NATO plays in the reinforcement of [Turkey's] national security is great and exhilarating".[30] Regarding economic considerations, it is often stated that any foreign aid required for the country's growth could be obtained from "the international organisations of which Turkey is a member and

---

29 As the study focuses on the most influential narratives, it does not provide insights into the critical stances or counter-narratives that challenge the ones presented here. It does not provide information on, for instance, the views of the Islamist/ultra-nationalist parties or the critical Marxists or delve into their specific type of conservatism, support for a certain type of modernisation and scepticism towards Europeanization and Westernization processes.

30 Bayar, Celal. On Birinci Dönem İkinci Yasama Yılı Açış Konuşması, Speech, The Grand National Assembly of Turkey, Ankara, 01.11.1958. Original quote: "Hür yaşamaya azmetmiş milletlerin vücuda getirdikleri müstesna eser olan NATO'ya sadakatla bağlıyız. NATO'nun, millî emniyetimizin takviyesi bakımından oynadığı rol büyüktür, inşirah vericidir."

from friendly and allied countries in the sense of economic stability and Western democracy".[31]

Issues concerning cooperation or integration with the EU and Turkey's position in the Western bloc are often conflated in *Westernisation*. For Turkish actors, the desire to preserve this position to some extent makes permanent their aim of maintaining a relationship with the EU. Moreover, this narrative involves multiple linkages to a variety of actors and wide-ranging drivers focusing on political, economic and security aspects of relations rather than cultural, historical, or identity-related debates. While placing considerable emphasis on Turkey's 'Westernness', the narrative's target-oriented nature leaves little room for fluctuations arising from speculations or conjectures on Turkey's credentials for EU membership. Consequently, even at times of serious bilateral disputes, Turkish political actors' inclination to locate Turkey in the West, hence together with the EU, persists throughout the years.

The *Europeanisation* narrative, which starts to gain influence in the late 1980s but becomes especially dominant from the second half of the 1990s, strongly emphasises Turkey's 'rightful' place among European countries. The country is regarded as a natural part of continental Europe for palpable geographical and historical reasons; a modern, civilised state that to a certain extent is already integrated into the European economic and political system. According to this narrative, Turkey and the EU need each other for strategic as well as security-related reasons. During the Cold War, this need was mainly derived from the turbulent international environment, but since 1990, it has become more to do with economic and political opportunities offered by the new global order together with challenges that the parties ought to face together. According to Turkish actors, Turkey and the EU share a common destiny as well as joint interests and concerns across a broad spectrum of issues.

Even at the very beginning of relations in 1959, Turkish actors seemed eager to take part in any form or level of European integration, but this desire becomes stronger as the EU institutionalises, thereby gaining power and influence. In this context, extensive constitutional reforms that have been carried out by focusing on the country's political, legal, economic

---

31 İnönü, İsmet. 27. Cumhuriyet Hükümeti'nin (IX. İnönü Hükümeti) Programını Millet Meclisi Genel Kurulu'na Sunuş Konuşması. Speech. The Grand National Assembly of Turkey. Ankara, 02.07.1962. Original quote: "Bu suretle, iktisadi istikrar ve Batılı demokrasi anlayışı içinde, kalkınmamızın lüzumlu kıldığı dış yardım ihtiyacının, üyesi bulunduğumuz Milletlerarası teşekküller ile dost ve müttefik memleketlerden temin edebileceğine kaani bulunmaktayız".

and social systems throughout the years have reportedly been designed to be compatible with European institutional architecture. EU membership is asserted as being "a means, rather than an end, to bring the Turkish nation up to the level of contemporary civilisation it deserves".[32]

Europeanisation is the narrative that most explicitly promotes and supports Turkey's EU membership since it overwhelmingly centres upon the Union (rather than broader alliances such as the Western bloc). With its centuries-old, deep interactions and relations with countries throughout the continent, Turkey is claimed to be an indisputable member of the European family. As the EU postpones Turkey's membership and continually imposes new preconditions, in the eyes of Turkish actors, not only are the sincerity and objectivity of relations increasingly questioned, but the demand for equal treatment and transparency becomes more explicit. Nevertheless, Europeanisation remains central to Turkish narratives, with the goal of membership still being asserted by many actors as a key priority within the country's foreign policy.

The *Eurasianisation* narrative emerging immediately after the Soviet Union's collapse, pays significant attention to smaller, newly formed Eastern states, such as Belarus, Georgia, Armenia and the like. It leaves Turkey's one-sided foreign policy orientation toward the West aside and establishes Turkey as an influential regional power, a bridge between the West and the East. While acknowledging the state's self-evident connections to Europe, the central premise here presents Turkey as a key player with a strategic geopolitical position and a complex character that is compatible with both Western and Eastern values. Prime Minister Bülent Ecevit, serving four terms between 1974 and 2002, for instance, contended that Turkey is European "with its culture, history, and geography" but 'Europeanness' alone does not define Turkey since the country also belongs to "Central Asia, Middle East, Eastern Mediterranean, Black Sea, Balkans, and partly Africa".[33] In this narrative, Turkey is a guide, a successful model

---

32 Erdoğan, Recep Tayyip. Türkiye ve Avrupa Birliği Arasındaki İlişkiler Konusunda Genel Görüşme Hakkında Hükümet Adına Yaptığı Konuşma. Speech. The Grand National Assembly of Turkey. Ankara, 29.05.2003. Original quote "Biz, Avrupa Birliği'ne üyeliği, bir amaç olarak değil, Türk Halkını hak ettiği çağdaş uygarlık seviyesine ulaştırmak için bir araç olarak görüyoruz".

33 Ecevit, Bülent. 57. Cumhuriyet Hükümeti Programının Millet Meclisi Genel Kurulu'nda Yapılan Görüşmeleri Sırasında Yaptıkları Konuşma, Speech, The Grand National Assembly of Turkey, Ankara, 07.06.1999. Original quote: "Biz, kültürümüzle, tarihimizle, coğrafyamızla Avrupalıyız; ama sadece Avrupalılığa da sığmayız. Biz, aynı zamanda, bir Orta Asya ülkesiyiz, bir Ortadoğu ülkesiyiz, bir Doğu Akdeniz ülkesiyiz, bir Karadeniz ülkesiyiz, bir Balkanlar ülkesiyiz,

for the other countries in the region as it is a "great county that has understood the modern world with its established democratic tradition; its experience on the free-market economy application".[34]

In this context, Turkish identity is understood as a complex, multi-layered phenomenon (maybe more so than that of the EU). It is also considered adaptable and fluid as the country stands prepared to merge its historical heritage (through which it bears a resemblance to its Eastern neighbours) with modern competencies (through which it stands close to the EU). In this understanding, civilisation is nurtured by democratisation, liberalisation and securitisation. It is an accumulation of knowledge, which is not necessarily produced by the West (or Europe per se) but can be relayed from there to the East through Turkey. Assuming that the EU would seek political and economic links or even integration of a sort with Eurasian actors, this narrative not only sees Turkey as a role model for these countries through its ability to blend West and East, but also argues that Turkey's much-delayed membership to the EU is a first step for the European project's possible widening in the region.

The Turkey as 'the Heir' narrative essentially revolves around the supposed clash of Turkish and European identities as propounded by Europeans from time to time. As Turkey develops closer relations with Middle Eastern and Central Asian countries, becoming noticeably more conservative under AKP rule since 2002, references to Turkey's imperial legacy and alleged organic links to Turkic dynasties (starting from the Anatolian *beyliks* from the 11th century) seem to increase significantly. Following the waning of an EU membership perspective and the continuing impasse in accession negotiations, over time empathy and admiration give way to attitudinal ambivalence and scepticism.

While this narrative envisages Turkey as the grandiose heir and highlights the glory of former empires, it does not necessarily share the idea of conflicting Turkish and European identities. On the contrary, it often asserts that Turkey is European *because* of its past and accuses European

---

kısmen Afrika ülkesiyiz ve bu kökenleri çok iyi bağdaştırabildiğimiz için de, Avrasyalaşma sürecinin anahtar ülkesi konumuna gelmiş bulunuyoruz".

34 Demirel, Süleyman. On Dokuzuncu Dönem Beşinci Yasama Yılı Açış Konuşması. Speech. The Grand National Assembly of Turkey. Ankara, 01.10.1995. Original quote: "Türkiye, köklü demokratik gelenekleriyle, serbest pazar ekonomisi uygulamasında edindiği birikimlerle, çağdaş dünyayı anlamış büyük bir devlet olarak, bu ülkeler için bir ışıktır, bir penceredir; bu ülkelere yön verme imkânına da en iyi şekilde sahiptir; bunların dünyayla bütünleşmeleri için ideal bir köprü konumundadır".

counterparts of exploiting the historical divergences among parties in creating arbitrary obstacles to oppose its joining the Union. Even though it promotes Turkey's greater engagement with countries that were once part of the Ottoman Empire, it still stresses Turkey's ultimate objective of full membership to the EU.

In this narrative, Turkey is visualised as heir not only to the formidable Ottoman Empire, but also the preceding Turkic empires. Thus, the narrative captures more than Neo-Ottomanism: It merges elements from both Balkanism and Turkism, underlining that the Ottoman Empire "in fact developed as a Balkan state in its founding period" and became a "multicultural, multinational, multi-religious European and Mediterranean power"[35] with Istanbul as the capital. Turkey's President Recep Tayyip Erdoğan, for instance, insists that "Turkey is not a guest but the host in Europe",[36] stating:

> "I do not go as far back as the Turkic states that were established in Europe in the 400s, 500s, 600s, 700s; the times before we honoured [Europe] with Islam. I simply refer to the times since our ancestors, Ottomans, expanded into the European continent in the 1350s, when I say we have been in existence in Europe with our country, our culture, and our civilisation for more than 650 years and we will continue to do so".[37]

In the *Turkey as 'the Heir'* narrative, one can identify a more profound claim that European actors bring up so-called identity-related differences, strategically using Turkey's past and thereby masking their own underlying reluctance for further integration. According to former Prime Minister

---

35 Demirel, Süleyman. Yirmi Birinci Dönem İkinci Yasama Yılı Açış Konuşması, Speech, The Grand National Assembly of Turkey, Ankara, 01.10.1999. Original quote: "Osmanlı Devleti, kuruluş döneminde esas itibariyle bir Balkan devleti olarak gelişmiştir ve İstanbul'un başkent olmasıyla birlikte, çok kültürlü, çok uluslu, çok dinli bir Avrupa ve Akdeniz gücü olarak tarih sahnesindeki yerini almıştır".

36 Erdoğan, Recep Tayyip. 30. Muhtarlar Toplantısında Yaptıkları Konuşma. Speech. Ankara, 01.12.2016. Original quote: "Biz Avrupa'da misafir değil, ev sahibiyiz".

37 Ibid. Original Quote: "Daha eskilere, İslamiyet'le şereflendirdiğimiz o günlerin öncesine, 400'lü, 500'lü, 600'lü, 700'lü yıllarda Avrupa'da kurulmuş olan Türk devletlerine kadar gitmiyorum. Ecdadımız Osmanlı'nın 1350'li yıllarda Avrupa kıtasına geçişinden itibaren ele alarak söylüyorum: 650 yılı aşkın süredir kesintisiz bir şekilde Avrupa'da devletimizle, kültürümüzle, medeniyetimizle varız, var olmaya devam edeceğiz".

Mesut Yılmaz, "the Turkey-phobia, which those who were sitting at the table have had since the very beginning"[38] is the main reason why Turkey was not accepted together with Eastern European applicants as a candidate state by the European Council Summit of Luxembourg in 1997. These allegations about the intentional, prevalent negative image of the Turkish state and nation in fact goes back a long way in the history of European-Turkish relations.[39]

In this narrative, Turkey is portrayed as an honourable but victimised party in the relationship. Even though it exerts itself to the utmost and keeps all of its promises, it cannot escape unfair, disrespectful and deceptive treatment by the EU. Despite everything, Turkish actors still expect the EU to make the right decision and pursue an objective, transparent, impartial policy towards Turkey. They maintain a forgiving, noble attitude whilst, unlike the previous narratives, at the same time offering assurances that Turkey will be just fine by itself if the EU fails to come through. In this respect, Turkish actors still hold membership as a goal, but only under certain conditions.

The *Turkey as a 'Great Power'* narrative, which emerged in the early 2000s and has gradually gained prominence since then, envisages Turkey as a powerful political and economic actor with a pivotal regional role that entails various strategic opportunities. It pictures Turkey and the EU as equals, asserting that accession negotiations should continue in a more transparent and impartial manner while concurrently criticising the EU for not showing the interest, respect and enthusiasm that Turkey deserves.

Hence, as Turkey grows stronger, the sense of cooperation and collaboration seemingly gives way to the notion of quid pro quo. In this narrative, Turkish actors dismiss thoughts of an asymmetrical relationship between Turkey and the EU. A free and powerful 'New Turkey' does not have to comply with the EU's rules, or desperately try to make room for itself among the existing members. It proclaims a capacity to wield influence and sit down at the table under equal terms. Instead of accepting what is offered, it is envisaged as having the means of negotiating and fighting for

---

38 Yılmaz, Mesut. 1998 Mali Yılı Bütçe Kanunu Tasarısını Sunuş Konuşması. Speech. The Grand National Assembly of Turkey. Ankara, 25.12.1997. Original quote: "Lüksemburg zirvesinde ortaya konulan neticenin, bizi tatmin etmeyen o kararların müsebbibi, ne Türkiye Cumhuriyeti Devletidir ne de aziz milletimizdir. Bu kararların, bu neticenin tek müsebbibi, bir taraftan, o masanın etrafında oturan ülkelerden bazılarının, ezeli olarak taşıdıkları Türkiye fobisidir".

39 Cf. Aydın-Düzgit, Senem et. al. Turkish and European Identity Constructions in the 1815–1945 Period. FEUTURE Online Paper No. 4. Cologne, July 2017, p. 6.

what is fair. It is easy to spot this new vision during talks on the infamous Turkey-EU Agreement of 18 March 2016. Turkey's Chief Negotiator Ömer Çelik stated that Turkey's performance on the issue of migration prevented "one of the biggest crises to upset the geopolitical order and political map"[40] which is why, "visa liberalisation is not a gesture to Turkey but an outcome that should be reached as a requirement of the agreement that has already emerged".[41]

The *Turkey as a 'Great Power'* narrative comprises a seemingly ossified 'Us' versus 'Them' dichotomy, which is not inherently antagonistic. It initially serves to picture Turkey and the EU as two distinct sides with different bargaining positions and powers on a variety of issues. However, the rhetoric gradually becomes more aggressive and confrontational in light of a series of events that bring forward the parties' increasingly diverging and sometimes opposing interests.

Leaving aside the somewhat paradoxical coexistence of Turkey's fierce criticism and perpetual commitment towards the EU, this narrative successfully illustrates the time factor's relevance within EU-Turkey relations. When linked with changes within the structure of relations and drivers over time, tiredness from decades-long 'stalling' has resulted in a narrative unlike any other: *Turkey as a 'Great Power'* is the first to contain such a level of despair and anger. It is the only narrative within which Turkish actors "do not recognise"[42] or respect decisions reached by the European institutions. It is also alone in considering other international institutions, such as the Shanghai Cooperation Organisation, as alternatives to EU membership.[43] In that sense, this particular narrative arguably best demonstrates how a shift in the present dominant narrative might be critical in terms of resolving Turkey's future destiny with the EU and vice versa.

---

40   Çelik, Ömer. Arguments Compiled Based on the Statements by the Minister for EU Affairs and Chief Negotiator Ömer Çelik. No: 4 Syrian Issue and Refugee Crisis. 2016, p. 5. Original quote: "Bu [Mülteci krizi] da jeopolitiği ve siyasi haritayı altüst edecek en büyük krizlerden bir tanesidir".

41   Ibid. Original quote: "Dolayısıyla vize serbestisi bize yapılacak bir jest değil, zaten ortaya çıkan anlaşmanın bir gereği olarak varılması gereken bir sonuçtur".

42   Erdoğan, Recep Tayyip. İSEDAK 32. Toplantısı Açılış Oturumunda Yaptıkları Konuşma. Speech. Istanbul, 23.11.2016, https://www.tccb.gov.tr/konusmalar/353/61109/isedak-32-toplantisi-acilis-oturumunda-yaptiklari-konusma [23.10.2020].

43   Cf. "Erdoğan: 'Şanghay Beşlisi içerisinde Türkiye niye olmasın?' diyorum". In: Spuknik News, 20.11.2016, https://tr.sputniknews.com/turkiye/201611201025892702-erdogan-ab-sanghay-beslisi/ [23.10.2020].

3.2 Narratives in the EU

As with Turkish narratives, those being propagated by EU institutions and actors have also changed, becoming more divergent over time. Whilst mutual perceptions have undergone transformation (to varying degrees), the same can be said about the number of competing perspectives and different goals formulated as part of the stories narrated. In the latter aspect, they differ from Turkish narratives outlined above, which all tend to share the formal goal of membership to the EU, or at least do not abandon this option altogether.

According to the *Membership* narrative, Turkey should become a member of the EU. There are different drivers that motivate this over time, such as geopolitical arguments stressing Turkey's importance for regional security or the emphasis that Turkey is an important trading partner. The prospect of contributing to democratisation in Turkey via the enlargement process is another regular element within this narrative, relating to an overall vision of the Union's mission in the international system (as expressed in Art. 21 in the Treaty on European Union).

Regarding underlying identity representations, this view places greater value on common features that Turkey shares with Europe, as prominently captured by the oft-quoted speech of first Commission President Walter Hallstein when the Ankara Agreement was signed in 1963. On that occasion, he stressed that "Turkey is a part of Europe",[44] arguing that in particular Kemal Atatürk's efforts to reform "every aspect of life" radically and strictly along "European lines" contributed to rendering the country more "European" and that this modernisation process was a characteristic that Turkey shared with Europe.[45] A resolution by the European Parliament from 1970 argued in a similar vein that the Association's key objective was "the full membership of Turkey in the Community".[46]

This kind of perception in placing Turkey's identity within the European 'family' has, though, only rarely been present in official statements from EU actors and institutions. This was mostly linked to the Ankara Agreement, but never emerged again as a dominant perception after

---

44 Hallstein, Address by Prof. Dr. Walter Hallstein, 1963.
45 Ibid.
46 European Parliament. "Entschliessung zu den vom Gemischen Parlamentarischen Ausschusses EWG-Türkei in Zusammenhang mit dem Fünften Jährlichen Tätigkeitsbericht des Assoziationsrates angenommenen Empfehlungen". Resolution, adopted on 8 July 1970. Amtsblatt der Europäischen Gemeinschaften Nr. C 101129. Brussels, 04.08.1970.

1970.[47] Indeed, this narrative had lost its impetus by the end of the 1970s, particularly after the military coup in Turkey on 12 September 1980. Thereafter, one can identify an increase in the number of conflictual elements within the discourse, as captured below by the *Distant Neighbour* narrative. At that time, Community institutions harshly criticised the human rights situation and military rule. In light of these developments, it comes as no surprise that official documents dropped any explicit mention of Turkish membership during the 1980s.

At the other end of the political discourse spectrum, the *Distant Neighbour* narrative perceives Turkey as an estranged and faraway, or even hostile neighbour, expressing a preference for keeping the country at arm's length. In regard to implications for the institutional side of relations, references to the freeze or suspension of relations and/or an abandoning the accession process represent the most drastic consequence or postulation-forming part of this narrative in its contemporary form. It can also imply a distancing from political tendencies and authoritarian trends, but is also often linked to emphasising the EU primarily as a community of values. In recent years, this narrative has gained in relevance and particularly so since the purges in Turkey after the coup attempt of 2016. Since then, EU actors have often argued that Turkey is moving "away in giant strides from Europe".[48]

From a perspective of identity and culture, this narrative tends to perceive Turkey more as 'the Other' and hence also as too different from 'Europe' to become an EU member. In this sense, Turkey is rather situated outside European 'borders'. Besides possible geographic arguments, representations also tend to refer to the differences in a cultural and religious sense, for example, by underlining an alleged Islamic character of Turkish society. Representations of Turkey as 'Other' also frequently bear orientalist features, as outlined by Eduard Said, or by adopting a patronising view of Turkey (and the Middle East) as less developed than EU countries.[49]

However, possibly the most constant element in EU institutions official rhetoric, which also forms part of different narratives, has been the emphasis on Turkey's high geostrategic relevance for Europe. This links to an understanding of Turkey as reflected by the *Strategic Partner* narrative. Arguments inherent in this narrative usually relate strongly to the security

47 Hauge et al., 2019, p. 33.
48 Juncker, Jean-Claude. President Jean-Claude Juncker's State of the Union Address 2017. SPEECH-17-3165. Brussels, 13.09.2017.
49 Said, Edward. Orientalism. New York, 1978.

dimension but also to Turkey's growing economic importance and the increasing trade relations, as well as to its role in the neighbourhood.

It goes without saying that the international context is also an influential factor for the relevance of this narrative. In many instances, Turkey's role as a partner of the 'West' and bulwark against expansion of the Soviet Union was acknowledged or even underlined by political elites. In concluding the association agreement with Turkey in 1963, the President of the Council of Ministers at the time, Joseph Luns, voiced the agreement's contemporary mutual interests and motives, by making this point: "For Turkey, this agreement effectively represents another proof that it is European in its nature. For our community, this agreement represents recognition of the prominent position that Turkey assumes today in the free world (...)".[50]

There are also numerous more recent instances in which this narrative can be identified. The EU-Turkey statement of November 2015 was an example of the *Strategic Partner* narrative's logic. It also exemplifies another facet of this narrative, namely that it can also include references to a (desired) form of the EU-Turkey relationship, which accordingly is framed as a partnership or strategic partnership. Although the EU-Turkey statement still included a formulation that the accession process should be revitalised, cooperation within the Joint Action Plan on migration management, as well as the visa liberalisation process, was in the foreground of this agreement.[51] Similarly, the March 2016 statement foresaw high-level meetings and summits as means of strengthening cooperation in the fields of migration, counter-terrorism, energy and business.[52] Recent EP resolutions also include elements that link to a form of strategic partnership. For example, in 2016 the EP supported "a structured, more frequent and open high-level political dialogue on key thematic issues of joint interest such as migration, counter-terrorism, energy, economy and trade".[53]

---

50 European Parliament, "Assoziierung EWG-Türkei". Debate. Brussels, 28.11.1963.

51 Cf. Saatçioğlu, Beken. Turkey and the EU: Strategic Rapprochement in the Shadow of the Refugee Crisis. In: *E-International Relations*, 21.01.2016.

52 Cf. European Council. Meeting of Heads of State or Government with Turkey – EU-Turkey statement. Brussels, 29.11.2015, http://www.consilium.europa .eu/en/press/press-releases/2015/11/29/eu-turkey-meeting-statement/pdf [24.10.2020]; European Council. EU-Turkey statement. Press Release 144/16. Brussels, 18.03.2016, http://www.consilium.europa.eu/en/press/press-releases/ 2016/03/18/eu-turkey-statement/pdf [24.10.2020].

53 European Parliament. European Parliament resolution of 14 April 2016 on the 2015 report on Turkey. Resolution. P8_TA(2016)0133. Brussels, 14.04.2016,

Despite the high level of conflict in diplomatic relations recently as well as harsh criticism and concerns voiced by EU institutions, representations of a perspective stressing Turkey's strategic importance for the EU are embedded in most of the statements, rendering it a dominant perception.

Another relevant narrative from recent decades is that depicting Turkey as a *Special Case (or Candidate)*. This argues that the country has specific characteristics, giving rise to remarks about its relatively large size, geography or economy, which prompt questions regarding the EU's absorption capacity. Also included here are issues to do with cultural or religious differences. This line of argumentation often raises concerns about Turkey's difficulties in fulfilling the Copenhagen Criteria and hence implementing the acquis, leading to an emphasis that its association and later candidacy are not only different but also more difficult than other cases. A central notion places emphasis on the 'open-ended' character of accession negotiations and an inability to guarantee their outcome. This was an expression used and repeated by all EU institutions when referring to the opening of accession negotiations.

With few representations in the European Community's official discourse during preparations for the Ankara Agreement about Turkey's economic situation creating cause for concern, this narrative did gain more relevance in the late 1980s. It was then 'institutionalised' at the European Council summit of 1997 in Luxembourg, during which the EU put forward a specific "European Strategy" for Turkey alone and also decided not to grant candidacy status to the country (unlike the policy for Eastern European applicant states).[54] A few days before this meeting, Commissioner van den Broek justified this strategy by saying that "[i]t is only natural that Turkey should pursue its own path towards integration with Europe given that its historical experience has been so different from that of the countries in the former communist bloc".[55] Elements of this narrative continue to be part of the EU's discourse, even following the opening of accession negotiations in 2005.

---

https://www.europarl.europa.eu/doceo/document/TA-8-2016-0133_EN.pdf [23.10.2020].

54 Cf. European Council. Luxembourg European Council (12 and 13 December 1997). Presidency Conclusions. Luxembourg, 13.12.1997, https://www.europarl.e uropa.eu/summits/lux1_en.htm [23.10.2020].

55 Van den Broek, Hans. The Prospect for EU Enlargement. Conference organised by the International Press Institute "The future of Europe". SPEECH/97/264. Brussels, 27.11.1997.

Linked to this kind of narrative, in some instances there is a perception of Turkey as "liminal", which has manifested over time, thus "a partly-self, partly-other" position,[56] particularly dominant in the 1980s and 1990s[57] which coincides with the *Special Case* narrative. Consequently, it is worth explaining this dynamic in more detail. For instance, one could argue that Turkey's alleged liminal identity is related to different kinds of discourses.

On the one hand, there is argumentation that concludes from this distinct character that Turkey is not fit to be part of the EU. For example, Huntington defines Turkey as a torn country caught between Western and Eastern civilisations, which hence cannot become an EU member state.[58] Even at the time of the establishment of the Republic of Turkey in 1923 and subsequent reforms undertaken by Atatürk, some actors were attesting to Turkey's "hybrid system comprising both Oriental and Western features".[59] This liminal status, as Rumelili has argued, can also contribute to a perceived threat, not least because it may induce a more pressing necessity to "clarify and articulate the differences between Turkey and Europe".[60]

Related to this perception, but rather interpreting Turkey's special character in a positive sense, there is on the other hand a common frame depicting the country as a bridge or gate between Europe and the Middle East.[61] In light of the so called 'Arab spring', but also before, political actors went even further and regularly stressed the role of Turkey as a model for the Islamic World, in successfully combining democracy and Islam. Modernisation and reform packages of the 1990s and early 2000s further supported this view that Turkey could act as a model and bridge to those countries in the Arab world which were seen as moving towards the principles of statehood, society and economy prevalent in democratic 'Western' states.

Our analysis of narratives presented over a sixty years period reveals that identity and mutual perceptions do indeed represent a defining fea-

---

56 Cf. Rumelili, Negotiating Europe, 2008.
57 Cf. Aydın-Düzgit et al., Turkish and European Identity Constructions in the 1946–1999 period, 2018, p. 20.
58 Cf. Huntington, Samuel P. Clash of Civilizations and the Remaking of World Order. New York, 1996, p. 146.
59 Aydın-Düzgit et al. Turkish and European Identity Constructions in the 1815–1945 Period. 2017, p. 10.
60 Rumelili, Bahar. Liminal identities and processes of domestication and subversion in International Relations. In: *Review of International Studies*, 2012, Vol. 38, p. 506.
61 Cf. Lindgaard et al., Turkey in European Identity Politics, 2018, p. 2.

ture of narratives in current and past debates on EU-Turkey relations. All documents analysed from both sides were generally rather of an official character and thus, especially in the case of EU institutions, the formulations adopted carried a more neutral tone. However, the speeches and statements by Turkish political leaders have at times been couched in less diplomatic language and hence often presented greater opportunities for conclusions on perceptions of self and the other, in this case the EU.

4. Conclusion: What about the Future?

Narratives, or collective stories told by political actors, carry many functions, such as: constructing social reality; generating and transmitting knowledge; discursive framing of events; providing context for storytellers' actions; and eliciting emotions and reactions among audiences. They comprise images and experiences from the past, inform and get informed by the dynamism and uncertainties of the present, and at times orient towards the future. Above all, they present descriptions of characters (with goals, beliefs, desires and expectations) as a dichotomy between the self and the other(s).

Similarly, and more specifically, narratives regarding EU-Turkey relations contain character representations, primarily to do with the EU and Turkey but also others, around which the story revolves. These representations neither exist independently nor are fixed in structure; they are renegotiated and reconstituted continually through intersubjective interactions. The character aspects that stand out in these representations or show salience over time and the conflicts or congruence between them can provide us with important clues about the current state and denouement of the actual relationships between storified characters.

This chapter has focused comparatively on these narratives from the perspective of political actors in Turkey and the EU, examining the historical roots and evolution of identity perceptions as well as characterisations. Since such narratives do not exist in a complete story form per se, it has relied on textual analyses of official documents collected and qualitatively coded separately for both sides of the relationship between 1958 and 2017. Ultimately, the chapter has concluded with several considerations on the present and possible future of this relationship, drawn from our reflections above on narratives and identity representations based upon a trans-historical perspective.

The ups and downs of the relations since Turkey's application for an association agreement with the ECC indicate that change itself is the key continuing feature. As we have shown here, this is also found to be true for relationship narratives. Identity perceptions and character descriptions in both Turkish and European narratives, as with the relationship itself, seem to have changed and transformed over time since 1958. This inference aligns with conclusions drawn by Aydın-Düzgit et al., who go back further in the common history of Turkey and Europe and propound the fluidity of identity constructions as the most characterising feature in this relationship.[62] How actors view themselves and others has continued to change throughout history. As the circumstances and conditions that determine a relationship (for example, the international context and interactions with each other and third parties) have differed, so have inextricably linked political stories. Hence, it is quite likely that change itself will persist as a fixed and fundamental element in the perceptions of mutual identity and character descriptions in narratives.

Yet, this state of constant change as a dominant characteristic does not exclude patterns of continuity or the re-appearance of certain identity elements. The perceptions and considerations, which have either remained salient for a long time or resurfaced sporadically in discourses are also of major importance. We argue that such continual or cyclical elements form the key apparatus when reflecting on the relationship's possible future scenarios, in that they represent discursive constituents which transcend temporal identity boundaries. Since what has occurred consistently or frequently up to now is likely to be carried forward, this makes possible informed forecasting for the future.

As a quite striking result, mutual recognition of importance and significance is the most prominent example of such perpetuity. Actors in Turkey view the EU in a number of different ways: as a strong and normatively superior actor in its own right; as an influential member of larger partnerships; or as an equivalent partner to Turkey. In the same vein, European actors display complete ambivalence, sometimes embracing Turkey as one of their own but at other times portraying it as an alien and hence completely dissimilar to them. Yet, no matter what rhetoric is encountered, both parties constantly acknowledge and express the geopolitical and geostrategic importance to each other, which consequently determines the need for some level of dialogue and cooperation. As a result, mutual acknowledgment and emphasis on both sides of the relationship, along with the factor of change, stand out as possible dominant features of future narratives.

---

62 Cf. Aydın-Düzgit et al. Turkish and European Identity Constructions in the 1815–1945 Period, 2017, p. 16.

Finally, our empirical study confirms that conflict within and between Turkish and European narratives is not a new phenomenon, but rather a recurrence. The absence of conflict between reciprocal characterisations in these narratives is observed only for a limited time during the 1960s and 1970s. As outlined earlier, *Westernisation* and particularly *Europeanisation* narratives in Turkey found their corresponding 'counterpart' then in one of the European narratives, namely *Membership*. The two parties seemingly reached a consensus in terms of their expectations, demands and wishes from each other; hence they were able to envision a common identity that separates them from the others in the universe of extended relations. This allowed for a 'convergence' of narratives for a period, which was paralleled by statements describing Turkey as part of Europe – a notion that has been contested ever since.

Even though in the context of narratives conflict has been present for a long time, our study confirms that the level of animosity and rivalry has gradually increased to reach an unprecedented level, especially in the last few years. Turkish narratives, *Turkey as 'the Heir'* and *Turkey as a 'Great Power'*, which have emerged in the 2000s, have no equivalent on the European side. The ways in which Turkey, the EU and the relationship itself are described in these narratives are certainly not reciprocated in European stories. These two Turkish narratives are shaped, more by ambivalence and scepticism than sympathy and admiration towards Europe. Paradoxically, despite Turkish actors continuing to pursue their objective of EU membership, criticism directed towards the EU has increased substantially. Similarly, the *Distant Neighbour* narrative on the EU side, which has gained relevance more recently, reveals an increasingly conflict-laden tone, which goes hand in hand with a perception of Turkey moving away from the EU and thus from the values ascribed therein.

A vaguely articulated but deeply felt sense of Europeanness is a prominent facet of self-identity descriptions in all Turkish narratives. When this identity feature, which is obvious and indisputable in the eyes of actors in Turkey, is questioned or not recognised by the European actors, any underlying eagerness for cooperation and the ultimate goal of full integration become threatened. Recognition of Turkey's identity as European appears as a necessary condition for both the relationship and associated narratives to move beyond the current conflictual situation. While this is possible over time through mutual trust, dialogue and cooperation, a rapid and effective change in this perception on the EU side seems unlikely in the next couple of years. Hence, conflict (at some level) is identified as the third feature in predictions for narratives within the foreseeable future.

A Charged Friendship: German Narratives of EU-Turkey Relations in the Pre-accession Phase, 1959–1999

Anke Schönlau, Mirja Schröder

1. Introduction: Diving into Germany's Role in EU-Turkey Relations

After the Second World War, Turkey and countries of 'the West' did not lose any time in establishing a common, post-war institutional architecture: Turkey gained membership to the Council of Europe in 1949 and the North Atlantic Treaty Organisation (NATO) in 1952. Moreover, the country signed an Association Agreement with the European Economic Community (EEC) as early as 1959. This so-called Ankara Agreement entered into force in 1963. Since then, Ankara and Berlin have maintained a close association with each other through trade relations and the high number of people of Turkish origin living in Germany. This chapter's guiding assumption is that German-Turkish relations have always had a particular influence on Turkey's relations with the European Union (EU) and its institutional predecessors. By analysing the German Government's institutional preferences towards Turkey and how these were reflected in the government's narratives before Turkey became a candidate country to the EU in 1999, our study contributes to a better understanding of this *Unique Relationship* that extends well beyond high-level political relations by deeply affecting lives of citizens in both countries.[1]

Over recent years scholarly attention has mainly been focused on Germany's role in Turkey's EU accession process, with full membership negotiations having been initiated in October 2005. This is especially so in relation to the EU-Turkey statement in 2015.[2] However, it is important to

---

1 Cf. Turhan, Ebru/ Seufert, Günter. German Interest and Turkey's EU Accession Process: A Holistic Perspective. Istanbul, 2015; Turhan, Ebru. With or Without Turkey? The Many Determinants of the Official German Position on Turkey's Accession Process. In: Ebru Turhan (Ed.). German-Turkish Relations Revisited. The European Dimension, Domestic and Foreign Politics and Transnational Dynamics. Turkey and European Union Studies. Vol. 2. Baden-Baden, 2019, pp. 59–90.

2 Cf. Reiners, Wulf/ Tekin, Funda. Taking Refuge in Leadership? Facilitators and Constraints of Germany's Influence in EU Migration Policy and EU-Turkey Affairs during the Refugee Crisis. In: *German Politics*, 2020, Vol. 29; Hauge, Hanna-Lisa/

note that today's discourse about "the most difficult enlargement ever"[3] or "the never-ending story"[4] of Turkey's accession to the EU has its roots in the pre-accession phase stretching back over 40 years before the actual 'granting' of candidacy. Turkey's application for association with the EEC in 1959 and its subsequent Association Agreement of 1963 served as the main institutional basis of EU-Turkey relations. This Ankara Agreement aimed at establishing a Customs Union and freedom of movement for workers within a three-step approach to preparation, transition and finalisation.[5] While the Customs Union was achieved in 1995, Turkey is still waiting for workers' freedom of movement.

After laying out the analytical framework of this chapter, we undertake an analysis of German narratives in government declarations chronologically, decade by decade, from 1959 to the 1990s. Thus, we have been able to disentangle the various complex developments during this period. By contextualising and comparing the official narrative of EU-German-Turkish relations with the German Government's factual intentions and interests, we seek to answer how and why the German Government employed certain narratives over time and to what extent these converge with its interests.

Wessels, Wolfgang. EU-Turkey Relations and the German Perspective. In: Elif Nuroğlu, Ela Sibel Bayrak Meydanoğlu, Enes Bayraklı (Eds.). Turkish German Affairs from an Interdisciplinary Perspective, Frankfurt am Main, 2015; Turhan, Ebru. The European Council Decisions Related to Turkey's Accession to the EU: Interests vs. Norms. Baden-Baden, 2012.

3 Grigoriadis, Ioannis N. Turkey's Accession to the European Union: Debating the Most Difficult Enlargement Ever. In: *SAIS Review of International Affairs*, 2006, Vol. XXVI, No. 1, pp. 147–160.

4 Müftüler-Baç, Meltem. The never-ending story: Turkey and the European Union. In: *Middle Eastern Studies*, 1998, Vol. 34, No. 4, pp. 240–258.

5 Cf. European Economic Communities. Agreement establishing an Association between the European Economic Community and Turkey (signed at Ankara, 12 September 1963). In: *Official Journal of the European Communities*, No. L 217, 29.12.1964.

2. The Analytical Framework: Official Narratives and German Interests

This section summarises the analysis' database, context and limitations.

2.1 Method

Narratives provide an "insight on how different people organize, process, and interpret information and how they move toward achieving their goals", suggesting "how the speakers make sense of the commonplace".[6] Furthermore, narratives can reveal speakers' perceptions of certain situations. They reflect "the speaker's view of what is canonical" – the mere mention of anything "unusual and exceptional" will immediately draw listeners' attention.[7] In the context of this chapter, though, we assume that the contrary may also be true; this means that the "spaces and silence"[8] in carefully selected and assessed language of official communications such as government declarations may not only convey what is "canonical",[9] but also what is considered sensitive or problematic and hence demanding special analytical attention. Thus, as adapted for our analysis, narratives by the German Government are defined as interpretations of the evolution, drivers, obstacles and goals associated with German/EU-Turkey relations, in other words justification strategies for certain behaviour.[10] Narrative analysis is based on the assumption that narratives play a critical role in the construction of political behaviour.[11] We pay particular attention to rather explicit attributions, such as 'friend' or 'bridge' that resonate for years and hence have strong potential to be remembered (and quoted) over time.[12]

---

6 Patterson, Molly/ Renwick Monroe, Kristen. Narrative in political science. In: *Annual Review of Political Science*, 1998, Vol. 1, p. 316.

7 Ibid.

8 Ibid.

9 Ibid.

10 Cf. Hauge, Hanna-Lisa, et al. Narratives of a contested relationship: Unravelling the debates in the EU and Turkey. FEUTURE Online Paper No. 28. Cologne, February 2019.

11 Cf. Tekin, Funda/ Schönlau, Anke. The EU-German-Turkish Triangle. A Conceptual Framework for Narratives, Perceptions and Discourse of a Unique Relationship. In this volume, pp. 9-30, p. 20.

12 Cf. Weise, Helena/ Tekin, Funda: German Narratives, Strategies and Scenarios of EU-Turkey Relations 2002–2018: Towards a Unique Partnership – Yet to be defined. In this volume, pp. 79-109, p. 80.

Analysis of the German official narrative is based on a qualitative document analysis of 30 government declarations dealing with Turkey between 1959 and 1999, thus prior to the country becoming a candidate for joining the EU (pre-accession phase). Government declarations in Germany are speeches by government members before the parliament that not only aim to specify the executive's political actions and policy proposals but also have a symbolic character.[13] Our data set comprises both declarations by chancellors as well as ministers responsible for foreign and internal affairs. In general, we assume that government declarations contain no spontaneous reactions, but rather have been carefully prepared in advance utilising diplomatic language. These declarations convey how the government 'makes sense' of the relations and deliberately leaves out what it does not want to discuss publicly. Hence, the official narrative does not necessarily correlate with public discussion or a single speaker's personal opinions, but instead is aimed at steering the government's actions as a whole. We thus imply an intentional use of narratives, driven by the unintentional sense-making of policy makers' reality at given points in time, dependent on the current cultural context.

To put the conveyed messages or narratives into context, we compare them with the German Government's factual intentions and interests. How are these intentions and interests expressed in official narratives, what goals and justifications in narratives are conveyed and what goals are pursued? Our analysis seeks to reveal whether the official narrative does indeed reflect all interests or whether there are (intentional) blind spots . To determine German interests – in other words, what kind of institutional arrangements it wants the EU to have with Turkey and why – this chapter draws on the *Akten zur Auswärtigen Politik der Bundesrepublik Deutschland* (AAPD): This is an edited compilation of files on the Foreign Policy of the Federal Republic of Germany that includes various kinds of confidential internal documents and reports declassified by the Federal Foreign Office after 30 years by law. It serves as a comprehensive source for background information on drivers of the German attitude towards Turkey,[14] complemented by a systematic secondary literature review.

---

13 Cf. Hoffebert, Richard I./ Klingemann, Hans-Dieter. The policy impact of party programmes and government declarations in the Federal Republic of Germany. In: *European Journal of Political Research*, 1990, Vol. 18, pp. 277–304, p. 280, p.285.

14 The editions consist of reports, personal letters, meeting minutes etc., giving insights and decisive added value to the analysis of the official documents. The Federal Foreign Office has commissioned the research centre *Institut für Zeitgeschichte* with publishing secret and non-secret files in commented volumes after 30 years

2.2 Four Narrative Dimensions in EU-German-Turkish Relations

We presume that German-Turkish bilateral relations have had a major impact on the development of EU-Turkey relations.[15] Hence German statements both on EU-Turkey relations and the bilateral state of relations are analysed. Our analysis is structured along the four decades between Turkey's bid for EEC Association in 1959 and EU candidacy in 1999, namely the 1960s, 1970s, 1980s and 1990s. Owing to the major political turning point of transition from Helmut Kohl's chancellorship (1982–1998) to Gerhard Schröder in 1998, the 1990s are divided into two separate sections. To enhance the comparability of official narratives over time, we distinguish four dimensions of content: In the specific historical context of this chapter, firstly, geostrategic arguments deal with Turkey's geopolitical significance for the European continent. Security related topics are the most important rationale from this perspective, such as Turkey's vital role as a pillar in NATO's security architecture due to its geographic characteristics. Secondly, Germany's value as Turkey's main trading partner would be reflected in the economic dimension in the official narrative. This category subsumes all references made to bilateral and multilateral trade, but also economic support schemes such as 'development aid'.[16] Thirdly, political aspects of discourse play a decisive role in the context of accession talks, referring to the first Copenhagen Criterion (political criteria), namely democracy, the rule of law, human rights as well as respect for and protection of minorities. Fourthly and finally, the societal dimension works with ascriptions of what Turkey's and Turkish identity actually 'is'. Religious, cultural identification and ascriptions determining norms, values and behaviour of individuals and groups as well as societal categories applied by the narrators, for instance 'us' vs. 'them', are reflected in this category. A prominent image here refers to Turkey and Turkish people serving as a bridge between Western and Eastern civilizations.

---

of closure. At the time of writing, files up to 1987 were accessible. Hereafter, footnotes will abbreviate the Akten zur Auswärtigen Politik as 'AAPD'.

15 Cf. Tekin/ Schönlau, The EU-German-Turkish Triangle, 2022, p. 9-30.

16 The contemporary term 'development cooperation' aims to underline partnership and equality of the involved actors.

3. *Germany and EU-Turkey Relations – Pre-dominant Narratives over Time*

The following analysis, covering four decades of German official narratives and interests in EU-Turkey relations, identifies resemblances, continuations and gaps therein. The 1960s were mainly driven by security interests and hence all developments in bilateral German-Turkish relations have to be viewed in this context. Although security cooperation continued, a strain was put on the relationship through a fear of further labour migration from Turkey to Germany in the face of Germany's stuttering economy following the oil crisis. Whilst reservation about migration from Turkey forms no part of the 1970's official narrative, this does become increasingly visible in the 1980s and 1990s, at which time Turkey gained more presence in the official German narrative. While Turkey was mentioned 25 times in total between 1959 and 1989, the words 'Turkey' or 'Turkish' appear 133 times in government declarations during the 1990s alone. Both the length and relevance of statements on Turkey increase. Accordingly, with the decisive change of administration from Kohl to Schröder, the 1990s take the major share of analysis in this chapter.

3.1 *The 1960s: Turkey as Partner of the West*

Germany's emerging post-war economy (*Wirtschaftswunder*) needed additional workers to supply its companies: A German-Turkish bilateral recruitment agreement came into force in 1961, Germany already having become Turkey's main importer of goods in 1949 and 1950. Although the recruitment of Turkish guest workers was certainly in Germany's interests,[17] such considerations were only one part of its enhanced engagement with Turkey.

Internationally, the 1960s landscape was characterised by evolving bipolarity during the Cold War era, with Turkey and Germany becoming part of the Western security architecture. Both countries supported each other's inclusion in multilateral frameworks: Turkey opted for Germany's inclusion in NATO, which was achieved in 1955, whilst Germany supported

---

17 Cf. Mayer, Matthias M. Germany's preferences on the Ankara Agreement: Ministerial actors between Cold War security concerns, Turkish European ambitions and the Wirtschaftswunder. Paper to be given at Fourth Pan-European Conference on EU Politics of the ECPR – Standing Group on the European Union, 2008, p. 19; AAPD 1962. Botschafter Grewe, Washington, an das Auswärtige Amt. Dok. No. 230, pp. 1030f.

Turkey's bid for EEC Association for which it applied on 31 July 1959.[18] When Turkey and Greece applied for association to the EEC at roughly the same time in 1959,[19] the Council tried to handle the Greek and the Turkish application as equally as possible. While other members of the Community and the Commission argued that more time was needed to assess these particular applications,[20] the German delegation promoted acceleration of this process for Turkey.[21]

The German Government's focus was on geopolitical, security-related aspects of German-Turkish relations and Turkey's position in NATO: Against a background of increased Union of Soviet Socialist Republics (USSR) activity in the Cyprus conflict and partly converging interests between the USSR and Turkey, for instance, Germany and the United States opted to grant defence assistance for Turkey to keep it closely attached to the West.[22] Germany contributed about 58.5 million US Dollars[23], one third of the EEC's financial package, to aid financially troubled Turkey within the framework of the Association Agreement and provided additional monetary support within the 'OECD Consortium to Aid Turkey'.[24]

---

18 Schreiben der Botschaft der Türkischen Republik, Herr Hikmet BENSAN, an den Präsidenten der Kommission der Europäischen Wirtschaftsgemeinschaft, Herrn Professor Hallstein, vom 31. Juli 1959, betrifft Assoziierung der Türkei mit der Europäischen Wirtschaftsgemeinschaft. Brussels, 5 September 1959. In: Archives Historiques, Conseil de la Communauté Économique Européenne, Conseil de la Communauté Européenne de l'Energie Atomique, CM 2/1963, No: 0841.

19 Greece in June 1959, Turkey in July 1959.

20 Italy and France were particularly reluctant in regard to Turkey's association; Rat der Europäischen Wirtschaftsgemeinschaft. Einleitende Aufzeichnungen, 7. Oktober 1959, R/739/59, pp. 4f; AAPD 1962. Gespräch des Bundesministers Schröder mit dem französischen Außenminister Couve de Murville in Paris. Dok. 272, pp. 1209f.

21 Cf. Rat der Europäischen Wirtschaftsgemeinschaft. Einleitende Aufzeichnungen. 9. September 1959, R/644/59.

22 Cf. AAPD 1962. Botschafter von Broich Oppert, Ankara, an das Auswärtige Amt. Dok. No. 52, pp. 256f; AAPD 1965. Aufzeichnungen des Botschafters von Walther. Dok. No. 71, p. 302; Dok. No. 451, p. 1863; AAPD 1967. Dok. No. 419, pp. 1603f. In fact, the Cyprus conflict came with some tricky implications for Bonn: Against the background of its own division in Eastern and Western Germany, it aimed at finding a balanced position between Turkey and the Cypriots.

23 Cf. Mayer. Germany's preferences, p. 19.

24 Cf. AAPD 1964. Dok. No. 21, pp. 115f; Dok. No. 47, p. 232.; A consortium established by the OECD to coordinate financial donors in support for Turkey; A similar consortium was established for Greece, cf. Kuchenberg, Thomas C. The OECD Consortium to Aid Turkey. In: *Studies in Law and Economic Development*, 2(1), pp. 91–106.

Furthermore, the Federal Foreign Office behind closed doors justified economic support for Turkey with its position as a "cornerstone within our system of defence"[25] and frequently underlined this position with its partners, such as France.[26]

Germany's official narrative at the time largely converges with its interests. As such, no special attention is given to Turkey in government declarations: Only 2 out of 64 government declarations in the 1960s refer to Turkey.[27] If Turkey is mentioned at all, it is within the geostrategic dimension, underlining Turkey's importance in the context of "multilateral constructions"[28] and "bordering the Soviet Union".[29] Chancellor Kurt Georg Kiesinger describes German-Turkish relations as "traditionally friendly".[30] The economic dimension, namely the Association Agreement, was mentioned only once.[31] The recruitment agreement itself did not form part of any government declaration. Political reservations about the Turkish political system's volatility and identity ascriptions of Turkish people did not play a major role at that time. The Turkish military coup of 27 May 1960 did not affect the German Government's official narration of Turkey at all, to the extent that it was not even mentioned in official declarations.

Although we will argue within this chapter that the German Government deliberately avoided any mention of labour migration in its official narrative over the following years, the low number of references in government declarations from the 1960s does not yet allow us to draw such conclusions. At this stage it is more likely that relations with Turkey were not an issue of public priority, given that migration was only just about to start. The focus on geostrategic and economic considerations in the official narrative followed a general trend in Europe at that time. *Aydın-Düzgit et. al.* conclude from their analysis of public discourse that the fear of "losing Turkey to Soviets"[32] overrode any value-based differentiation.

---

25 Bundesarchiv. 72. Kabinettssitzung am 8. April 1963, https://www.bundesarchiv. de/cocoon/barch/1000/k/k1963k/kap1_2/kap2_17/para3_7.html [30.11.2019].
26 Cf. AAPD 1964. Dok. No. 47, p. 232; Dok. No. 48, p. 237; Dok. No. 188, p. 779.
27 In 2016, about 80 percent of German government declarations mentioned Turkey. Cf. Weise/ Tekin, German Narratives, Strategies and Scenarios of EU-Turkey Relations 2002–2018, 2022, p. 105.
28 Deutscher Bundestag. Regierungserklärung. 87. Sitzung, 5.11.1959, p. 4692.
29 Deutscher Bundestag. Regierungserklärung.185. Sitzung, 25.09.1968, p. 10053.
30 Ibid.
31 Cf. Deutscher Bundestag. Regierungserklärung. 90. Sitzung, 18.10.1963, p. 4198.
32 Aydın-Düzgit, Senem et al. Turkish and European Identity Constructions in the 1815–1945 Period. FEUTURE Online Paper No. 4. Cologne, July 2017, p. 7.

3.2 The 1970s: Military Alliances in Times of Conflict

The Cold War and oil crisis very much shaped the 1970s international agenda. Turkey's occupation of Northern Cyprus in 1974 became a security issue for NATO.[33] Moreover, a gradual alignment of Turkey and the USSR with ongoing financial offers by the latter led to tensions within NATO.[34] Greece's decision to drop out of military engagement within NATO after the second phase of Turkey's intervention in Cyprus left German officials in fear of leaving NATO's 'southern flank' exposed. Despite its controversial actions, military assistance to Turkey was perceived as strengthening NATO in the region.[35]

At the same time, German officials were aiming to prevent broader public discussion on military shipments to Turkey against this background.[36] This strategy was perhaps based on a government impression that German citizens would rather support Greece in the conflict after Turkey's second intervention phase. Furthermore, the German Government was seeking to prevent a public perception in which the country needed to step into the (financial) breach in place of the US which had imposed an arms embargo on Turkey (1975–1978) in response to the conflict.[37] While financial and military support continued, with Germany further consolidating its role

---

33 Richter, Heinz A. Historische Hintergründe des Zypernkonflikts. In: *Aus Politik und Zeitgeschichte*, 12/2009, pp. 3–8.

34 Cf. AAPD 1977. Gesandter Peckert, Ankara, an das Auswärtige Amt. Dok. No.75, pp. 380f.

35 Between 1964 and 1995, Turkey and Greece received (material) grants of about 9 billion German Mark in total through four bilateral agreements, which underlines the German *Sonderrolle* (special role). The importance of this dimension to the Turkish-German relations is underlined by the fact that Germany has continuously been Turkey's biggest European distributor of arms, only surpassed by the United States, despite the fact that the US did not deliver for a long time. Cf. AAPD 1974. Dok. No. 271, pp. 1201f; Deutscher Bundestag. Unterrichtung durch den Bundesrechnungshof. Drucksache 13/2600, 1998, pp. 85f; Kramer, Heinz/Reinkowski, Maurus. Die Türkei und Europa. Eine wechselhafte Beziehungsgeschichte Stuttgart, 2008, p. 142; SIPRI Stockholm International Peace Research Institute Arms Transfer Database, https://www.sipri.org/databases/armstransfers/background [22.08.2019].

36 Cf. AAPD 1974. Dok No. 271, p. 1201, Footnote No. 5; AAPD 1975. Dok. No. 32, pp. 175f; Dok. No. 226, p. 1054. During 1975, the arms embargo held up by American congress posed an increasing threat to NATO, up to inoperability of the Turkish forces due to lack of supplies. The American Government's bid to Germany to step into the breach contradicted Germany's commitment to friendly, balanced relations with both sides in the conflict.

37 Cf. AAPD 1974. Dok. No. 238, pp. 1034f.

as Turkey's advocate in Europe,[38] domestically, the German Government started to seal itself off from Turkish migration. Between 1961 and 1974, nearly 650,000 workers had migrated from Turkey to Germany. Migrants from Turkey living in Germany accounted for approximately 80 percent of more than 1 billion US Dollars in foreign remittances to Turkey during the early 1970s.[39] Over the course of the 1970s, this issue of labour migration increasingly caused strains within the relationship. In the Additional Protocol to the Ankara Agreement of 23 November 1970, the Member States and Turkey had agreed to implement step by step the freedom of movement of workers between 1976 and 1986. Germany in particular as number one destination for Turkish workers became increasingly hesitant due to its own labour market situation.[40] In 1973, the German Government terminated the bilateral recruitment agreement and was looking to restrict family reunion – a fact that was not reflected in German Government declarations.[41] Although frequently discussed amongst the Member States, this issue has not been mentioned at all in the declarations.

Germany's official narrative about Turkey focused on the Cyprus conflict's impact and its geopolitical implications. In summary, the narrative was one on a *Complicated Military Ally*. Foreign Minister Hans-Dietrich Genscher carefully underlined that bilateral financial assistance for Greece[42] following its military regime was aimed to balance relations with both countries as a contribution to stabilisation of this conflictual region: "Support for Greece is not meant to be against Turkey, an ally, with whom we have friendly and close relations for many years without interruptions."[43] On the instruments of membership and association,

38 Kramer/Reinkowski. Türkei und Europa, p. 142, p. 146.

39 Cf. Akkuş, Güzin Emel. The Contribution of the Remittances of Turkish Workers in Germany to the Balance of Payments of Turkey (1963–2013). In: Elif Nuroğlu, Ela Sibel Bayrak Meydanoğlu, Enes Bayraklı (Eds.): Turkish German Affairs from an Interdisciplinary Perspective. Frankfurt am Main 2015, pp. 185–212, pp. 197f.

40 AAPD 1976. Dok. No. 421, pp. 1118f; Dok. No. 422, pp. 1120f; Dok. No. 261. pp. 1194f; Dok. No. 283, pp. 1297f.

41 Bade, Klaus J. Als Deutschland zum Einwanderungsland wurde. In: Zeit Online, 24.11.2013, https://www.zeit.de/gesellschaft/zeitgeschehen/2013-11/einwanderung -anwerbestopp [01.12.2019].

42 To support a new democratic beginning in Greece, Genscher offered to consider financial assistance (*Kapitalhilfe*) to the new Greek Government of 60 million euro and further support of the same amount (*Projekthilfe*) in the two consecutive years.

43 Deutscher Bundestag. Hans-Dietrich Genscher. Plenary Protocol 7/115. Bonn, 18.09.1974, p. 7700.

Chancellor Helmut Schmidt stated that bringing countries such as Greece, Portugal, Spain and Turkey closer to the Community would promote their economic development and thereby develop or stabilise their democratic order.[44] While this statement suggests the political dimension's increasing importance in discourse, one has to note that the second military intervention by Turkey in 1971 gained little German attention. Even though the German Bundestag held a debate on 12th March 1971 about Turkish *Gastarbeiter* (guest workers) in Germany, the coup was not mentioned in this or the following debate two weeks later.[45]

In conclusion, Germany's interest in Turkey during the 1970s became more ambivalent compared with the 1960s, a development not fully reflected in government declarations from that time. However, it is possible to identify the geostrategic dimension's continuing importance. The sensitive issue of labour migration is not reflected in government declarations of the 1970s, although labour migration played a major role in bilateral relations. Turkey did not play a role in government declarations (only 2 out of 93 declarations mentioned Turkey), though the situation in Cyprus and its implications for NATO continued to be of serious concern for the German Government and its (transatlantic) partners. First indications of an increase in the importance of democratic order did not lead to addressing negative developments in the official narrative. Hence, we argue that the German Government subordinated all concerns regarding migration or political order to balanced relations with the Turkish Government in view of geostrategic considerations. Consequently, general issues of concern were not addressed, but instead geostrategic aspects were underlined.

3.4 The 1980s: Growing Conflict

The military coup in Turkey on 12 September 1980 and the following military rule had consequences for the country internationally. The Parliamentary Assembly of the Council of Europe discussed the possibility suspending Turkey's representation.[46] Countries with former military regimes such as Spain, Portugal and Greece argued that Turkey's new military leaders could use membership in the Council of Europe as legitimisation

---

44 Cf. Deutscher Bundestag. Helmut Schmidt. Plenary Protocol 8/5. Bonn, 16.12.1976, p. 48.
45 Cf. Deutscher Bundestag. Plenary Protocol 6/108. Bonn, 12.03.1971; Deutscher Bundestag. Plenary Protocol 6/109. Bonn, 24.03.1971.
46 Cf. Council of Europe. Statue of the Council of Europe. Art. 8.

of their control. From Germany's point of view, though, the Council of Europe would lose its main instrument for exerting influence on Turkey if it stopped the dialogue and hence pushed to keep relations open.[47] During its Council of the European Communities (EC) presidency in 1983, the German Government tried to end the blockade of EC financial assistance ('fourth financial protocol') to Turkey by promoting Turkish economic and social development as well as investments in industry and infrastructure. However, all efforts failed to convince other EC Members and the European Parliament.[48] Moreover, the German Government gave its consent to retain ongoing NATO deployment, explaining that continuation would be in the interests of the alliance's unity, which was of foremost importance.[49]

While Germany took over a strong position in European and international arenas to maintain good relations primarily due to security considerations, at a bilateral level Germany suspended its visa exemption for Turkish nationals in 1980. France soon followed Germany's example.[50] The establishment of an area of freedom of movement in 1986, as foreseen by the Ankara Agreement, was regarded a "sword of Damocles"[51] by German authorities: In light of a tight German labour market situation and based on perceived "difficulties regarding the integration of foreigners"[52] the German Government was eager to provide Turkey with measures that were aimed to support the Turkish Government in ceasing its labour

---

47 Cf. Szatkowski, Tim. Die Bundesrepublik Deutschland und die Türkei 1978 bis 1983. Oldenbourg, 2016, pp. 78f.
48 Cf. Wessels, Wolfgang. Die Europäische Politische Zusammenarbeit. In: Werner Weidenfeld/ Wolfgang Wessels (Eds.): Jahrbuch der Europäischen Integration 1983. Baden-Baden, 1984, pp. 227–239, p. 235.
49 Cf. AAPD 1980. Gesandter Pfeffer, Brüssel (NATO), an Auswärtiges Amt. Dok. No. 269, p. 1387.
50 Cf. Council of Europe. Minutes of the 67th Session of the Committee of Ministers, held on 16 October 1980, 1980, CM (80) PV 4, p. 26; Parliamentary Assembly of the Council of Europe. Situation in Turkey, 1980, Recommendation 904.
51 Pfuhl, Detlef. Außenbeziehungen. In: Werner Weidenfeld/Wolfgang Wessels (Eds.): Jahrbuch der Europäischen Integration 1986/1987, Baden-Baden, 1987, pp. 222–231, p. 227.
52 AAPD 1985. AA Referat 411, 13 September 1985. In: AAPD 1986, Aufzeichnung des Ministerialdirigenten Trumpf, p. 57: „Arbeitsmarktlage und Schwierigkeiten bei der Integration von Ausländern haben die Bundesregierung dazu veranlaßt, den Anwerbestopp zu erlassen und später auch den Familiennachzug einzuschränken."

emigration.[53] The German Government facilitated a revival of association talks and release of financial assistance, because it perceived Turkey's application for EC membership on 14 April 1987 as buying time so that final decisions could be made on freedom of movement.[54]

In bilateral meetings with British Prime Minister Margaret Thatcher and Turkish Prime Minister Turgut Özal, German Chancellor Kohl stated that problems with Turkish guestworkers in Germany were based on their cultural background. He pointed to different religious identities, stressing that Germany would not become an immigration country.[55] This was at a time when anti-immigrant sentiments and talk of guestworkers returning to their country of origin characterised German public debate.[56] Kohl's stance was to remain unchanged during the 1990s.[57] In this context, Foreign Minister Genscher warned the Turkish Ministry of Foreign Affairs in 1986, that early application for EC membership and the related migration issue could become a point of discussion in the upcoming German elections.[58]

In Germany's official narrative, Turkey was mentioned in eight government declarations between 1980 and 1983, while the declarations in the following years until 1990 do not contain a single reference. All references made from 1980 to 1983 belong to the geostrategic dimension, accompanied by economically coined arguments.[59] Support for Turkey, amongst other countries, was part of a "Western strategy to strengthen

---

53 Cf. AAPD 1987. Aufzeichnung der Ministerialdirektoren Jelonek und Freiherr von Richthofen, p. 695.

54 The EC-Turkey Association Council had met last time before the Coup of 12 September 1980. Cf. AAPD 1986. Aufzeichnung des Ministerialdirigenten Trumpf, pp. 58f; AAPD 1987. Aufzeichnung der Ministerialdirektoren Jelonek und Freiherr von Richthofen, p. 697.

55 Cf. AAPD 1985. Dok No. 129, Gespräch des Bundeskanzlers Kohl mit Ministerpräsidentin Thatcher in Chequers, p. 654; AAPD 1985. Dok. No. 185, Gespräch des Bundeskanzlers Kohl mit Ministerpräsident Özal in Ankara, p. 987.

56 Cf. Der Spiegel. ‚Nimm deine Prämie und hau ab' Ausländerpolitik: Koalitionsstreit um die Wende, No. 34/1983, pp.26 – 31.

57 Cf. Müftüler-Baç, Meltem. Through the Looking Glass: Turkey in Europe. In: *Turkish Studies*, 2000, Vol. 1, pp. 21–35; Turhan. European Council decisions, p. 172, 200.

58 Turhan. European Council decisions, pp. 98f; Secretariat du Conseil des Communities Europeennes. Letter of Prime Minister Turgut Özal to the President of the Council of Ministers of the European Communities, Léo Tindemans. Ankara, 14th April 1987.

59 Cf. Deutscher Bundestag. Helmut Schmidt. Plenary Protocol 8/203. Bonn, 28.02.1980, p. 16171.

the independence of states that want to assert their independency against a new hegemony",[60] stated Foreign Minister Genscher in January 1980. Turkey is characterised as a "important partner" due to its "strategic location".[61] Culturally infused sentiments in domestic politics regarding Turkish migration were clearly compartmentalised away from strategic interests: "(T)his allied country (Turkey) as a participant of the Islamic Conference of Islamabad is a proof that the pursuit of Islamic interests and objectives and the objectives of the Western Defence Alliance are not opposites but compatible".[62]

During the 1980s, the political component in the German official narrative gains strength: Accession of Spain and Portugal and association of Turkey would "strengthen Europe's stability".[63] The state of Turkey's political system caused worries in Germany.[64] Foreign Minister Genscher addressed Turkey's role within NATO as a "community of values", calling Turkey to "come back to democracy",[65] referring to the coup of 1980. As outlined in the sections above, the military coups of the previous two decades had not been addressed in government declarations.

Germany followed a rather dual approach during the 1980s. While the 1973 coup had not gained much attention, the narrative of *political concern* becomes more present in the 1980s. Narratives belonging to the geostrategic dimension (*important partner*) remain the most important in official discourse followed by those related to economic issues, with both dimensions are being closely intertwined. As with the prior decade, constraining Turkish migration to Germany and its rationale were not part of official discourse, although arguments referring to political and identity issues were slowly gaining in importance.

---

60 Deutscher Bundestag. Hans-Dietrich Genscher. Plenary Protocol 8/196. Bonn, 17.01.1980, p. 15599.
61 Deutscher Bundestag. Helmut Schmidt. Plenary Protocol 8/203. Bonn, 28.02.1980, p. 16188.
62 Deutscher Bundestag. Hans-Dietrich Genscher. Plenary Protocol 8/203. Bonn, 28.02.1980, pp. 16188f.
63 Deutscher Bundestag. Helmut Kohl. Plenary Protocol 10/4. Bonn, 04.05.1983, p. 69.
64 Cf. Turhan. European Council decisions, p. 108.
65 Deutscher Bundestag. Hans-Dietrich Genscher. Plenary Protocol 10/13. Bonn, 15.06.1983, p. 691.

3.5 A Rocky Road to Candidacy: The 1990s Under Helmut Kohl

Whilst some have argued that Turkey's membership bid "fell on deaf ears"[66] after the end of Cold War, Turkey's geostrategic importance in the Western security architecture remained emphatically relevant. With emerging conflicts in the Balkans,[67] the Caucasus and the Middle East,[68] it could be said that the country was at the crossroads of almost every conflict affecting Europe.[69] Hence, Germany finds itself now in a position of constant conflict between its strategic interests[70] in Turkey and domestic politics – considerations that were of less importance in previous decades.

Although Helmut Kohl's chancellorship began in 1982, Turkey was in fact not part of government declarations until the early 1990s, at which time there was a sharp increase in the number of mentions.[71] During that period, EU-German relations with Turkey became increasingly important in domestic politics. This development was mainly driven by an 'integration debate' amongst the German public, especially in relation to the 'Kurdish question', while at the same time there was a surge of right-wing block activities in the shape of violent attacks on foreign nationals or people of foreign descent living in Germany.

For the first time in 1992 Kohl added the identity dimension to a government declaration. He stated that "Turkish people living and working here (were) important 'bridges' between our peoples",[72] but added that the government would not accept domestic Turkish conflicts as issues that should be dealt with on German territory. This was set against the Kurd-

---

66 Müftüler-Baç, Meltem. Turkey's Role in the EU's Security and Foreign Policies. In: *Security Dialogue*, 2000, Vol. 31, pp. 489–502, p. 489.

67 Cf. Deutscher Bundestag. Gerhard Schröder. Plenary Protocol 14/41. Berlin, 08.06.1999, p. 3485.

68 Cf. Hauge, Hanna-Lisa et al. Mapping milestones and periods of past EU-Turkey relations. FEUTURE Working Paper, 2016, p. 14.

69 Cf. Tirman, John. Improving Turkey's "Bad Neighbourhood" Pressing Ankara for Rights and Democracy. In: *World Policy Journal*, 1998, Vol. 15, pp. 60–67, p. 61.

70 Cf. Deutscher Bundestag. Helmut Kohl. Plenary Protocol. 12/2. Bonn, 14.01.1991, p. 22; Deutscher Bundestag. Helmut Kohl. Plenary Protocol. 12/5, Bonn, 30.01.1991, p. 68.

71 The following section is mainly based on secondary literature. By the time of writing, the *Akten zur Auswärtigen Politik* were available until 1987.

72 Deutscher Bundestag. Helmut Kohl. Plenary Protocol 12/87. Bonn, 02.04.1992, p. 7176; Deutscher Bundestag. Klaus Kinkel. Plenary Protocol 12/218. Bonn, 13.04.1994.

ish-Turkish conflict having recently become an issue of German domestic security:

"Like the two million Turkish citizens who live here in Germany, the several hundred thousand Kurdish people among them are welcome guests and fellow citizens in Germany who can count on our care. But it is evident that there are basic rules of hospitality in every country of the world: Whoever makes use of it has to respect the law and order of the host country".[73]

In the full original German quote, the term 'hospitality' appears four times. As such, Kohl's statement not only creates proximity between Turkish (and Kurdish, in this context) and German people, but also at the same time a certain distance. This distance is reflected in a quote of Foreign Minister Klaus Kinkel in which Turkey is regarded as being *European with exceptions:*

"Turkey belongs to the European family. But at the same time we owe an open word to our Turkish friends. We must not conceal either the problem of freedom of movement or the major problems, such as the human rights situation or the Kurdish question, which Turkey in particular is called upon to overcome in order to create the necessary conditions for this".[74]

A unique feature of the Kohl administration's government declarations in the 1990s – compared with all other administrations – is its explicit attribution of the word 'friend' to Turkey. From the 1960s to 1991 Turkey was mentioned only five times as one or one of many 'friends' or 'friendly states'.[75] Such expressions were also used by the Kohl administration to underline Turkey's geostrategic relevance amongst domestic critics and express grief as well as humility towards Turkey and the Turkish community in the context of arson attacks[76] against people of Turkish descent

---

73 Deutscher Bundestag. Klaus Kinkel. Plenary Protocol 12/218. Bonn, 13.04.1994, p. 18865.
74 Deutscher Bundestag. Klaus Kinkel. Plenary Protocol 13/210. Bonn, 11.12.1997, p. 19112.
75 Cf. Deutscher Bundestag. Kurt Georg Kiesinger. 5/185. Bonn, 25.09.1968, p. 10053; Deutscher Bundestag. Hans-Dietrich Genscher. 7/115. Bonn, 18.09.1974, p.7700; Deutscher Bundestag. Helmut Schmidt. 9/34. Bonn, 07.05.1981, p. 1712; Deutscher Bundestag. 10/4. Bonn, 04.05.1983, p. 69; Deutscher Bundestag. Helmut Kohl, 12/2. Bonn, 14.01.1991, p.21.
76 In the early 1990s, Germany's right-wing movement gained strength, culminating in attacks in different German towns. Between 1990 and 1992 alone, 42 people

in Germany.[77] Most of the time, though, this notion has been used only within messages containing criticism, mainly on the political dimension concerning Turkey's human rights situation. Accordingly, the notion of 'friend' can be assessed as justification strategy, putting Germany into the position of being able to criticise Turkey. It appears most frequently at a time of rather tense bilateral relations and in speeches by members of the Kohl government that was known to have a critical stance towards Turkey's accession to the European Union.[78]

In the 1990s, relations with Turkey and their portrayal in the official narrative became increasingly complex, linking different dimensions with each other, such as the geostrategic and the political, especially in 1992 with the "escalation of violence in southeast of Turkey" where "violence may not be a means of politics".[79] In view of the deteriorating human rights situation in Turkey, Germany even suspended its arms deployment there in 1995. "As part of the Western community of values – as member of NATO, the Council of Europe and Commission on Security and Cooperation in Europe (CSCE) – Turkey itself must be measured against European standards and obligations",[80] Kohl said.

In summary, the early 1990s are characterised by a diffuse picture towards Turkey. The Kohl administration was a proponent of the EU-Turkey Customs Union and stated to be further interested in an expansion of bilateral (trade) relations but continued to oppose Turkish accession to the community. Secondary literature and alleged statements from Kohl suggest that his personal rejection was based on cultural grounds and

---

died in right-wing attacks. Cf. Bundeszentrale für Politische Bildung. 25 Jahre Brandanschlag in Solingen, https://www.bpb.de/politik/hintergrund-aktuell/1619 80/brandanschlag-in-solingen [05.03.2020].

77 Cf. Deutscher Bundestag. Helmut Kohl. Plenary Protocol 12/162. Bonn, 16.06.1993, p. 13855f; Deutscher Bundestag. Klaus Kinkel. Plenary Protocol 12/218. Bonn, 13.04.1994, p. 18864f.

78 Cf. Deutscher Bundestag. Helmut Kohl. Plenary Protocol 12/78. Bonn, 02.04.1992, p. 7176; Deutscher Bundestag. Klaus Kinkel. 12/118. Bonn, 13.04.1994, pp. 18864f; Deutscher Bundestag. Klaus Kinkel. 13/145. Bonn, 05.12.1996, pp.13057f; Deutscher Bundestag. Klaus Kinkel. Plenary Protocol 13/210. Bonn, 11.12.1997, pp. 19112f.

79 Deutscher Bundestag. Hans-Dietrich Genscher. Plenary Protocol 12/20. Bonn, 17.04.1991, p. 1255; Deutscher Bundestag. Helmut Kohl. Plenary Protocol 12/87. Bonn, 02.04.1992, p. 7177; Deutscher Bundestag. Helmut Kohl. Plenary Protocol 12/162. Bonn, 16.06.1993, pp. 13855f; Deutscher Bundestag. Klaus Kinkel. Plenary Protocol 12/218. Bonn, 13.04.1994, p. 18864.

80 Deutscher Bundestag. Helmut Kohl. Plenary Protocol 12/87. Bonn, 02.04.1992, pp. 7176f.

concerns about Turkish migration. These issues are touched on, but not extensively covered in the narratives conveyed through government declarations. The usage of the 'friend' notion as justification strategy for criticism is an outstanding feature of the 1990's Kohl government.

3.6 A Turning Point: The 1990s Under Gerhard Schröder

The change of governments from Helmut Kohl to Gerhard Schröder in 1998 is said to represent a "catalyst of Turkish accession to the EU"[81]: While Kohl preferred an association with Turkey (and the Commonwealth of Independent States) under the exclusion of membership prospective, Schröder was a staunch supporter of Turkey's accession.[82] After a failed attempt to achieve Turkey's candidacy status at the German Council Presidency Cologne Summit in June 1999, Schröder worked extensively on achieving this goal at the following summit. In a personal letter to Prime Minister Bülent Ecevit, he expressed his desire to keep the channels for talks open and bring Turkey into the community.[83]

Between Schröder's election and the European Council's Helsinki Summit in 1999, when Turkey was granted candidate status, Turkey was mentioned in a number of speeches, two by Chancellor Schröder, one by Foreign Minister Joschka Fischer and one by Interior Minister Otto Schily (out of 16 government declarations in total). The fact that Schily was the first Minister of the Interior to have mentioned Turkey in a government speech underlines the importance that Turkey carried at that time in matters of German domestic security.[84] The issue of Turkish-Kurdish conflicts remained on the agenda as it had in the Kohl era. Unlike his predecessor, until the 1999 Helsinki Summit the Schröder government never used the 'friendship' notion. Schröder rather preferred to speak about (geopolitical) interests and responsibility when advocating for Turkey's integration:

---

81 Turhan, Ebru. Turkey's accession process: do member states matter? In: *Journal of Contemporary European Studies*, 2016, Vol. 4/24, pp. 463–477, p. 466.

82 Cf. Schwarz, Hans Peter. Helmut Kohl. Eine politische Biografie, 2nd edition, München, 2012, pp. 714f.

83 Cf. Schöllgen, Gregor. Gerhard Schröder. Die Biographie, München, 2015, pp. 453f.

84 Cf. Deutscher Bundestag. Otto Schily. Plenary Protocol 14/20. Bonn, 23.02.1999, p. 1385.

References to the geostrategic dimension continued under Schröder and became especially relevant in regard to the Kosovo crisis.[85] For him, Turkey remained an "important and weighty partner"[86] for Europe as well as the whole region. He revives the narrative of a *geostrategic partner*. Schröder's narrative, however, has a different 'moral of the story'[87] than his predecessor Kohl's: Europeans had an interest in supporting Turkish democrats and winning them over to 'European ways', in terms of policies and shared values.[88] Schröder held that one cannot emphasise Turkey's strategic importance for Europe and NATO without offering a membership perspective beyond the Customs Union. As such, statements in the political dimension dominate both Schröder's chancellery and the 1990s more generally, with the EU perceiving itself "not as a Club of the Christian Occident, but as a community of values".[89] A Turkey, that not only admits but really applies these values, would be welcomed as a member of the EU, Schröder said.[90] Even though he favoured Turkey's accession, he emphasised his preference for a "European Turkey".[91]

4. Conclusion

Analysis of the EU-German-Turkish triangle can present itself as a cumbersome process, given the relationship's age and complexity. Narrative analysis of selected documents has served as a useful tool for structuring the multifaceted nature of this relationship. Supported by the AAPD's insights into German foreign policy, it has been possible to show how German interests regarding Turkey's rapprochement process with the EU was manifested in official narratives throughout different decades.

Having said that, 1960s and 1970s provided few examples of declarations which could be analysed, despite Germany's clear interests and active contributions to a relationship that was dominated by geostrategic consid-

---

85 Cf. Deutscher Bundestag. Gerhard Schröder. Plenary Protocol 14/41. Berlin, 08.06.1999, p. 3487.

86 Ibid.

87 Cf. Tekin/ Schönlau, The EU-German-Turkish Triangle, 2022, p. 120.

88 Cf. Deutscher Bundestag. Gerhard Schröder. Plenary Protocol 14/41. Berlin, 08.06.1999, p. 3487.

89 Deutscher Bundestag. Gerhard Schröder. Plenary Protocol 14/79. Berlin, 16.12. 1999, p. 7215. Argument repeated on page 7220.

90 Cf. Deutscher Bundestag. Gerhard Schröder. Plenary Protocol 14/79. Berlin, 16.12.1999, p. 7215.

91 Schöllgen. Gerhard Schröder, p. 454.

erations. The Cold War alone seemed sufficient explanation for Germany to support Turkey's economic development and stability through EC association.

Turkey's geostrategic position has been its most significant asset during the pre-accession phase – even though it could not balance the political and societal/identity related concerns and 'drawbacks'. German attempts to restrict migration from Turkey to Germany became more of an issue in the mid-1970s. From that time on, this sensitive topic was of great concern to the German authorities, albeit not directly addressed in government declarations. This duality continued in the 1980s: the geostrategic role dominated discourse, but political aspects such as Turkey's state of democracy started to gain in importance, with early indications being identified during the 1980s, reflecting the EC's evolving self-conception from an economic actor into a community with shared values. Those factors were increasingly associated with Turkey's stability, with regard both to its economy and geostrategic position, while the migration issue – and closely linked thereto the identity dimension – is left out of the official narrative. An expectation of increasing migration from Turkey to the EC effectively put a brake on bilateral institutional development, which was driven by the German perspective. The German side was aware that the perceived cultural incompatibility was a sensitive issue and avoided addressing such concerns in the official narrative for a long time. Accordingly, narrative analysis is necessarily incomplete when looking only at what is being said. Equally important is to look at what is not being said.

The 1990s differ from previous decades. Firstly, the quantity and quality of statements related to Turkey increased in official discourse. This increase underlines a growing relevance for the German audience, especially in relation to German domestic politics, not least with the Turkish-Kurdish conflict being raised as a question of German domestic security. Secondly, all four dimensions are considered to be relevant. During both Kohl cabinets in the 1990s, the focus shifts to arguments in the political and identity dimensions, though geostrategic discourse remains important: Turkey stood "on the crossroads of almost every issue of importance",[92] such as conflicts in the Balkans, Cyprus, Iraq, Russia and the post-Soviet states. The economic and geostrategic dimensions appear to be intertwined, albeit economic issues do not play a major role. Use of the *friendship narrative* is very characteristic for the two terms: When the

---

92 Richard Holbrook cited in: Tirman. Improving Turkey's "Bad Neighbourhood", p. 61.

government aimed to address an issue delicate to the Turkish state – such as migration or the state of democracy – the friend notion appeared to justify that Germany had raised its voice on these matters.

This is in sharp contrast to the stance taken by Chancellor Schröder, who openly promoted Turkey's accession to the EU. He was a decisive proponent of Turkey's EU membership bid and facilitated the European Council's decision to grant Turkey candidate status. His narrative was geostrategic-political: Generating political stability in Turkey through accession was in the Union's geostrategic interest. From Schröder's perspective, Turkey needed the EU to take over responsibility – not a friend providing admonishing words. When Angela Merkel (CDU) became Chancellor in 2005 she continued this pragmatic enlargement policy towards Turkey only in the spirit of 'pacta sunt servanda' and in light of the close bilateral relationship.

German Narratives, Strategies and Scenarios of EU-Turkey Relations 2002–2018: Towards a Unique Partnership – Yet to be defined

Helena Weise, Funda Tekin

1. Introduction

Since the beginning of institutionalised relations between the European Union (EU) and Turkey in 1959, Germany has been seen as a key actor with decisive influence on the course of EU-Turkey relations.[1] Particularly under Gerhard Schröder's chancellorship, there were repeated references to the German potential as a 'driver' in starting and accelerating accession negotiations to the EU. Today, more than 20 years after the European Council's decision to grant Turkey the status of an EU accession country and more than 15 years after the start of these negotiations in 2005, Turkey's accession to the EU seems to be a highly unlikely scenario, although negotiations have not officially been suspended or cancelled. In 2018, the then-EU Commissioner for European Neighbourhood Policy and Enlargement Negotiations, Johannes Hahn, even referred to the accession procedure as an obstacle to a new, realistic form of strategic cooperation.[2]

This study aims to trace Germany's position on EU-Turkey relations both at parliamentary and governmental level in order to identify dominant narratives, preferred strategies and possible scenarios for Germany as an influential EU Member State. Germany and Turkey share a long-standing, exceptional connection. Not only is Germany home to the largest number and greatest share of people with Turkish roots living in Western

---

1 Cf. Schröder, Mirja/ Tekin, Funda. Institutional Triangle EU-Turkey-Germany: Change and Continuity. In: Ebru Turhan (Ed.). German-Turkish Relations Revisited. The European Dimension, Domestic and Foreign Politics and Transnational Dynamics. Turkey and European Union Studies. Vol. 2. Baden-Baden, 2019, pp. 31–57.

2 Cf. EU-Kommissar für Ende der Beitrittsgespräche mit der Türkei. In: Welt-Online, 06.11.2018, https://www.welt.de/newsticker/dpa_nt/infoline_nt/brennpunkte_nt/article183339692/EU-Kommissar-fuer-Ende-der-Beitrittsgespraeche-mit-der-Tuerkei.html [22.12.2020].

European countries, but also one of Turkey's main trading partners.[3] Our analysis of parliamentary debates and governmental declarations dealing with Turkey between the years 2002 and 2018 seeks to document and reflect both the Federal Government's official attitude and the fight for political opinion leadership in the Bundestag. Particular attention will be paid to discontinuities in the course of debates: How did perceptions as well as narratives on Turkey change and in response to which events? Hence, which strategies of cooperation can be derived from the respective views articulated in the German Parliament (Bundestag) and to which scenarios of institutionalised relationship do they point?

The chapter follows a constructivist approach, assuming that social reality comprises perception and experience. Accordingly, objective knowledge is not relevant. Following this conceptual view, articulated perceptions or stories told by relevant actors shape the reality of relations. Hence, the interpretations by German parliamentary representatives on EU integration and Turkey's development are assessed as forming a relevant cornerstone in the EU's stance towards this third country. The following section delineates the key concepts narratives, strategies and scenarios and provides information on the operationalisation of the analysis. Section 3 traces the key narratives in five identified periods between 2002 and 2018 in view of discontinuities that have been identified within governmental declarations and parliamentary debates as well as milestones from EU-Turkey relations. Section 4 provides a conclusive assessment of the findings and an outlook on future scenarios of EU-Turkey relations.

2. Narratives, Strategies, Scenarios

2.1 Conceptual Definition and Delineation

Within the framework of this analysis, 'narratives' are defined as collective stories or interpretations by German political actors relating to the evolution, drivers and actors of EU-Turkey relations.[4] These stories are examined, firstly, by their expression and language such as 'explicit attribu-

---

3 Cf. Schröder/ Tekin, Institutional Triangle EU-Turkey-Germany, 2019, pp.35 f.
4 Cf. Özbey, Ece Ebru et al. Narratives of a Contested Relationship: Unravelling the Debates in the EU and Turkey. In: Beken Saatçioğlu/ Funda Tekin (Eds). Turkey and the European Union. Key Dynamics and Future Scenarios. Turkey and European Union Studies. Vol. 3. Baden-Baden, 2021, pp. 31–56.

tions' (for instance *friend* or *key partner*). Secondly, we look at their 'plot', meaning a range of topics relating to four dimensions: political, economic, geopolitical and identity/ societal. As the research conducted has shown, these dimensions present themselves to varying degrees depending on events and topics, reacting to actions by the respective other within our examined triangle of Germany, Turkey and the EU.

Thirdly, stories demand an analysis of their underlying aims, which finds expression in voiced strategies towards certain scenarios. By evaluating the findings on explicit attributions and plots, one can identify three different 'strategies' that representatives of the German Government and Parliament articulate: (1) continuing EU accession negotiations, (2) breaking-off accession negotiations (or respectively not even opening them for the years before 2005) and finally (3) a twin-track strategy, suggesting a continuation of negotiations, while at the same time introducing new forms of institutional cooperation between the EU and Turkey. It is crucial to add that although topics and arguments from the four dimensions applied are used to promote strategies, there is no direct link between them. For example, a political argument does not necessarily speak for membership, an identity-based argument does not necessarily speak for breaking off negotiations, and so on.

All these strategies are linked to the same question: What is the shape of future cooperation with Turkey and how can it be implemented? This means that the three strategies are pointing to different possible 'scenarios' of a more or less institutionalised relationship between the two actors, with: (1) EU membership as the most institutionalised form, (2) a Unique Partnership as a form of strategic cooperation which includes certain privileges for Turkey, or (3) a relationship with Turkey as a neighbouring country that is marginally institutionalised and geared to short-term cooperation in certain areas of interest.

As with dimensions, strategies are used to pursue different aims or scenarios. For example, a party can demand the cancellation of accession negotiations either to stop any form of institutional cooperation or build a Unique Partnership in the long run. Similarly, accession negotiations can be advocated either to accomplish eventual membership or recognise that for the time being no other strategy is available for EU-Turkey cooperation. Consequently, this chapter differentiates between 'strategy' and 'scenario' when analysing stories emanating from the Bundestag. While strategies represent the underlying aim of a certain narrative, scenarios serve as models for the potential shape of an EU-Turkey relationship in the future. These scenarios do not serve as descriptive but rather analytical tools, mapping out variations of oversimplified realities that can serve as terms of reference for a scholarly assessment of future relations.[5]

Figure 2: The Concepts of Narratives, Strategies and Scenarios

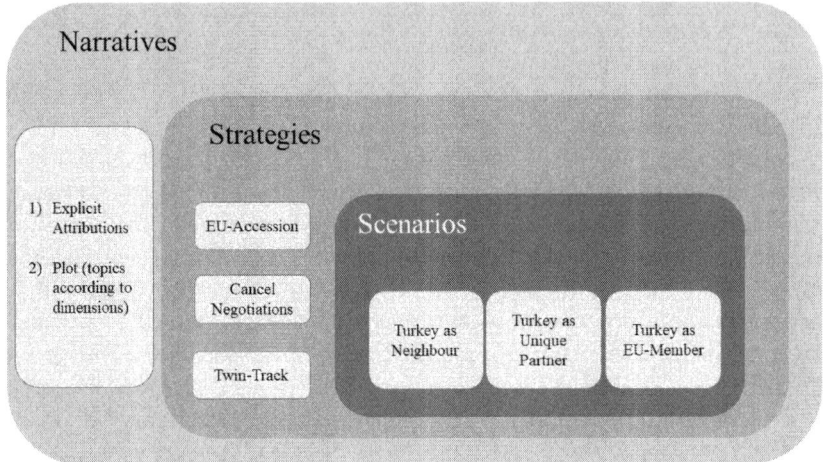

Source: own compilation.

In considering German narratives on EU-Turkey relations, there are certain practical reasons that limit the explanatory power of our analysis which stem from the overall contexts within which this relationship is set. Firstly, on a domestic level the Bundestag as actor of interest is a heterogeneous sum of parties' and individuals' voices, which influences the course of German Government, but does not determine it. Secondly, on the EU level, despite its influential role within the EU discourse on Turkey, Germany cannot take decisions alone but as party to agreements reached by 27 Member States. Thirdly and finally, how EU-Turkey relations unfold also depends heavily on developments, strategies and narratives originating from within Turkey itself,[6] albeit the EU's position does not necessar-

---

5 Cf. Tekin, Funda. The Future of EU-Turkey Relations: Exploring the Dynamics of Relevant Scenarios. In: Beken Saatçioğlu/ Funda Tekin (Eds). Turkey and the European Union. Key Dynamics and Future Scenarios. Turkey and European Union Studies Vol. 3. Baden-Baden, 2021, pp. 11–27, pp. 20 f.

6 Cf. Özbey et.al. Narratives of a Contested Relationship: Unravelling the Debates in the EU and Turkey. FEUTURE Online Paper No. 28. Cologne, February 2019.

ily have to match that adopted by Turkey.[7] That being said, this study provides a detailed analysis of one influential voice within the complex EU-Turkey relationship and the fight for dominant political opinion that stands behind it.

2.2 Operationalisation

Our study analyses plenary protocols from all debates in the Bundestag dealing with Turkey as well as governmental declarations between 17 October 2002 and 31 December 2018. A combination of data from governmental and parliamentarian levels, facilitates insights into official discourse as well as less diplomatically formulated debates involving Members of Parliament, which are publicly available, but nevertheless take place away from the public eye. The analysis requires consideration of full legislative periods in the Bundestag. It starts with the 15th period that begins on 17 October 2002, which coincidentally includes the European Council's announcement in 2004 about the opening of accession negotiations with Turkey[8] and ends at the beginning of the 18th period in 2018. This time frame of 16 years corresponds to 493 debates and 25 declarations which were coded and evaluated using the data analysis software MAXQDA. Our analysis is based on a quantitative approach in which segments are allocated to topics and dimensions with the help of a code system which was constantly expanded parallel to the coding, so that all relevant terms and topics addressed could be considered. A quantitative matrix of the plot was drafted by analysing how often which topics were discussed in the Bundestag. This matrix hints at irregularities in the debates, such as quantitative peaks or lows of specific topics and terms that deserve reconsideration to explain the change of story. The quantitative analysis was completed by an in-depth qualitative examination of every coded segment referring to Turkey so as to provide further knowledge about how the Bundestag positioned itself on certain topics and events. This

---

7 Cf. Ibid; Schröder, Mirja /Wessels, Wolfgang. The Energy Geopolitics of Turkey – From Classical to Critical Reading. In: Mirja Schröder / Marc-Oliver Bettzüge / Wolfgang Wessels (Eds.): Turkey as an Energy Hub? Contributions on Turkey´s Role in EU Energy Supply. Turkey and European Union Studies. Vol. 1. Baden-Baden, 2017, pp. 27–48.

8 Cf. Council of the European Union. Copenhagen European Council 12 and 13 December 2002. Presidency Conclusions. 15917/02. Brussels, 29.01.2003, https://www.consilium.europa.eu/media/20906/73842.pdf [22.12.2020].

qualitative analysis fills the gaps resulting from our quantitative research and is illustrated in this chapter by use of literal quotations in support of quantitative observations.

3. Tracing German Narratives on EU-Turkey Relations

3.1 Parliamentary Debates on the Opening of Accession Negotiations 2002– 2005: Sustainable European Perspective versus Privileged Partnership

At the 1999 European Council meeting in Helsinki, Turkey was officially granted candidate status for EU accession. Three years later at the European Council meeting in Copenhagen, the EU announced its decision to open accession negotiations in 2004. During these years, the possibility of EU accession was not only the exclusive topic of governmental declarations by Chancellor Gerhard Schröder in dealing with Turkey but also the most discussed issue within the thematic dispute on Turkey from a deeply polarised German Bundestag. While the coalition government of the Social Democratic Party (SPD) and the Greens strongly supported Turkey's EU membership bid, the Christian Democratic Union/Christian Social Union (CDU/CSU) as second largest faction in the Bundestag and opposition leader was generally critical towards prospects of Turkish EU accession. Under the leadership of Chancellor Angela Merkel, the CDU/CSU introduced the concept of a 'Privileged Partnership' with Turkey as an alternative model for full membership. It was not further specified but intended to deepen economic and security relations. "When you are talking about Europe these days, I believe it is a mistake considering the accession of Turkey to the European Union. Drop it! It is not for the benefit of the European Union",[9] stated Angela Merkel in October 2002.[10] In addition to the candidate state's weak economic performance or its high inflation rate[11] this position related more substantially to questions of identity and values. As Michael Glos (CSU) stated in December 2002: "Turkey is neither economically nor politically ready for an EU-accession. We are convinced that Europe is based on a common cultural and religious heritage.

---

9 Deutscher Bundestag. Dr. Angela Merkel. Plenary Protocol 15/4. Berlin, 29.10.2002, p. 68.

10 All literal quotations come from the plenary minutes of the Bundestag debates and were translated into English by the authors.

11 Cf. Deutscher Bundestag. Michael Glos. Plenary Protocol 15/4. Berlin, 29.10.2002, p. 88.

Turkey does not belong to the European cultural circle".[12] His colleague Georg Nüßlein was even more explicit in the parliamentary debate of November 2003: "The Christian-Jewish heritage remains the main source of identity for the European community of values. That is one reason why I am against Turkey's full membership".[13]

Contrary to this cultural and value-based refusal, the SPD-green coalition under Chancellor Gerhard Schröder felt some responsibility to offer Turkey a membership perspective after 40 years of association within the framework of the economics-driven Ankara Agreement in 1963. As early as his governmental declaration of 3 December 1999, Schröder stated:

> "Europe also has a responsibility towards Turkey. We cannot repeatedly emphasise its strategic importance for Europe, place a heavy burden on it within the North Atlantic Treaty Organisation (NATO), court it as an important regional power and commit it to European standards if we are not willing to offer a clear European perspective that goes beyond the existing Customs Union".[14]

He pursued the vision of a reconciliation process between non-fundamentalist Islam and European Enlightenment values.[15] Within this process, the governing parties were convinced that EU membership or at least the opening of accession negotiations could further enhance the reform process in Turkey. The Liberal Democratic Party (FDP) supported this view, observing that Turkey had clearly embarked upon a path of European values such as the rule of law, human dignity and democracy – a 'catch-up process' that was considered far more decisive than religion or geography and that had to be taken into consideration.[16] The key question was subsumed by the German Foreign Minister Joschka Fischer in 2002: "Can secular modernisation succeed on the basis of democracy and the rule of law in Turkey as one of the largest Islamic states?"[17] If so, this was seen as the answer to the strategic security question covering the entire

---

12 Deutscher Bundestag. Michael Glos. Plenary Protocol 15/13. Berlin, 04.12.2002, p. 874.

13 Deutscher Bundestag. Dr. Georg Nüßlein. Plenary Protocol 15/72. Berlin, 06.11.2003, p. 6178.

14 Schröder, Gerhard. Governmental Declaration, 03.12.1999, p. 7062.

15 Cf. Schröder, Gerhard. Governmental Declaration, 30.04.2004, p. 9587.

16 Cf. Deutscher Bundestag. Dr. Werner Hoyer. Plenary Protocol 15/148. Berlin, 16.12.2004, p.13790.

17 Deutscher Bundestag. Joschka Fischer. Plenary Protocol 15/4. Berlin, 29.10.2002, p. 96.

region, especially in light of a European perception that the fight against international terrorism after 9/11 should concentrate mostly on the EU's Eastern external borders.[18] Despite Turkey's major contribution to the EU's future stability within the geopolitical dimension, the proponents of a Turkish EU membership advocated democratic reforms in line with the EU's Copenhagen Criteria to be necessary prerequisites for any form of cooperation. This was also confirmed by Angelica Schwall-Düren, deputy chairwoman of the SPD faction for European affairs in the Bundestag, who said: "The existence of a stable democracy as well as the protection of human and minority rights have absolute priority over geostrategic considerations".[19]

For the period of these years prior to the opening of accession nego-tiations, this political dimension was by far the most dominant in the Bundestag, largely due to the debate on Turkey's EU accession and its democratic standards. The geopolitical dimension including frequently mentioned topics such as 'Securityand Stability' and 'NATO' as well as the identity dimension, including the topics of 'Religion' along with 'Euro-pean Values and Family', were at about equally important, constituting the thematic pools from which the parties derived their corresponding arguments. The SPD and Greens made use of the geostrategic argument in relation to Turkey's relevance for security and stability to advertise a sce-nario of EU membership. However, they subsumed this security gain un-der the political dimension. Only if Turkey implemented political reforms and succeeded in modernising could it guarantee a security advantage for the EU. In order to match the preferred scenario of full membership with a political diagnosis of the problem, they pursued the strategy of accession negotiations which would commit Turkey to reforms and European val-ues. Even though the CDU/CSU shared the assessment of all governing parties that problems in the areas of democracy, human rights and the rule of law were dominant, they used a different identity-based narrative. As can be seen in Figure 3 below, issues about Turkish religion and be-longing to the European family of values were raised more frequently by the CDU/CSU than any other party and were used to argue against the country's EU membership. Consequently, delegates spoke out against the

---

18 Cf. Deutscher Bundestag. Joschka Fischer. Plenary Protocol 15/13. Berlin, 04.12 2002, p. 922.

19 Deutscher Bundestag. Dr. Angelica Schwall-Düren. Plenary Protocol 15/16. Berlin, 19.12.2002, p.1193.

strategy of accession negotiations. Instead, from the outset they proposed a 'Privileged Partnership' that would meet the EU's geopolitical interests.

Figure 3: Identity Dimension by Party 2002–2005

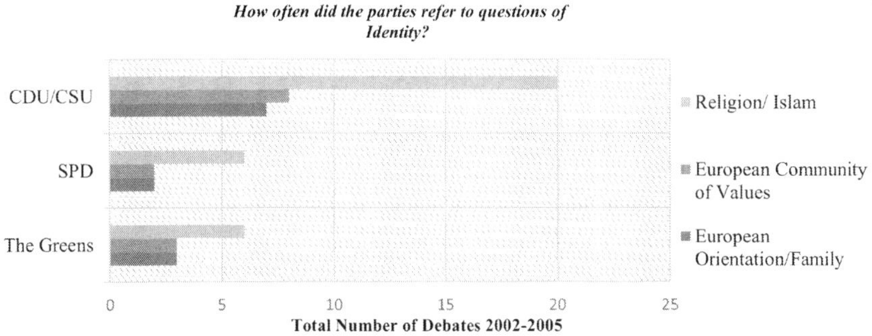

How often did the parties refer to questions of Identity?

CDU/CSU

SPD

The Greens

■ Religion/ Islam

■ European Community of Values

■ European Orientation/Family

0   5   10   15   20   25

Total Number of Debates 2002-2005

Source: own compilation.

In 2004, the European Commission eventually recommended that accession negotiations should be opened, based on the opinion that Turkey fulfilled the political criteria sufficiently.[20] Negotiation talks started in October 2005, only one month after German parliamentary elections in which the CDU/CSU gained a narrow majority of the votes and entered into a grand coalition with the SPD under Chancellor Angela Merkel. In her very first governmental declaration on 30 November 2005, Merkel immediately addressed Turkey's candidacy by underlining that negotiations were being conducted with an open outcome that did not necessarily guarantee EU membership:

> "If the EU does not have the capacity to absorb a new member or if Turkey should not be in a position to meet all the obligations of membership, the country must be linked as closely as possible to European structures in a way that allows it to develop further its privileged relationship with the EU".[21]

This statement was fully in line with the CDU/CSU position but sent a radically different signal regarding Turkish membership than Schröder had sent previously and moreover lacked any commitment to offer a

---

20 Cf. Council of the European Union. Brussels European Council 16/ 17 December 2004, Presidency Conclusions. 16238/1/04 REV1. Brussels, 01.02.2005, http://data. consilium.europa.eu/doc/document/ST-16238-2004-REV-1/en/pdf [22.12.2020].

21 Merkel, Angela. Governmental Declaration, 30.11.2005, p. 89.

medium-term European perspective. As the newly elected Chancellor, she stayed close to the EU's course and even adopted the official negotiating framework formulations.[22] She advocated the motto 'pacta sunt servanda' – agreements must be kept – but in the next sentence she quickly emphasised that this process of accession negotiations had to be observed with special attention.[23] Against the background of her statements as a CDU Member of Parliament in the Bundestag, it was no secret that she was taking over a project from her predecessor, which she very much doubted would end with a positive conclusion. Hence, whilst she followed the official government line on accession negotiations, she was by no means the driving force for eventual Turkish EU membership that Gerhard Schröder had been.

3.2. The Years After the Start of Accession Talks (2005–2012)

It was not just from a German perspective that the dynamics of accession lost momentum. Additionally, shortly after the start of accession negotiations in October 2005, the Turkish Parliament refused to ratify the Ankara protocol, which was an additional provision extending the Customs Union to ten new EU Member States including Cyprus.[24] After the EU had repeatedly announced that it would suspend accession negotiations if Turkey did not ratify the protocol by the end of 2006, the European Council decided in December 2006 to suspend eight negotiating chapters until that question had been resolved. The coalition government of CDU/CSU and SPD was again divided over this decision. While CDU/CSU delegates perceived this development as confirmation that it had been wrong to take up membership negotiations, SPD representatives supported this suspension but continued advocating the accession process. CDU delegate Ursula Heinen, for example, commented that the European Commission's progress report from September 2006 had "brought to light what many

---

22 Cf. Council of the European Union. Negotiating Framework. Enlargement – Accession Negotiations with Turkey: General EU Position. 12823/1/05 REV 1. Brussels, 12 October 2005, https://www.ab.gov.tr/files/AB_Iliskileri/Tur_En_Reali tons/NegotiatingFrameowrk/Negotiating_Frameowrk_Full.pdf [22.12.2020].
23 Cf. Merkel, Angela. Governmental Declaration, 30.11.2005, p. 89.
24 The Ratification of the Ankara protocol would have meant the recognition of Cyprus, which Turkey refuses to do. The reasons go back to the Cyprus territorial conflict in the 1970s between Turkey and Greece.

feared would happen: the reform process in Turkey is stalling".[25] Chancellor Merkel, albeit more cautiously, also dealt in detail with the lack of reforms and noted in her governmental declaration of December 2006: "This is not a matter of triviality, but of the self-evident fact that accession candidates and EU Member States recognise each other politically and diplomatically".[26]

Foreign Minister and SPD delegate Frank-Walter Steinmeier in contrast replied to the question asked by the Greens on how the Government judged the Commission´s report:

> "On the one hand, in the further process one cannot ignore non-ratification of the Ankara Protocol and thus the non-opening of ports and airports on the Turkish side to Cypriot ships and aircraft. On the other hand, the Commission proposal states that it cannot be in the European interest to stop the process of Turkey's rapprochement with Europe and makes operational proposals on how to maintain this process at a lower level".[27]

In line with the SPD's support for continued membership negotiations, his party colleague Lale Akgün also supported the EU's procedure: "It is a sound decision that does justice to both sides, Turkey and the EU. [...] But – and this is just as important – the negotiations must now be continued with the greatest care. Freezing must not become synonymous with a creeping end to the negotiations, even if some might wish to".[28] Hence, the SPD promoted explicitly maintaining the strategy of negotiations in order to preserve the aim of Turkish EU membership despite diplomatic conflict. The Greens supported this course optimistically. Renate Künast, the leader of the Greens faction in the Bundestag, also expressed confidence regarding the EU´s normative power: "I am sure of one thing: the European Union will succeed in exporting the rule of law even to Turkey".[29]

---

25 Deutscher Bundestag. Ursula Heinen. Plenary Protocol 16/66. Berlin, 22.11.2006, p. 6578.
26 Merkel, Angela. Governmental Declaration, 14.12.2006, p. 7210.
27 Deutscher Bundestag. Dr. Frank-Walter Steinmeier. Plenary Protocol 16/70. Berlin, 30.11.2006, p. 6936.
28 Deutscher Bundestag. Dr. Lale Akgün. Plenary Protocol 16/73. Berlin, 14.12.2006, p. 7231.
29 Deutscher Bundestag. Renate Künast. Plenary Protocol 16/88. Berlin, 22.03.2007, p. 8845.

But over the years growing impatience has developed, especially amongst those who were critical of Turkey's accession from the very beginning. CDU delegate Gunther Krichbaum criticised recent efforts of the Turkish Government to limit press freedom and warned: "Turkey must return to the path of virtue".[30] In January 2010, his colleague Andreas Schockenhoff noted that Turkey had been refusing to apply the Ankara Protocol for more than three years, which raised the question of what Turkey had actually expected from the EU in the first place. He also called for preventive strategic thinking on what to do if negotiations came to a full stop.[31] This included a renewed reference to the 'Privileged Partnership', which the CDU/CSU had increasingly grown fond of but had stopped promoting explicitly. When a few months later, in September 2010, the majority of Turkish people in a referendum voted for constitutional amendments that aimed at bringing the Turkish Constitution into line with EU standards, only the Greens assessed this referendum as "Turkey's most serious step towards accession and reform in decades".[32] Neither the rest of the Bundestag nor the Government paid any particular attention to this issue. Whilst the SPD had been a great supporter of Turkey's EU membership under Chancellor Gerhard Schröder, its position was now weakened by the coalition partner CDU/CSU. As presented in Figure 4 below, even though the Bundestag continued to discuss Turkey and German-Turkish relations on a regular basis, the topic of EU accession seemed to be off the table. This coincides with an observation that the Bundestag's interest in Turkey's EU accession was generally declining. While in 2004, Turkey's membership bid was discussed in 22 out of 30 debates that were dealing with Turkey, it did not occur in more than eight debates per year between 2007 and 2013. General perception prevailed that it was now Turkey's call to advance its accession to the EU by continuing its reform procedure. While the strategy of accession negotiations was still officially being pursued, it had lost its drive and consequently the scenario of membership was temporarily side-tracked.

---

30 Deutscher Bundestag. Gunther Krichbaum. Plenary Protocol 16/211. Berlin, 19.03.2009, p. 22729.
31 Cf. Deutscher Bundestag. Dr. Andreas Schockenhoff. Plenary Protocol 17/15. Berlin, 20.01.2010, p. 1299.
32 Deutscher Bundestag. Kerstin Müller. Plenary Protocol 17/58. Berlin, 15.09.2010, p. 6085.

Figure 4: Comparison of Percentage Share of Debates on Turkey and Turkey's EU Accession 2003–2018

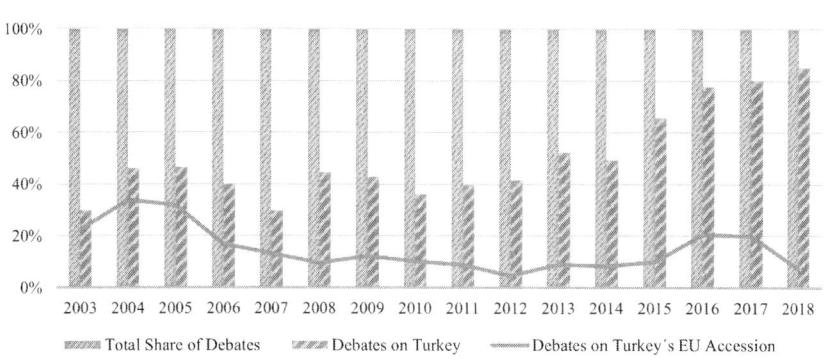

Source: own compilation.

This was also reflected at governmental level: Chancellor Angela Merkel mentioned Turkey only once during her governmental declarations between 2007 and 2013. The rare references to Turkey appeared in the context of her criticism of the difficult cooperation between NATO and European security policy in view of the unsolved Cyprus conflict in 2009.[33] This low point for EU-Turkey or German-Turkish relations is represented not only by a void within governmental declarations, but also by the general lack of discussion on the topic in the Bundestag. In March 2011, the Greens submitted a motion to "revive the EU accession negotiations"[34] without any effect. It was not discussed in the Bundestag, merely referred to the committees responsible and subsequently rejected by the coalition of CDU/CSU and FDP as well as the Left Party in the following October.

3.3 Positive Agenda 2012 and Gezi Protests 2013 – Test and Turning Point

After several years of a slow to temporarily faltering accession process, in May 2012 the EU Commission and the Turkish Ministry of European Affairs[35] launched the so-called Positive Agenda, a concept to bring "fresh

---

33 Cf. Merkel, Angela. Government Declaration, 26 April 2009, p. 23125.
34 Deutscher Bundestag. Claudia Roth. Plenary Protocol 17/96. Berlin, 17.03.2011, p. 11087.
35 The Ministry of European Affairs was a Ministry of the Turkish Government responsible for Turkey's European policy from 29 June 2011 to 8 July 2018,

dynamics into EU-relations"[36] by enhancing cooperation and promoting reforms in Turkey so as to establish a technical dialogue below the threshold of chapter openings. The aim was to facilitate progress in areas of common interest such as alignment with EU legislation, visa and migration, trade and energy together with counterterrorism. But even though this was the first joint step towards a Turkish membership bid since 2005, neither German governmental declarations nor parliamentary debates mentioned the Positive Agenda once. Furthermore, the overall topic 'EU-Membership and Accession' reached its absolute low regarding the frequency of mentioning in Bundestag debates for the years 2002 to 2018.

By contrast, the occurrence of nationwide Gezi protests in Turkey in 2013[37] was an extensively debated Bundestag topic, especially in light of the Turkish Government's resulting harsh treatment of demonstrators and participants, which was heavily criticised by the EU. For the majority of German Parliamentarians, who were already showing clear signs of exhaustion with regard to the accession process at that time, this was "probably the greatest test of the Turkish Government since Erdoğan's party took office",[38] as Foreign Minister Guido Westerwelle put it. In his opinion, the Turkish Government sent the 'wrong signal to Europe' and had to prove to Europe and the world that it was indeed guided by the European principles to which it had previously committed.

Following the protests, both the CDU/CSU and FDP asked for an immediate parliamentary debate on the current situation in Turkey, in which delegates expressed their concerns regarding the Turkish Government's lack of compliance with democratic standards and their doubts regarding Turkey's future in the EU. At the same time, most Parliamentarians made a clear distinction between the Turkish Government and Turkish society, which conversely had demonstrated a strong understanding of democracy and freedom of expression. In order to support Turkish societal demands and commit the country's government to meeting them, SPD and Green

---

before being incorporated into the Ministry of Foreign Affairs on 9 July 2018 with the start of the new legislature.

36　European Commission. Positive EU-Turkey agenda launched in Ankara. Press Release. MEMO/12/359. Brussels, 17.05.2021, http://europa.eu/rapid/press-release _MEMO-12-359_en.htm [22.12.2020].

37　The Gezi protests started in Istanbul in May 2013, initially as a peaceful protest campaign against the urban development plan for the Gezi Park in the Taksim quarter. After the police had violently broken up the sit-in blockade, a nationwide wave of protest against the AKP government spread.

38　Deutscher Bundestag. Dr. Guido Westerwelle. Plenary Protocol 17/245. Berlin, 12.06.2013, p. 31173.

Party delegates spoke in favour of revitalising accession negotiations and 'opening new chapters', such as Chapter 23 on 'Justice and fundamental rights'. SPD delegate Johannes Kahrs even referred to the vibrant civil society which would result from accession negotiations, stating that the values demanded by the Turkish demonstrators were, to a large extent, reflected in the accession process. He underlined this argument by stating "it is important to say today that we do want the EU accession process to continue, that we call on Turkey to press ahead with it and that we also want the European states to press ahead with this process".[39] Nevertheless, he also emphasized that no one wanted Turkey as it was now to become a member of the EU.

This statement reflects the Bundestag's uncertainty vis-à-vis the turn of developments in Turkey and thus the future of EU-Turkey relations. On the one hand, delegates (even individual delegates from the CDU/CSU)[40] did not want to dash Turkish society's hopes of being part of the European community one day. On the other hand, doubts about the Turkish Government's will to advocate democracy was becoming stronger and more expressible. In this sense, 2013 marks the start of open and regular criticism of the Turkish Government by the entire Bundestag and thus an increasingly sceptical view on Turkey within the political dimension. At the same time, from this point onwards most members of the Bundestag clearly distinguished between the Turkish Government and civil society, increasingly supporting the Turkish people. The corresponding strategies for EU-Turkey relations varied depending on party affiliation. While proponents of Turkish EU membership from the SPD and Greens focused on the strategy of accession negotiations to commit Turkey to human rights standards, the CDU/CSU used the generally critical mood to argue once again in favour of suspending accession negotiations. In their view, the opening of additional negotiation chapters would represent a reward for Erdoğan's regime and signify a betrayal of the protestors. Thus, the setbacks in Turkey should be consistently sanctioned in order for the EU to remain credible.[41]

Regarding the Gezi protests and how to adjust the political course towards Turkey, the debate was at that time confined to the political

---

39 Deutscher Bundestag. Johannes Kahrs. Plenary Protocol 17/245. Berlin, 12.06.2013, p. 31174.

40 Cf. Deutscher Bundestag. Ruprecht Polenz. Plenary Protocol 17/245. Berlin, 12.06.2013, pp. 31174 f.

41 Cf. Deutscher Bundestag. Thomas Silberhorn. Plenary Protocol 17/245. Berlin, 12.06.2013, pp. 31180 f.

dimension. However, the Arab Spring, the Syrian civil war and the threat posed by the Islamic State of Iraq and Syria (ISIS) brought the geopolitical dimension back to the fore (see Figure 5, below).

Figure 5: Dimensions in German Parliamentary Debates between 2003 and 2018

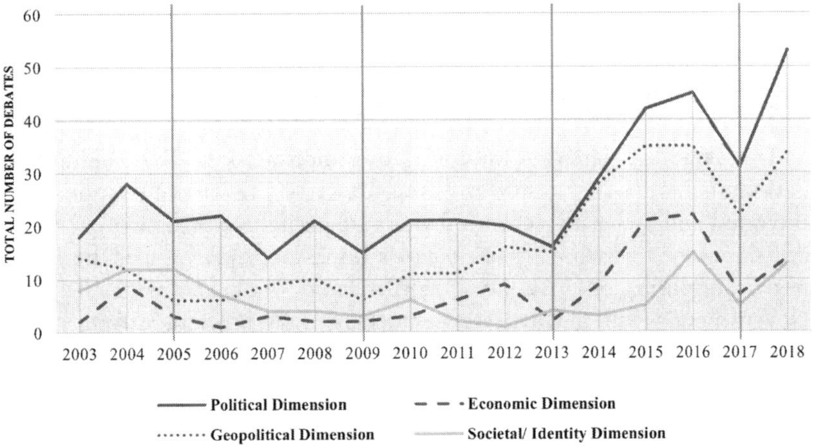

Source: own compilation.

This was primarily due to Turkey requesting patriot defence missiles from its NATO allies in 2012 so as to secure its border with neighbouring Syria. This topic was much debated in the Bundestag before Foreign Minister Guido Westerwelle eventually pledged Germany's support. Thus, Turkey was increasingly perceived as a key partner in geostrategic and security terms.

3.4 A Peak in every Respect – Geostrategic Relevance and Political Crisis in 2015/2016

The geostrategic relevance that Turkey had continually gained since the destabilisation in the Middle East, became decisive for its relations with the EU in 2015 and 2016. The growing number of refugees from Syria posed a challenge to the EU's Common European Asylum System and created conflict between Member States regarding the distribution and limit to the number of refugees who could be accepted. In the context of this crisis, EU Heads of State or Government together with Turkey agreed on a Joint Action Plan in November 2015 to solve the migration issue, which included an EU declaration to step up its political and financial engagement.[42] Furthermore, both sides agreed on re-energising Turkey's EU accession process by establishing more frequent and structured meetings as well as opening Chapter 17 of the accession process on further economic integration with Turkey.[43] In March 2016, the EU and Turkey also concluded the EU-Turkey statement on Migration with the aim to ending irregular migration via Turkey to the EU. This was to be achieved through a 1:1 mechanism, whereby for each illegal Syrian migrant returned from the EU back to Turkey, another was to be legally relocated to the EU. Furthermore, Turkey promised to take all necessary measures to prevent further irregular migration, whilst in return the European Council agreed to set up a Refugee Facility for Turkey equipped with a total of 6 billion euros before the end of 2018 for projects in the areas of health and education. Most importantly, the Council also reconfirmed its commitment to re-energise the accession process, upgrade the Customs Union and facilitate visa liberalisation for Turkish citizens by the end of June 2016, provided that "all benchmark criteria have been met".[44]

During these months between September 2015 and March 2016, the German Government published six declarations, all of which highlighted Turkey´s "key role"[45] in the context of growing security threats emanating from ISIS and the general destabilisation in the Middle East as well as the migration crisis. Chancellor Angela Merkel continually stressed that the migration issue was a global problem that needed to be dealt with on international and multilateral levels. In her statement of 16 December 2015, she commented on the EU-Turkey statement on migration:

> "It is in everyone's interest to reduce the number of people seeking refuge in Europe. That is in the interests of Germany, that is in the interests of Europe and that is also in the interests of the refugees themselves, so that they do not have to embark on a life-threatening journey across Europe. That is why, at the EU-Turkey Summit on 29

---

42 Cf. Reiners, Wulf/ Tekin, Funda. Taking Refuge in Leadership? Facilitators and Constraints of Germany's Influence in EU Migration Policy and EU-Turkey Affairs during the Refugee Crisis (2015–2016). In: *German Politics*, 2020, Vol. 29, Issue 1, pp. 115–130.

43 Cf. European Council. Meeting of the EU Heads of State or Government with Turkey, 29.11.2015, https://www.consilium.europa.eu/en/meetings/international-summit/2015/11/29/ [22.12.2020].

44 European Council. EU-Turkey statement, 18 March 2016. Press Release. Brussels, 18.03.2016, https://www.consilium.europa.eu/en/press/press-releases/2016/03/18/eu-turkey-statement/, [22.12.2020].

45 Merkel, Angela. Governmental Declaration, 15.10.2015, p.12557.

November [2015], we laid the foundations for a long-term migration partnership with Turkey".[46]

Thus she classified the statement as a result of mutual interests facilitating a form of long-term cooperation. In addition to this multilateral form of cooperation, Merkel addressed the topic of migration as a bilateral issue: As she explained in her declaration on 17 February 2016, the German Government had been pursuing three approaches in this regard by: (1) combatting the causes for flight, (2) protecting the EU's external border and (3) controlling refugee migration in police and technical cooperation with Turkey. She went on to say that: "We have agreed bilateral cooperation with Turkey in many areas. [...] and I may say, by the way, that this bilateral cooperation is developing very well".[47]

Regarding the political dimension, one month before the EU-Turkey Statement on Migration was concluded in March 2018, Merkel acknowledged in front of the Bundestag that Turkey was expecting a revival of accession negotiations in return for cooperation on the refugee issue. In this regard, she assured that talks on the migration partnership also included a critical examination of areas such as journalistic freedom in Turkey, the Kurds and the Turkish youth.[48] The decisive factor would be whether and if so how a balance of interests could be achieved that corresponded to European values. The EU-Turkey Statement on Migration was essentially co-determined by the German Chancellor[49] and reveals for the first time a strategy defined in this chapter as 'twin-tracked'. By continuing or even revitalising accession negotiations, a parallel track of interest-based cooperation was initialised through the migration partnership. Thereby, the strategy of continued accession negotiations was not necessarily aimed at the medium-term scenario of EU accession, but served primarily to maintain an already existing, highly institutionalised form of relationship with Turkey.

Parts of the Bundestag, including the CDU/CSU as well as the Left Party, were highly critical of this so-called EU-Turkey migration deal. The Left Party denounced the agreement as a "dirty deal [with] Erdoğan, the godfather of terrorism",[50] through which the EU has made itself vulnerable to blackmail in its fundamental democratic values. Left Party delegates demanded the

---

46 Merkel, Angela. Governmental Declaration, 16.12.2015, p.14283.
47 Merkel, Angela. Governmental Declaration, 17.02.2016, p.15133.
48 Cf. Ibid.
49 Cf. Reiners/ Tekin, Taking Refuge in Leadership?, 2020.
50 Cf. Deutscher Bundestag. Sevim Dağdelen. Plenary Protocol 18/160. Berlin, 16.03.2016, p. 15760.

cancellation of accession negotiations as well as any form of transactional cooperation based on mutual interests. CDU/CSU delegates seemed to be more convinced than ever that Turkey would never fully share EU values and should, therefore, no longer be offered the prospect of accession.[51] The question of the right strategy for EU-Turkey relations became more and more central in light of the migration issue. While CDU/CSU members were in favour of closer cooperation to manage refugee flows, their representatives in the Bundestag did not see accession negotiations as an appropriate strategy:

> "It is one thing to meet the Turks halfway, naturally always retaining the criteria that we have established, for example with regard to visa liberalisation. However, only one thing should not be put on the agenda, because it has no relevance in this regard, and that is the question of Turkey's accession to the European Union".[52]

This is consistent with the observation that in 2015 and 2016 the CDU/CSU described Turkey most often as a *strategic partner*, in comparison both to previous years and the other parties – a term that points away from EU accession and towards a Unique Partnership, as shown in Figure 6 below.

Figure 6: Turkey as a Strategic Partner – Explicit Attributions by Parties in the Bundestag 2003–2018

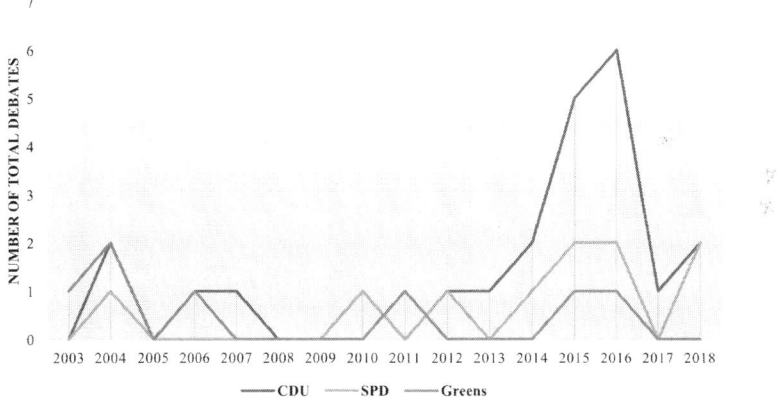

Source: own compliation.

---

51 Cf. Deutscher Bundestag. Dr. Johann Wadepuhl. Plenary Protocol 18/154. Berlin, 17.02.2016, p. 15182.
52 Deutscher Bundestag. Dr. Hans-Peter Friedrich. Plenary Protocol 18/130. Berlin, 15.10.2015, p.12572.

According to the SPD and Greens, the opposite was true. In January 2016, Dorothee Schlegel from the SPD, Committee for the Affairs of the European Union, recalled that the EU as well as Germany under SPD Chancellor Gerhard Schröder had originally sought Turkey's accession for reasons of foreign and security policy. These interests were now more urgent than ever, despite the tense relationship. She called for the accession process to be seen as an opportunity because "the instrument of accession negotiations, to remain in military jargon, is the EU's 'sharpest sword'. For it is the primacy of peacekeeping that counts".[53] The Greens delegate Cem Özdemir also regretted the German Government's lack of interest in Turkey since Merkel took office, which, in view of the democracy and human rights situations in Turkey, was now taking its revenge.[54]

As can be seen from these statements, the Bundestag agreed on the fact that Turkey was becoming geostrategically more relevant during these years and that cooperation was certainly worthwhile. However, the question of whether or not the accession process would be an appropriate framework remained controversial. This debate became even more contentious in the course of 2016, which in retrospect is often referred to as the crisis year for bilateral relations between Germany and Turkey. The so-called Böhmermann affair in April[55] was followed by the Armenia Resolution in June, in which, at the request of the CDU/CSU, SPD and the Greens parliamentary groups, the Bundestag commemorated the genocide of Armenians and other Christian minorities in 1915 and 1916. The Turkish Government reacted with strong displeasure, referring to the vote as "a disgrace to the reputation of this body",[56] and calling the Bundestag "ignorant and disrespectful".[57] In the same month, the Turkish Government issued a ban on visits by members of the German Bundestag to the

---

53 Deutscher Bundestag. Dr. Dorothee Schlegel. Plenary Protocol 18/149. Berlin, 14.01.2016, p. 14689.
54 Cf. Deutscher Bundestag. Cem Özdemir. Plenary Protocol 18/129. Berlin, 14.10.2015, p. 12535.
55 The Böhmermann affair describes a conflict between the German TV presenter Jan Böhmermann and the Turkish President Recep Erdoğan. In March 2016, Böhmermann had read a satirical poem on German television, for which Erdoğan prosecuted him.
56 Turkish Ministry of Foreign Affairs. Press Release regarding the Resolution by the Parliament of the Federal Republic of Germany of 2 June 2016 on the Events of 1915, No. 125, 02.06.2016, http://www.mfa.gov.tr/no_-125_-2-june-2016_-press-rel ease-regarding-the-resolution-by-the-parliament-of-the-federal-republic-of-germany -of-2-june-2016-on-the-events-of-1915.en.mfa [22.12.2020].
57 Ibid.

Turkish military airbase in Incirlik,[58] whereupon the Left Party demanded the immediate withdrawal of German troops. The other parties criticised the Turkish Government's actions, but nevertheless stressed the necessity of bilateral military cooperation within NATO, which was fundamental for Germany. This illustrates perfectly the Bundestag's dilemma between geostrategic relevance and political conflict in its relations with Turkey at that point.

The relations between the two states were already strained when in July 2016 the Turkish military attempted a coup, which ultimately failed. In response, Erdoğan's government declared a state of emergency, under which it arrested tens of thousands of people and dismissed them from their offices suspecting them of being affiliated with the Gülen movement that was made responsible for the attempted coup. The German Government commented neither on the coup attempt itself nor on Turkey's action through its governmental declaration. Foreign Minister Frank-Walter Steinmeier made a statement in the Bundestag on 7 September 2016 – immediately after the parliamentary summer recess – in which he expressed his regret that the Turkish Government had accused Germany of not taking the failed coup attempt seriously, even considering it to have been staged. However, he also pointed out that not every critical demand from the German side regarding constitutional standards should be regarded as arrogance. Finally, he advocated a controversial, direct exchange with the Turkish side:

> "It is not up to us to decide whether Turkey is important or unimportant. [...] Turkey is a key country – not only because of the 2.5 million refugees in Turkey, and not only because there is a refugee agreement with Turkey. [...] That is why I strongly advise us to be critical where it is necessary, but not to pretend that relations with Turkey can in any way be avoided because of the critical points".[59]

Still, in the Bundestag the critical points were much debated, with reference to the Turkish Government's crackdown on persons who allegedly were part of the failed coup attempt. During 2016, the most discussed topics in addition to refuge and asylum were democratic standards, the

---

58 The Turkish Government had banned German members of the Bundestag from visiting the Turkish base Incirlik.
59 Deutscher Bundestag. Dr. Frank-Walter Steinmeier. Plenary Protocol 18/186. Berlin, 07.09.2016, p. 18451.

rule of law as well as human and minority rights. All of them belong to the political dimension, which consequently peaked in that year (see Figure 7).

Figure 7: Topics and Keywords in German Parliamentary Debates 2009–2018[60]

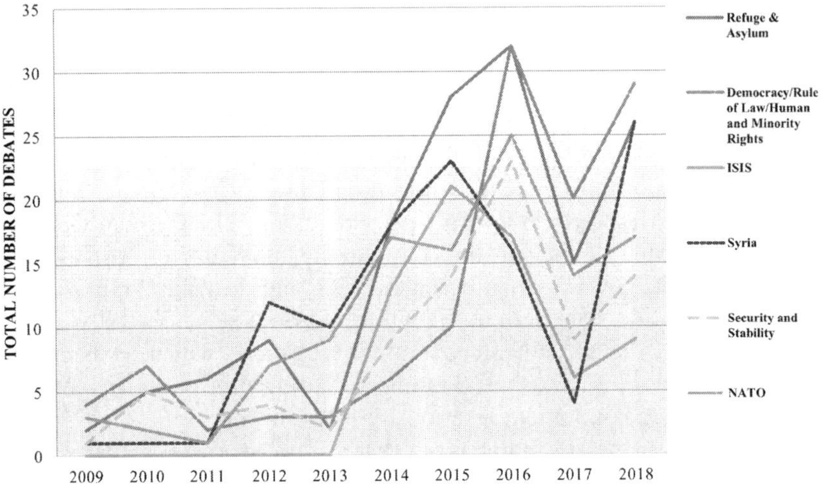

Source: own compilation.

CDU/CSU delegates Norbert Röttgen and Alois Karl perceaived Erdoğan's actions in the aftermath of the coup attempt as a way of distancing Turkey from Europe.[61] Thomas Oppermann from the SPD warned "if tens of thousands of civil servants, teachers and judges are arrested, who clearly have nothing to do with the coup, then this is an attack on the rule of law. We must not remain silent about this, ladies and gentlemen".[62] When Erdoğan announced shortly afterwards that he wanted to reintroduce the death penalty, the Bundestag set up a debate on the current situation in Turkey and defined this a red line for Germany to demand the accession

---

60 The chart shows a selection of the most frequently discussed topics in the Bundestag from 2012.
61 Cf. Deutscher Bundestag. Dr. Norbert Röttgen, Alois Karl. Plenary Protocol 18/186. Berlin, 07.09.2016, p. 18461, p. 18466.
62 Deutscher Bundestag. Thomas Oppermann. Plenary Protocol 18/186. Berlin, 07.09.2016, p. 18423.

talks to end with immediate effect.[63] Within a year's time, this was the second time since the start of accession negotiations in 2005 that the entire Bundestag had not only reached agreement on the Turkish situation, but more importantly on a common strategy for EU-Turkey relations.[64] Delegates equated a reintroduction of the death penalty with a rejection of the EU and its values. Michelle Müntefering (SPD), for example, observed that Turkey seemed increasingly turning away from its orientation towards the West and the course of modern civilization by stating

> "Turkey's revised policy and the changes made by President Erdoğan himself are now closing this door to Europe. We will continue to cooperate. We will continue to be neighbours, but at the same time something will change between our countries".[65]

Gunther Krichbaum stated "indeed, a country that introduces the death penalty and thus clearly wants to turn its back on EU values no longer has a place in Europe".[66] Even the Greens who had always been in favour of a Turkish EU Membership expressed doubts.[67] Foreign Minister Steinmeier noted

> "all the storms, all the turbulences, which Turkey experiences, point in my eyes quite clearly to one thing in the end, namely that Turkey stands at a crossroads. It is about the direction of the country: either towards Europe or away from Europe, towards a constituted democracy or away from it".[68]

As can be seen in these similar statements from different parties, the majority of the Bundestag seemed to identify Turkey as moving ever further away from Europe and the EU. This analysis reveals a change in narrative,

---

63 The same conclusion was reached by the Members of the European Parliament and the President of the European Commission, Jean-Claude Juncker, see also: https://www.euractiv.com/section/justice-home-affairs/news/juncker-death-penalt y-in-turkey-would-mean-end-to-eu-accession-talks/.

64 The first time was the Armenia Resolution in June of the same year.

65 Deutscher Bundestag. Michelle Müntefering. Plenary Protocol 18/199. Berlin, 10.11.2016, p. 19812.

66 Deutscher Bundestag. Gunther Krichbaum. Plenary Protocol 18/199. Berlin, 10.11.2016, p. 19810.

67 Cf. Deutscher Bundestag. Claudia Roth. Plenary Protocol 18/199. Berlin, 10.11.2016, p. 19808; Deutscher Bundestag. Tabea Rößner. Plenary Protocol 18/202, Berlin, 23.11.2016, p. 20196.

68 Deutscher Bundestag. Dr. Frank-Walter Steinmeier. Plenary Protocol 18/199. Berlin, 10.11.2016, p. 19803.

mentioned more or less explicitly by all the parties in the Bundestag. Political unpredictability and continuing tension were at this point translated into the identity dimension, in other words questions of belonging to and orientation towards Europe and the EU. While parliamentarians were committed to supporting Turkish civil society again, they also made the Turkish Government and its president personally responsible for creating distance between the EU and its Member States on the one side and Turkey on the other.

3.5 Still at the Crossroads? Developments after 2016

The year 2017 continued right where the year 2016 had left off. Bilateral tensions increased with the arrests in Istanbul of German-Turkish journalists Deniz Yücel and Meşale Tolu during February and April respectively, followed by human rights activist Peter Steudtner in July of the same year. Furthermore, in spring Turkish President Erdoğan accused the German Government of applying Nazi methods, after several German cities had banned Turkish politicians of the *Adalet ve Kalkınma Partisi (AKP)* from campaigning for the Turkish constitutional referendum. Chancellor Angela Merkel immediately responded by stating in front of the Bundestag "the comparisons between the Federal Republic of Germany and National Socialism must cease. They are not worthy of the close ties and relations between Germany and Turkey and our two peoples – politically, socially, as NATO partners and economically".[69] She called the statements "sad and depressing" and gave reassurances that she would continue to address fundamental issues regarding freedom of the press and freedom of expression. Despite the common European-Turkish interests and the "complicated but diverse connections" between Germany and Turkey she also noted "profound differences between the EU and Turkey as well as Germany and Turkey".[70] The Bundestag debate was initiated by President Norbert Lammert, who himself clarified some points and was applauded by the whole House: The meassage was that those who suspected Germany of using Nazi methods while its authorities and elected representatives were acting within the framework of the German constitutional order essentially disqualified themselves. In Germany, freedom of the press and freedom of expression were guaranteed – a partner country was expected

---

69 Angela Merkel, Governmental Declaration, 09.03.2017, p. 22066.
70 Ibid.

to guarantee the same rights that its representatives claimed in Germany. Finally, he emphasised once again what delegates had been addressing for months, namely that Turkey was developing into an autocratic state which was moving further and further away from Europe, its convictions and democratic standards.[71]

In April 2017, Turkey held a referendum on the Turkish constitution that included comprehensive changes towards a presidential system. When the amendments were adopted with a narrow majority by Turkish society, this also became an issue for debate in the Bundestag. Merkel expressed her concern about how the vote was conducted after Organisation for Security and Co-operation in Europe (OSCE) reports of irregularities. With recent events in mind, she stated

> "there is no doubt that developments over the past week have put a heavy strain on both German-Turkish and European-Turkish relations. [...] A final turning away of Turkey from Europe, but also – and I say this with caution – of Europe from Turkey would be neither in the German nor in the European interest".[72]

The coalition partner SPD also called for prudence. "I think Erdoğan himself must assume responsibility ahead of his people", said Thomas Oppermann in April 2017. "It's not we who slam the European door shut to Turkey, it is Erdoğan alone who is systematically leading his country away from the EU and European values".[73] But the grand coalition's attempt to keep a low profile regarding the future of accession negotiations proved difficult shortly before the upcoming Bundestag elections in September 2017. SPD Chancellor candidate Martin Schulz sent a strong signal during a publicly broadcasted TV debate with Angela Merkel when he made clear that EU accession talks with Turkey would end under his chancellorship.[74] This statement was atypical for an SPD delegate in view of the party's consistently supportive stance and came somewhat as a surprise for most of his colleagues – Merkel included. Nevertheless, the statement hinted at what was being discussed increasingly and in parts directly demanded in the Bundestag. There seemed to be little hope left for a political turnaround in

---

71 Deutscher Bundestag. Nobert Lammert. Plenary Protocol 18/221. Berlin, 09.03.2017, p. 22063.

72 Angela Merkel, Governmental Declaration 27.04.2017, p. 23180.

73 Deutscher Bundestag. Thomas Oppermann. Plenary Protocol 18/231. Berlin, 27.04.2017, p. 23186.

74 Cf. Bellinghausen, Yves. Schulz überrascht SPD mit hartem Türkei-Kurs. In: FAZ Online 04.09.2017.

Turkey after so much strain had been inflicted on bilateral and EU-Turkey relations.

In January 2018, Turkey launched its military offensive 'Operation Olive Branch' against Kurdish militias in the Syrian town of Afrin, whereupon the Bundestag once again appeared united in its condemnation of the attack as being contrary to international law. Chancellor Angela Merkel unreservedly condemned the operation as "unacceptable"[75] in her March governmental declaration and subjected the relationship with Germany's "European neighbour and NATO partner"[76] to a general examination by contrasting the geopolitical and economic with the political dimension:

> "We have a lot in common with Turkey: over three million people in our country have Turkish roots, our economies are closely linked; we stand together in the fight against terrorism; we work together reliably on migration. But in the recent past, the relationship between our two countries has been under the greatest strain, not only because of what is happening in Afrin, but also consider the arrests of Deniz Yücel, Peter Steudtner,[77] Meşale Tolu and others".[78]

The Left Party demanded an immediate parliamentary debate on 1 February 2018 to discuss Turkey's approach to Afrin, whilst also considering German arms exports. Within this debate, delegates of the grand coalition expressed repeated concerns that Turkey might turn its back not only on the EU but also on NATO and thus the West as a whole. Consequently, it was stressed that even if EU accession was currently out of question for the vast majority of representatives in the Bundestag, military or political isolation should be avoided.[79] This statement summarises the Bundestag's position well and supports once again the twin-track strategy, through which accession negotiations should be maintained in order to keep Turkey as an important partner in geostrategic and economic terms. How to approach relations with Turkey in the future was again the topic of parliamentary debate in September 2018 during Erdoğan's state visit to Germany. In sev-

---

75 Angela Merkel, Governmental Declaration, 21.03.2018, p. 1813.
76 Ibid.
77 The German human rights activist Peter Steudtner was arrested in Turkey at the beginning of July 2017.
78 Angela Merkel, Governmental Declaration, 21.03.2018, p. 1820.
79 Cf. Deutscher Bundestag. Dr. Frank Steffel. Plenary Protocol 19/11. Berlin, 01.02.2018, p. 873.

eral motions[80] delegates argued about 'Operation Olive Branch', erosion of the rule of law in Turkey and the reception for President Erdoğan himself. "The task is to reassess relations between Germany, the EU and Turkey in a changed environment",[81] stated CDU delegate Andreas Nick. Nevertheless, EU accession negotiations were still considered to be the most institutionalised form of cooperation with Turkey. Thus, even though the future scenario for EU membership was no longer feasible, conversely pushing Turkey out of all formats was not the preferred option, at least for the ruling grand coalition.[82]

4. Conclusions

During the years before negotiations started, the Bundestag was divided on whether or not Turkey should join the EU. Two narratives dominated at that time. The first, as promoted by the CDU/CSU, is identity-based in claiming that Turkey does not belong to the European family. This narrative referred to topics such as religion and cultural heritage, implying an assumption that even if Turkey implemented reforms within the political dimension, it would never fit into the European community. Hence, party members were opposed to the strategy of opening accession negotiations and entering into the scenario of potential EU membership. Instead, from the outset they pursued the concept of a 'Privileged Partnership', which pointed in the direction of a Unique Partnership as the future scenario for EU-Turkey relations. The second dominant narrative was presented by the governing SPD and the Greens coalition who introduced the idea of Turkey as a geostrategic asset in their advocating the opening of accession negotiations and the future scenario of EU membership. The Government under Chancellor Gerhard Schröder hoped that the strategy of accession negotiations would bind a geostrategic partner in the long term, whilst at the same time reforming and modernising it accordingly within the political dimension. However, with the German parliamentary elections in 2005 and Merkel's assumption of office as Chancellor, the mood turned.

---

80 The Bundestag never debated more on Turkey than during the years 2017 and 2018. In around 80 percent of all the parliamentary debates Turkey was an issue – compared to around 30 percent in 2003.

81 Deutscher Bundestag. Dr. Andreas Nick. Plenary Protocol 19/52. Berlin, 27.09.2018, p. 5419.

82 Cf. Deutscher Bundestag. Dr. Nils Schmid. Plenary Protocol 19/52. Berlin, 27.09.2018, p. 5427.

Without supporting the scenario of Turkey's EU accession herself, she assumed responsibility for a long-term negotiation process according to the motto 'pacta sunt servanda'.

Since Turkey became an official EU candidate in 1999 and the EU announced that it would decide on the opening of accession negotiations in 2004, the Bundestag had debated extensively the future of EU-Turkey relations. All actions, statements and interests were evaluated against the background of possible EU accession and Turkey was measured against the benchmark of a future EU member. The scenario of Turkey as only a neighbouring country without a much institutionalised form of co-operation was never a debated issue in the Bundestag. Over the years, though, the German perception of Turkey and EU/German-Turkish relations changed significantly und thus also respective dominant narratives, strategies and future scenarios.

A loss of momentum on the German side coincided with diplomatic conflict between Europe and Turkey over the Ankara Protocol at the end of 2005, with further division between the parties in regard to Turkey's EU accession. CDU/CSU delegates seized the conflict as an opportunity to repeat their doubts on Turkey's ability to reform based in the identity narrative. As a precaution, they called for the development of a new strategy in case accession negotiations failed. The SPD and the Greens remained positive about continuing the strategy of accession negotiations aimed at realising EU membership. Relying on the narrative of Turkey as a geostrategic asset, they tended to reinforce the reform process whenever the relationship faced political difficulties – true to the motto: 'Now more than ever'. However, due to the Bundestag's new composition, the voices in support of Turkey's future as EU member became more silent and hence the topic was relegated into the background of parliamentary debates. Thus, even though most Bundestag representatives did not outspokenly oppose either the strategy of accession negotiations or the scenario of EU membership, the topic had temporarily lost its urgency whilst the Bundestag seemed to await developments in Turkey.

In 2012, the EU and Turkey tried to revitalise the accession dynamic by launching the Positive Agenda, but with no impact. Instead, it was replaced by an increasingly critical stance within the political dimension, triggered by the Gezi protests in Turkey in 2013. The Bundestag distinguished explicitly between the Turkish Government, which it openly criticised as being undemocratic, and civil society, who on the contrary had expressed a strong will for democracy and needed to be supported. The year 2013 can thus be considered a turning point regarding the Bundestag's confidence in the Turkish Government's democratic will. It can be summarised under a narrative of increasing political unpredictability, that all parties referred to. In addition to the already weakened scenario of EU accession, the dominance of this narrative had the effect of also turning the strategy of accession negotiations into a point of contention. CDU/CSU members outspokenly demanded the cancellation of negotiations, referring to it as a reward for the Turkish Government's approach in its betrayal of the Turkish society. The SPD and Greens in contrast again insisted on the geostrategic relevance of Turkey which was possibly increasing in light of the Arab Spring, the Syrian civil war and the ISIS. In their view this implied a necessity to continue negotiations in order to bring back an important partner to a democratic negotiating basis with the help of available funds.

The Joint Action Plan and EU-Turkey Statement on Migration in exchange for a revitalisation of accession negotiations in 2015 and 2016 had a decisive influence on the dominant narratives and their direction of thrust. While Government and Bundestag agreed on the fact that Turkey had a key role within the geopolitical dimension and migration issue, the parties were divided on whether or not the strategy of accession negotiations was still the most appropriate means of winning Turkey over to forms of transactional cooperation. CDU/CSU delegates added to their repertoire the narrative of Turkey as a geostrategic asset, referring more than any other party to a *strategic partner*. But unlike the SPD, they used the narrative to promote the cancellation of accession negotiations. They were in favour of closer cooperation in migration terms, but out of geopolitical concerns did not want to compromise in the area of EU accession. The SPD, by contrast, stuck to their same narrative to promote the continuation of accession negotiations, as they had previously in the early 2000 years, so as to link Turkey institutionally to the EU.

The twin-track strategy, introduced by Chancellor Merkel, was increasingly discussed though not explicitly named in this context. At this point, the future scenario of EU-Turkey relations stood in the shadow of strategic debates on how to keep a geopolitically important partner. For most parliamentarians, membership no longer seemed feasible and was increasingly side-lined by the demand for alternative formats of cooperation, subsumed under the term *Unique Partnership* for the purposes of this chapter. In Figure 8 below, this development is shown in a quantitative manner: The topic, namely the thematic code 'EU accession', has been compared to the explicit attributions *Strategic* or *Key Partner* and *Privileged Partner* used for Turkey within debates.

Figure 8: Contrasting Thematic Issues and Explicit Attributions: EU-Accession vs. Strategic Partnership 2003–2018

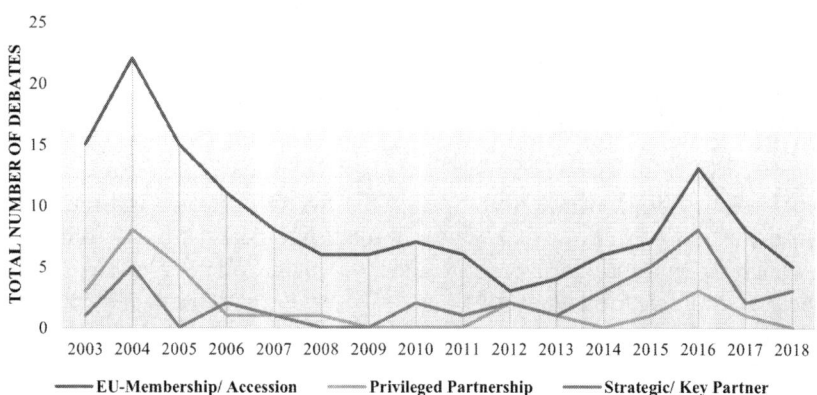

Source: own compilation.

Compared to 2004, one can observe an approximation of the terms by their use in the Bundestag for the years from 2013 with an increasing tendency for using the attribution *strategic partner* during 2018 and a decreasing tendency for the use of 'EU accession'. While the Bundestag was still divided on the strategic issue, the different parties' narratives converged not only within the geopolitical dimension but also in political and identity terms during the course of 2016, which marks the year of bilateral crisis. At the end of that year, all parties noted that Turkey was moving away from the EU and its values and was now at a crossroads, facing a move towards or away from democracy. This observation not only hints at the dominance of political unpredictability again, but also the return of an identity-based narrative. This time, the Bundestag did not use this narrative to give a character description of Turkey, as the CDU/CSU had done around 2004, but rather to describe a process of alienation and distancing from Europe and the EU. Consequently, parliamentarians agreed not only on Turkey's geostrategic asset but also on the narrative of a fundamental change in Turkey and in EU-Turkey relations that somehow had to be translated into an institutional reality.

Numerous incidents in 2017 and 2018 indicated that Turkey did not change its course away from the EU. The Bundestag agreed in various debates on autocratic developments within the Turkish political system and profound differences between Germany and Turkey, as well as between the EU and Turkey. Thus, the narrative concerning Turkey's political unpredictability as well as its alienation from the EU continued to be dominant and temporarily became even more dominant than the narrative referring to

Turkey as a geostrategic asset in Bundestag debates. This is supported by the Bundestag's three unanimous votes on Turkey regarding the Armenia resolution, the demand to end accession negotiations if Turkey should reintroduce the death penalty and the condemnation of the 'Operation Olive Branch' in Afrin. With regard to the future of EU-Turkey relations, the Government and Bundestag began to weigh Turkey's role in the political and identity dimension on the one hand against the geopolitical and economic dimension on the other. For a majority of members of the Bundestag, including those representing governing parties, the main challenge at that point was to keep institutionalised relations alive in order not to isolate an important partner, but at the same time to reassess relations in a changed environment. This frequently expressed concern points again, increasingly clearly towards the twin-track strategy and an as yet not defined form of Unique Partnership as a future scenario for EU-Turkey relations.

In summary, it can be observed that regarding Turkey and its relationship with the EU the Bundestag used three main narratives relating to the political, geopolitical and identity dimensions. The economic dimension, although referred to regularly, was not operationalised in the same way as the other dimensions in developing an argument so as to pursue a specific strategy and scenario. During the years around and after the start of accession negotiations, the identity-based narrative and the narrative of Turkey's geostrategic asset were most dominant in the debate between CDU/CSU on the one side and SPD and the Greens on the other. During 2012 and 2013 two specific narratives began to dominate: The idea of Turkey as a geostrategic asset gathered momentum due to a changing security environment coupled with increasing political unpredictability in view of Turkey. The Gezi Park protests and how the Turkish Government and state actors handled it mark the respective turning point. Moreover, these narratives were now used by most Bundestag representatives, regardless of party affiliation and the strategy of EU accession negotiations had a different aim. This means that after 2013 this strategy did not aim at facilitating Turkey's accession to the EU but rather realigning a geostrategically important partner to the EU. With the migration crisis in 2015, the narrative of Turkey as a geostrategic asset once again gained importance but was soon accompanied by the narrative of political unpredictability and the perception of Turkey alienating itself from Europe. This had the consequence that the governing parties in particular agreed on the twin-track strategy, which was intended to continue accession negotiations in order not to isolate Turkey, while at the same time reconsidering the future of institutionalised EU-Turkey relations.

So Close Yet So Far: Turkey's Relations with Germany in Recep Tayyip Erdoğan's Narratives (2003–2018)

Nurdan Selay Bedir, Ardahan Özkan Gedikli, Özgehan Şenyuva

1. Introduction

Turkey and Germany have had ongoing relations dating from well before the Republic of Turkey was founded in 1923. Today, Ankara and Berlin have close ties, especially through good trade relations and many people of Turkish origin, first, second and third generations, living in Germany. Bilateral relations, shaped by social, political and economic factors, have over recent years swung between periods of either convergence and harmony or divergence and discord. Turkish-German relations generally develop in tune with EU-Turkey relations, so that tensions or enhancements in one relationship translate into the other.[1] Similarly, the state of bilateral affairs shapes the perception and framing of Turkish-German relations in Turkey.

In broad terms, EU-Turkey relations have gone through three phases in the post-2000 era: the golden years (1999–2006), stagnation (2007–2013) and backsliding (2013-present).[2] Turkey was officially granted candidacy for EU membership at the European Council in Helsinki in 1999. The Justice and Development Party (AKP), which won the 2002 elections in Turkey, eagerly pursued an agenda aimed towards EU membership, implementing several reforms to meet the Copenhagen Criteria throughout this first period. Hence, in 2004 the European Council declared that Turkey fulfilled the political criteria for the accession process and negotiations started in October 2005. Thereafter, problems emerged from the long-term

---

1 Cf. Turhan, Ebru. With or Without Turkey? The Many Determinants of the Official German Position on Turkey's EU Accession Process. In: Ebru Turhan (Ed.). German-Turkish Relations Revisited: The European Dimension, Domestic and Foreign Politics and Transnational Dynamics. Turkey and European Union Studies. Vol. 2. Baden-Baden, 2019.

2 Cf. Soler I Lecha, Eduard. EU-Turkey Relations: Mapping landmines and exploring alternative pathways, 2019, pp. 4–6.

Cyprus issue[3] and the reluctance of new European conservative leaders – Angela Merkel and Nicolas Sarkozy– towards Turkey's EU membership. Thus, from 2006 the Council of the EU as well as Cyprus and France unilaterally blocked several accession negotiation chapters.[4] Following the 2013 Gezi Park protests, relations deteriorated even further starting with the harsh repression of protests and reaching a low point with the purges and detentions resulting from the 15 July 2016 failed coup attempt. The referendum for and entry into force of the new presidential system in 2017 and 2018 respectively[5] further increased Western suspicions and criticisms on Turkey's state of democracy.[6]

These developments were directly reflected in the narratives of Western/EU and AKP elites. The AKP government's initial pro-EU stance and reforms were praised by Western audiences, being reflected positively in Western narratives. Indeed, the then prime minister Erdoğan was portrayed as a "bridge builder"[7] and discussions emerged about whether the AKP represented a "model Muslim-democratic party"[8] for the broader Muslim world. Throughout these golden years, the AKP elite "placed a strong emphasis on democracy and human rights, advocated EU membership, supported globalisation and eschewed 'anti-Western' discourse".[9] Emerging problems in the second period were similarly reflected in narratives on both sides. Chancellor Merkel, who in 2004 had introduced the concept of "privileged partnership" as an alternative cooperation model,

---

3 Cf. Eralp, Doğu Ulaş/ Beriker, Nimet. Assessing the Conflict Resolution Potential of the EU: The Cyprus Conflict and Accession Negotiations. In: *Security Dialogue*, 2005, 36(2).

4 Cf. Weise, Helena/ Tekin, Funda. German Narratives, Strategies and Scenarios of EU-Turkey Relations 2002–2018: Towards a Unique Partnership – Yet to be defined. In this volume, p. 79-109 p. 102.

5 Aslan Akman, Canan/ Akçalı, Pınar. Changing the system through instrumentalising weak political institutions: the quest for a presidential system in Turkey in historical and comparative perspective. In: *Turkish Studies*, 2017, 18(4).

6 Cf. Tansel, Cemal Burak. Authoritarian Neoliberalism and Democratic Backsliding in Turkey: Beyond the Narratives of Progress. In: *South European Society and Politics*, 2018, 23(2), pp. 205–206.

7 Purvis, Andrew. Recep Tayyip Erdoğan: Turkey's Builder of Bridges. In: Time, 26.04.2004.

8 Tepe, Sultan. Turkey's AKP: A Model "Muslim-Democratic" Party?. In: *Journal of Democracy*, 2005, 16(3).

9 Aydın, Senem/ Çakır, Ruşen. Political Islam in Turkey, 2007, p. 1.

was stating by 2011 that the EU "does not want Turkey as a full member"[10] after a meeting with the then president Abdullah Gül. Parallel to developments after 2013, the EU increasingly voiced concerns about a variety of themes including human rights, freedom of speech and assembly, as well as the rule of law.[11] Indeed, Turkey increasingly began to be perceived as an "authoritarian and oppressive" country in the West, politicising a wide area of issues including Syrian refugees and smashing Western hopes for a "moderate and modernizing"[12] country. In response, the AKP elite narratives took on a Eurosceptic tone, presenting Turkey "as a victim of an international-scale conspiracy" while Erdoğan expressed several times "his distrust of European and Western partners".[13]

The AKP exemplifies a unique case in Turkish political history: On the one hand, it articulated "formal democracy, free market capitalism and conservative Islam",[14] which drove EU-Turkey relations essentially forward during the golden years. On the other hand, President Erdoğan and the AKP-government led EU-Turkey relations almost to a breaking point in the post-2013 period. During these years, Recep Tayyip Erdoğan has been indisputably the most important actor when it comes to politically framing EU-Turkey as well as Turkish-German relations. He served as prime minister from 2002 to 2014 and as the Turkish president ever since. In line with the developments referred to above, his stance on EU-Turkey relations has shifted dramatically over time. While he actively endorsed the EU accession process during the initial years, growing mistrust stemming from "perceived discrimination and EU double standards"[15] provoked his more sceptical stance towards the EU afterward. Thus, more recently, there has been increasing academic interest in Erdoğan's influence as well as links between discourse and foreign policy making within the Turkish

---

10 Merkel lehnt EU-Mitgliedschaft der Türkei ab. In: Welt-Online. 20.09.2011, https://www.welt.de/politik/deutschland/ article13614695/Merkel-lehnt-EU-Mitgliedschaft-der-Tuerkei-ab.html, [12.07.2021].

11 Cf. Pitel, Laura. Turkey's judiciary must protect rule of law, says Europe diplomat. In: Financial Times, 16.02.2018.

12 Goodman, Peter S. The West Hoped for Democracy in Turkey. Erdoğan Had Other Ideas. In: Ney York Times, 18.08.2018.

13 Soler I Lecha, EU-Turkey Relations, p. 6.

14 Tuğal, Cihan. The Fall of the Turkish Model: How the Arab Uprisings Brought Down Islamic Liberalism. London, 2016, p. 4.

15 Aydın, Senem/ Çakır, Ruşen, Political Islam in Turkey, p. 1.

context.[16] Whereas "systemic factors"[17] of the global order are crucial in assessing Turkish foreign policy, it has rightly been stated that domestic politics and the character of leadership both play determinant roles in foreign policy making.[18]

This research shares the view put forward by Görener and Ucal, who argue that any attempt to analyse recent Turkish foreign policy without considering Erdoğan's leadership will be found lacking due to his "preponderance in political life".[19] Aiming to put Turkish-German relations and the triangular relation between Turkey, Germany and the EU into a recent historical, contextual and conjunctural framework, this study examines narratives of Recep Tayyip Erdoğan regarding Germany and Turkish-German relations apropos EU-Turkish relations from 2003 to 2018. In social sciences, approaches to narrative analysis view narratives either as the object of research or as a strategy for conducting research.[20] This study combines these two approaches and accepts narratives as "the conversational units of communication".[21] Our analysis assesses how Erdoğan narrates Turkish-German relations and how in general terms he positions the EU and the West within this relationship. Thus, we seek to identify whether there is a change/turning point in President Erdoğan's narrative over time or any thematic prioritisation within the context of Turkish-German relations. A number of questions will be raised and answered: Why are some thematic dimensions referred to more often than others at a certain point in time? Are changes within and between thematic dimensions related

---

16 Cf. Benhaim, Yohanan/ Öktem, Kerem. The rise and fall of Turkey's soft power discourse: Discourse in foreign policy under Davutoğlu and Erdoğan, 2015; Erdoğan, Birsen. Turkish Foreign Policy: A Literature and Discourse Analysis, 2016; Kesgin, Barış. Turkey's Erdoğan: Leadership Style and Foreign Policy Audiences, 2019.; Saraçoğlu, Cenk/ Demirkol, Özhan. Nationalism and Foreign Policy Discourse in Turkey Under the AKP Rule: Geography, History and National Identity, 2014.

17 Özdamar, Özgür/ Devlen, Balkan. Man vs. the System: Turkish Foreign Policy After the Arab Uprisings, 2019, p. 178.

18 Cf. Cornell, Svante. What Drives Turkish Foreign Policy? Changes in Turkey, 2012.; Grove, Andrea. Foreign Policy Leadership in the Global South, 2017.

19 Görener, Aylin/ Ucal, Meltem. The Personality and Leadership Style of Recep Tayyip Erdoğan: Implications for Turkish Foreign Policy, 2011.

20 Cf. Hauge, Hanna-Lisa et al. Mapping periods and milestones of past EU-Turkey relations. FEUTURE Working Paper. Cologne, September 2016, p. 6.

21 Hauge, Hanna-Lisa et al. Narratives of a Contested Relationship: Unravelling the Debates in the EU and Turkey. FEUTURE Online Paper No. 28. Cologne, February 2019, p. 2.

and dependent on each other? What is the President's agenda, inferred from sub-dimensions he refers to mostly in each dimension and what is their distribution over time? Do dimensions in Erdoğan's narrative evolve between 2003 and 2018? If so, is this influenced by Erdoğan's position as Prime Minister, President or President of "New Turkey?"[22] What conclusions can be drawn for possible scenarios of conflictual and cooperative relations such as revitalised accession or Unique Partnership?[23] Which is dominant in Erdoğan's narrative: consistency or deviation?

This chapter proceeds as follows: In sections two and three we present our analysis's methodological and conceptual framework by elaborating the methodology and revisiting literature on the role of leaders and leadership in foreign policy analysis.[24] Our quantitative analysis findings are presented and contextualised in section four. This includes a discussion of which dimensions have dominated Erdoğan's speeches throughout different periods and how this can be assessed within national and international political contexts. We also examine which subjects in each dimension have dominated Erdoğan's narrative before presenting our conclusions in section five.

2. Methodology

This chapter's dataset comprises 154 documents, referring to Erdoğan's publicly delivered speeches which include references to *Germany* or *German* (see Figure 9).

Collected through an extensive and systematic web-based search, documents include media news between 2003 and 2018 as well as public statements between 2014 and 2018, which are available on the presidency's webpage.[25] Sources include formal and informal speeches as well as national and international statements.[26] Only direct quotes appear in the

---

22 Waldman, Simon/ Çalışkan, Emre. The "New Turkey" and Its Discontents, 2017.

23 Cf. Tekin, Funda/ Schönlau, Anke. The EU-German-Turkish Triangle. A Conceptual Framework for Narratives, Perceptions and Discourse of a Unique Relationship. In this volume, p. 9-30, p. 26.

24 Cf. Breuning, Marijke. Foreign policy analysis: A comparative introduction. New York, 2007.

25 Cf. T.C. Cumhurbaşkanlığı. Konuşmalar, https://tccb.gov.tr/receptayyiperdogan/k onusmalar/, [12.07.2021].

26 Cf. The discourse and narrative of populist leaders can be simple or more complex based on linguistic measures. Attempting to appeal to the average citizen, Erdoğan uses a very intermingled and vague discourse which has caused a trans-

database; hence, there are no indirect references to Erdoğan's speeches and statements by journalists and columnists. Between 2003 and August 2014, when Erdoğan served as the Prime Minister, we found 58 documents in total and for the years of his presidency (August 2014-December 2018) 96 documents. Figure 10 illustrates the dataset distribution throughout our analysis period.

Figure 9: Appearance of 'Germany' and 'German' in Erdoğan's Speeches Per Year

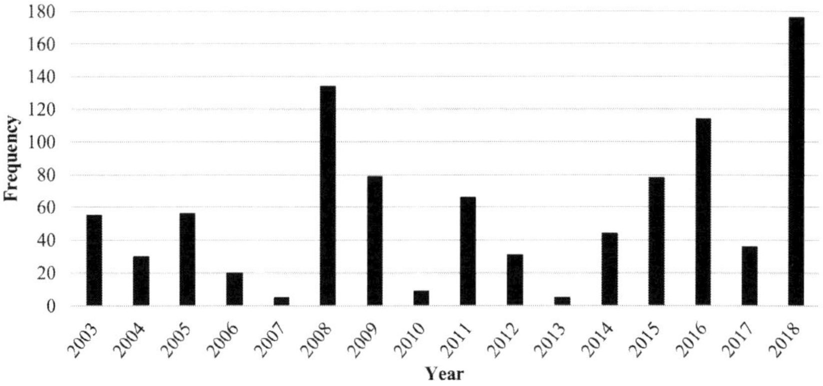

Source: own compilation.

If we combine data on the annual number of references to *Germany* or *German* (see Figure 9 above) with the increased number of relevant speeches as displayed in Figure 10, we can generally assume a gradual increase in Erdoğan's narratives on Germany. However, a detailed analysis is needed to provide comprehensive explanations for our research questions above. The relatively sharp decrease in references to Germany in 2017 stems from a lack of data as Erdoğan preferred to address the Western world and EU in general rather than specifically referring to Turkish-German relations throughout this period.

---

lation difficulty of his speeches into English. Indeed, right-wing populists often try to speak "the common man's language". For more detailed analyses see Mc-Donnell, D./ Ondelli, S. The Language of Right-Wing Populist Leaders: Not So Simple. In: *Perspectives on Politics*, 2020.; Bos, L., van der Brug, W./ de Vreese, C. An experimental test of the impact of style and rhetoric on the perception of right-wing populist and mainstream party leaders. In: *Acta Polit 48*, 2013.

Figure 10: Distribution of Data Sources

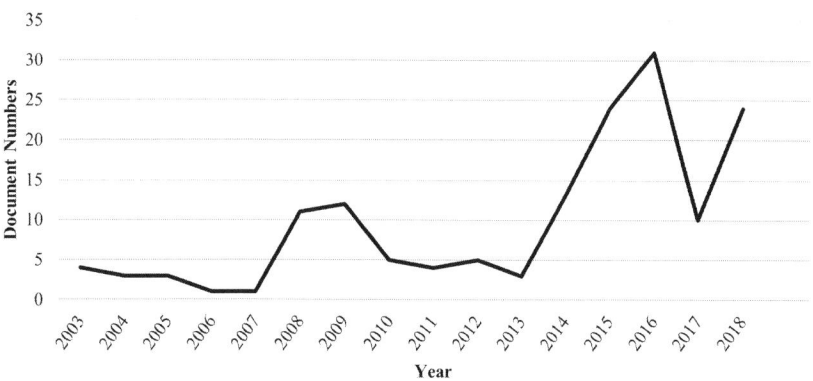

Source: own compilation.

The triangular relation of the EU, Germany and Turkey is multifaceted, combining many dimensions established through diverse interactions over several decades.[27] This study examines Erdoğan's narratives on the basis of four thematic dimensions, which are also introduced in this volume's overall framework: *political, economic, geopolitical* and *societal*.[28] Each thematic dimension comprises various sub-dimensions which refer to distinct themes. In addition, this study takes into consideration a fifth 'cross-cutting' dimension where Erdoğan takes Germany as a reference point. This dimension is characterised by competition – Germany as a rival rather than a model or an example for Turkey. Thus, this *cross-cutting dimension* constitutes a unique feature of Erdoğan's narratives that does not exist in those of other actors.

Sources have been manually coded and categorised according to these five dimensions (and their sub-dimensions)[29] through a MAXQDA analysis, a tool widely used within the context of quantitative methodology. Words and phrases written in *italics* throughout this chapter refer to thematic dimensions and sub-dimensions. Accordingly, each document has been associated with one or several thematic dimensions which have, in turn, provided data for our analysis and interpretation. Thus, sub-dimensions constitute the 'actual wording' identified in the original quotes

---

27 Cf. Aydın-Düzgit, Senem/ Tocci, Nathalie. Turkey and the European Union. Palgrave Macmillan, 2015.

28 Cf. Tekin/ Schönlau, The EU-German-Turkish Triangle, 2022, p. 24.

29 Cf. Annex.

and aim at categorising Erdoğan's speeches under the five dimensions explained above. For instance, *tourism, refugee aid, investment* and *economic cooperation* have been considered as *economic sub-dimensions*, and the speeches which featured these sub-dimensions have been categorised under the *economic dimension*. Based on this general concept, each analytical section of the thematic dimensions presents and discusses the relevant sub-dimensions below.

3. *Leaders and Foreign Policy: Why It Matters What They Say?*

Within our analysis of foreign policy, the role played by political leaders is subject to different approaches. Various factors within the structure of foreign policy (such as the institutional and constitutional design), the balance of power between institutions and class fractions, domestic constraints including accountability, level of democratic traditions and rule of law as well as international constraints, alliance set ups and diplomatic agreements can all be relevant in analysing a leader's influence on foreign policy in any given state.[30] Commonly, the leader's personality will be studied to understand and draw conclusions from foreign policy making. Leadership trait analysis, operational code and presidential character utilising extensive political psychology methodology as well as content and speech analysis constitute different strategies in this field.[31]

Leaders also play a crucial role in shaping and framing foreign policy issues in terms of public opinion.[32] As widely accepted, foreign policy is too complex and too detached from the everyday lives of citizens who would look for cues from leaders they trust in forming their own perceptions and positions on foreign policy issues.[33] Other authors argue that, rather than leading the public, leaders would take on positions (or create policy) in response to public preferences or in anticipation of future changes in public opinion.[34] Thus, charismatic, popular leaders and their communication on foreign policy issues are considered as vital inputs in analysing links between public opinion and foreign policy.

---

30 Cf. Breuning, Foreign policy analysis, 2007.
31 Cf. Ibid.
32 Şenyuva, Özgehan/ Çengel, Esra. Turkish Public Perceptions of Germany: Most Popular among the Unpopular. In this volume, p. 161-180, p. 172.
33 Cf. Lippmann, Walter. Public Opinion. New York, 1997.
34 Cf. Page, Benjamin/ Shapiro, Robert. Effects of Public Opinion on Policy, 1983.

The concept of elite dominance in public opinion purports that people respond to information and cues supplied by elites and leaders, as different studies have demonstrated.[35] This chapter draws on an approach by Zaller who defines elite domination "as a situation in which elites induce citizens to hold opinions that they would not hold if aware of the best available information and analysis".[36] Page and Barabas discuss the significant gap that exists between leaders and citizens, approaching this from a democratic theory perspective, stating that asymmetrical knowledge created an advantage for leaders to shape and frame foreign policy issues in a certain way.[37] This is also valid for Turkey since the vast majority of media has been "captured"[38] by the AKP today. This creates an essential advantage for the AKP elites who can control information supply to the public, thus to an important extent shape popular opinion.

Beyond the scope of this chapter, but relevant to the overall context, is the extensive body of research on different forms of relationships between and among the mass media, elites, the public, and the policy-making process.[39] Media is found to have considerable impact on people's agendas and priorities, particularly as widely reported issues become more significant in the eyes of the public. Research also reveals that media messages can affect or 'prime' the standards or criteria that individuals use in making evaluations.[40] While media's spreading of elite discourse is a subject that also deserves attention within the context of Turkey during the AKP era, this study focusses on a specific subject (Germany) as transmitted by an influential political leader (Recep Tayyip Erdoğan) over an extensive time period of 15 years.

---

35 Cf. Zaller. The Nature and Origins of Mass Opinion.; Iyengar, Shanto/ Kinder, Donald R. News that matters: television and American opinion. Chicago, 1987; Page, Benjamin., Shapiro, Robert Y./ Dempsey, Glenn R. What Moves Public Opinion?, 1987.

36 Zaller, The Nature and Origins of Mass Opinion, 313.

37 Cf. Page, Benjamin/ Barabas, Jason. Foreign Policy Gaps between Citizens and Leaders, 2000.

38 Balamir Coşkun, Gülçin. Media capture strategies in new authoritarian states: the case of Turkey. In: *Publizistik*, 2020, 65.

39 Cf. Brody. Richard. Assessing Presidential Character: The Media, Elite Opinion, and Public Support. Stanford, 1991; Page, Benjamin I./ Shapiro, Robert Y. The Rational Public. Chicago, 1992; Zaller, John R. The Nature and Origins of Mass Opinion. New York, 1992.

40 Cf. MacCombs, Maxwell. Setting the agenda: The mass media and public opinion. Cambridge, 2006.

4. Main Findings: Closer or Further Away?

This chapter analyses Erdoğan's narratives with a view to *economic, geopolitical, political, societal* and *cross-cutting (Germany as a reference point) dimensions* from 2003 up until 2018. As stated in the methodology section, Erdoğan became Prime Minister in 2003 and then President in August 2014. Turkey's governmental system then shifted from parliamentarian to presidential under his tenure in 2018. From the perspective of these different roles, the following sections examine each dimension with a comparative approach, relating them to each other. We also compare different sub-dimensions with each other within the thematic dimension in question and focus on how they evolved over time.

4.1. The Geopolitical Dimension

Because of the Bosporus, the straits which are perceived as a bridge between East and West, Turkey's geopolitical position is perceived as relying on its geographical position, national unity and border security (classical geopolitics)[41] more than social, economic, cultural and technological values (critical geopolitics).[42] Hence, matters including *security, terror/terrorism* (*FETÖ*[43], *PYD/YPG/YPJ/PKK*[44], *ISIS*[45]), the *Syrian issue* (e.g. *Afrin and İdlib interventions* – which is a cross-border military operation, known as Operation Olive Branch, conducted by Turkey with the Syrian National Army in the Kurdish Afrin District and entails a deal on a demilitarised buffer zone in Idlib [resulted in Sochi Agreement][46] in 2018), *energy, nuclear weapon, military cooperation* are designated as sub-dimensions under the geopolitical dimension. Reference to *terror/terrorism* appears as the most

---

41 Cf. Owens, Mackubin Thomas. In defense of classical geopolitics. Naval War College Review 52.4, 1999, p. 59–76.
42 Cf. Kuus, Merje. Critical geopolitics. In: Oxford Research Encyclopedia of International Studies, 2010.
43 Fethullah Gülen Terör Örgütü – Fethullah Gülen Terrorist Organisation.
44 Partiya Yekîtiya Demokrat – Democratic Union Party/Yekîneyên Parastina Gel – People's Protection Units/Yekîneyên Parastina Jin – Women's Protection Units/ Partiya Karkerên Kurdistanê – Kurdistan Workers' Party.
45 Islamic State of Iraq and Syria.
46 Cf. Petkova, Mariya. After the Sochi agreement, HTS is facing internal divisions. In: Aljazeera, 27.09.2018; Full text of Turkey. Russia agreement on northeast Syria, In: Aljazeera, 22.10.2019, https://www.aljazeera.com/news/2019/10/22/full-t ext-of-turkey-russia-agreement-on-northeast-syria/ [12.07.2021].

relevant sub-dimension within the *geopolitical dimension*. Especially after the failed coup attempt in July 2016, it is clear that Erdoğan's comparisons with and accusations towards Germany intensified (see Figure 11).

Figure 11: Narrative Distribution of Geopolitical Dimension

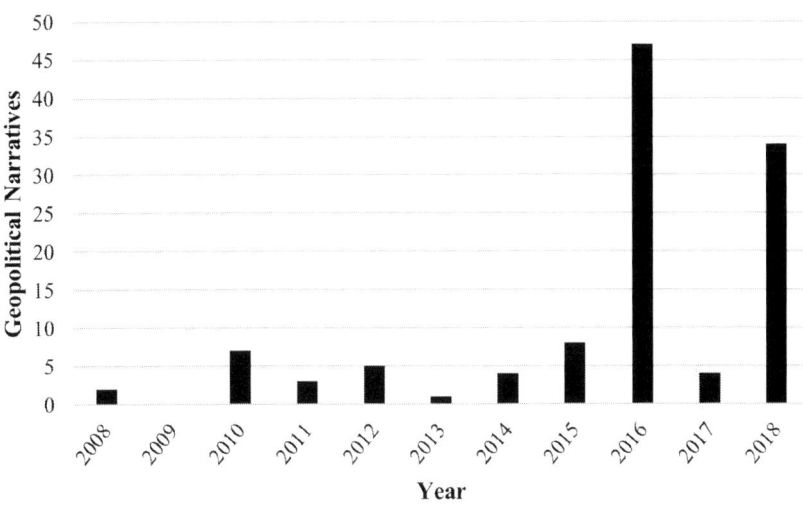

Source: own compilation.

It is important to note that Erdoğan mostly situates Germany within Europe and addresses several European countries when referring to Germany in his speeches. For instance, in the following 2017 speech he compares Turkey's counterterrorism policies with those of its European counterparts and directs harsh criticisms at major Member States, including Germany:

"While Turkey deports 5,000 terror suspects from Turkey – these are terror suspects, we deport them and report it – and prohibits 53,000 entry into Turkey, it did not receive serious intelligence support from European countries that are shaken with several incidents recently. On the contrary, these countries protected and granted asylum to names that have been reported as terror suspects from the Turkish side. Frankly, Germany is one of these countries".[47]

---

47 "Türkiye, 5 bin terör şüphelisini sınır dışı ederken, -bunlar terör şüphelisi, bunları sınır dışı ediyoruz ve haber de veriyoruz- 53 binine ülkeye giriş yasağı koyarken, maalesef bugün eylemlerle sarsılan Avrupa ülkelerinden ciddi bir istihbarat desteği alamamıştır. Tam tersine bu ülkeler Türkiye'nin terör örgütü üyesi olarak

It is known that some EU Member States such as Greece and Germany did not extradite people that Turkey accused of being related to the failed coup attempt or perceived as terrorists. For instance, Greece rejected Turkey's demand on extradition of eight Turkish soldiers who fled the country amidst the failed coup attempt.[48] Similarly, Germany insisted on more material evidence to meet Turkey's demand on extradition of the fugitive journalist Can Dündar and the members of the so-called terrorist organisations of FETÖ and PKK.[49] Hence, it is understood from Erdoğan's narrative here that Germany acts against Turkish interests, particularly when it comes to security-related issues after the failed coup attempt in July 2016.

Parallel to this, the *Syrian issue* finds a major place in Erdoğan's narratives, particularly on the issue of *foreign fighters*. He refers several times to people from various European countries who joined the armed struggle of ISIS in Syria as foreign fighters, as demonstrated in the following examples:

"Look, one of the greatest challenges of Turkey these days is the young people coming from the West to join these organisations.… The President of France says "One thousand people from my country joined this organisation", England says "600 people joined from my country", Germany is the same".[50] "We do not claim that currently there is no ISIS militants in Turkey. There are foreign fighters coming to Syria from France, England, Germany. Here, the National Intelligence Service, as our security intelligence, worked faster than others. If we had not worked fast, we would not have been able to make

---

bildirdiği isimleri korumuş, kollamış, hatta iltica başvurularını kabul etme yoluna gitmiştir. Almanya bunlardan bir tanesidir, bakın bu kadar açık konuşuyorum". T.C. Cumhurbaşkanlığı. 38. Muhtarlar Toplantısında Yaptıkları Konuşma, 2017.

48 Cf. Turkish anger as Greece rejects extradition of eight soldiers. In: BBC News, 26.01.2017, https://www.bbc.com/news/world-europe-38754821 [12.07.2021]; Bell, Bethany. Turkey coup attempt: Greek dilemma over soldiers who fled. In: BBC News, 19.07.2016.

49 Cf. Turkey-Germany: Erdoğan urges Merkel to extradite Gulen 'terrorists'. In: BBC News, 28.09.2018, https://www.bbc.com/news/world-europe-45684390.amp [12.07.2021].

50 "Bakın Türkiye'nin bu günlerde önündeki en önemli meselelerinden biri de Batıdan gelerek bu örgütlere katılan gençlerdir.[…] Fransa Devlet Başkanı "Benim ülkemden bin kişi bu örgüte katıldı" diyor, İngiltere "600 kişi benim ülkemden katıldı" diyor, Almanya bir o kadar". T.C. Cumhurbaşkanlığı. Uluslararası Uyuşturucu Politikaları ve Halk Sağlığı Sempozyumu'nda Yaptıkları Konuşma, 2014.

these detections. ... But if EU Member States transfer especially enough information to Turkey, Turkey all the time does what is necessary".[51]

However, the *Syrian issue* seems to be referred to in connection with the *political dimension* especially with regards to the *refugee issue* and its relevance for domestic politics. In 2018, Erdoğan argued that Germany was satisfied with and grateful to Turkey for keeping and taking care of Syrian refugees: "I think that we have the same sensitivities with Germany especially with regard to the Syrian crisis and irregular migration. The German authorities have always appreciated the Turkish nation's protection of the Syrian neighbours fleeing from persecution and that the Turkish nation shared their bread".[52] *The Syrian issue* is used by the Turkish president to deliver a message on EU/German dependency on Turkey in the region. At the same time, Germany is accused of acting against Turkish interests (see Dündar-case above), which fosters a narrative of unfair treatment in the *geopolitical dimension*, thus indicating a conflictual relationship.

Erdoğan's conflictual narrative of relations in the *geopolitical dimension* coincides with changing Western perceptions and narratives about Turkey's state of democracy, particularly after the failed coup attempt in 2016. In the aftermath, Western politicians and media increasingly criticised Turkey's shift to the presidential system as the beginning of a "more Islamist, nationalist and authoritarian"[53] era and Erdoğan as the "sultan of 21st-century Turkey" equipped with "an unprecedented amount

---

51 "Türkiye'de şu anda DAİŞ militanı yok, diye bir iddianın içerisinde değiliz. Fransa'dan, İngiltere'den, Almanya'dan Suriye'ye gelen yabancı savaşçılar var. Biz burada MİT, emniyet istihbaratı olarak diğerlerine göre hızlı çalıştık. Hızlı çalışmamış olsaydık bu tespitleri, yakalamaları yapamazdık. [...] Ama AB üyesi ülkeler özellikle yeterince bilgiyi Türkiye'ye aktarırlarsa Türkiye bunun gereğini her zaman yapar". Erdoğan'dan başkanlık sistemi açıklaması. In: Haber7., 30.03.2015, https://www.haber7.com/partiler/haber/1332804-erdogandan-bask anlik-sistemi-aciklamasi [12.07.2021].

52 "Suriye krizi ve düzensiz göç meselesi basta olmak üzere Almanya ile aynı hassasiyetlere sahip olduğumuzu düşünüyorum. Alman makamları Türk milletinin zulümden kaçan Suriyeli komşularına sahip çıkmasını, ekmeğini bölüşmesini daima takdir ettiler". Cumhurbaşkanı Erdoğan'dan Almanya'da flaş açıklamalar. In: Hürriyet, 29.09.2018, https://www.hurriyet.com.tr/gundem/cumhurbaskani-er dogandan-almanyada-flas-aciklamalar-40971180 [12.07.2021].

53 Erdoğan inaugurates a new political era in Turkey. In: The Economist, 28.06.2018, https://www.economist.com/europe/2018/06/28/erdogan-inaugura tes-a-new-political-era-in-turkey [12.07.2021].

of power".[54] Hence, it is especially after the failed coup attempt that the *geopolitical dimension* takes a broad place in his narratives (see Figure 12).

Figure 12: Narrative Distribution Immediately after the Failed Coup Attempt in 2016

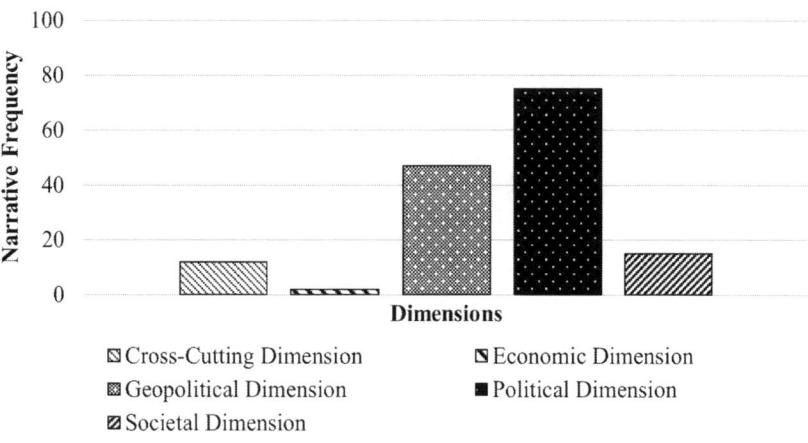

Source: own compilation.

This stems particularly from geopolitical issues such as the *Syrian issue* and the sub-dimension of *terror/terrorism* taking an extensive place in Turkey's political agenda throughout this era. Hence, Erdoğan's narrative in the *geopolitical dimension* becomes increasingly intermingled with Turkey's domestic affairs and takes a reactive approach in response to Western narratives on Turkey.

4.2. The Political Dimension

Generally, the *political dimension* is mostly referred to under thematic sub-dimensions such as *democracy/rule of law, triangular relation, friendship/cooperation/solidarity, EU membership/EU process, judiciary, coup attempt, asylum, fascism* and *Armenian genocide*. Throughout the early 2000s, Erdoğan emphasised the importance of *friendship/cooperation/solidarity* with the EU

---

54 Recep Tayyip Erdoğan: The sultan of 21st-century Turkey. In: Deutsche Welle (DW), 08.07.2018, https://www.dw.com/en/recep-tayyip-erdogan-the-sultan-of-21s t-century-turkey/a-44569548 [12.07.2021].

and Germany, expressing his desire for *EU membership*. However, with the emergence of problems in the EU accession process, his narratives indicate a growing mistrust and exhaustion towards the EU and European states. Hence, conflictual statements and criticisms become more frequent particularly in the post-2013 era over several issues such as democracy and rule of law, freedom of speech and the independence of Turkish judiciary. As visualised in Figure 13, this dimension takes a pre-dominant place in Erdoğan's speeches particularly after 2013 in comparison to other thematic dimensions. This is the year when Turkey starts to encounter criticisms concerning its state of *democracy and rule of law* with the eruption of Gezi Park Protests.

Figure 13: Distribution of Dimensions over Years[55]

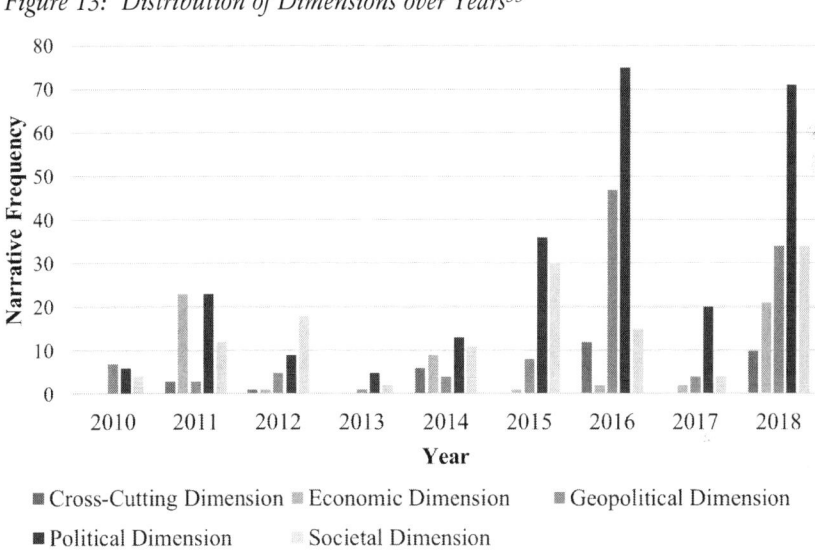

Source: own compilation.

Within this dimension, we interpret notions such as *friendship, cooperation and solidarity* as indicating Erdoğan's desire for cooperation. During the full timespan under investigation, 27 percent of sub-dimensions found in the political dimension indicate cooperative messages sent. These friendly notions are mostly present before 2010 although they continue to occupy

---

55 Since the figure aims to illustrate the domination of political dimension after 2013, the distribution between 2003–2009 was not included.

an important place in Erdoğan's speeches even after 2013. His narrative about German criticisms on Turkey's state of *democracy/rule of law and human rights* – particularly *freedom of press and expression* in Turkey – is built upon statements about Germany that indicate conflict and confrontation. After 2015, Erdoğan's narrative leans towards a conflictual bilateral relationship: The duality of cooperative and conflictual statements here creates a question of consistency in his overall narrative on Germany.

Especially after assuming presidential office in 2014, *democracy and the rule of law* are the sub-dimensions Erdoğan mostly refers to when he speaks on political matters (see Figure 14). When responding to Western criticisms and concerns regarding Turkey's divergence from liberal democratic norms, he aims to put the ball back into Germany's court. The quarrel on Germany's refusal to extradite former Cumhuriyet editor-in-chief Can Dündar to Turkey serves as an example. Referring to the convicted journalist, Erdoğan expressed the following words in 2018: "One of them is the so-called journalist who was sentenced to 5 years and 10 months. The so-called journalist took advantage of a gap, fled, and took refuge in Germany. He is currently in Germany. And he has been rewarded and held in high regard".[56] Furthermore, the Turkish President extensively refers to, or rather attacks *German/'Western' media* in the same period. Erdoğan criticises Western media with depictions of an anti-democratic actor stating: "I have seen that the countries which we thought are extremely powerful, are not being ruled by their politicians, but by the media. In my interviews, they say that "the media says this, the media says that". And I told them "leave the media aside, don't you care about what your people think?""[57] He does not deny or defend actions but turns these charges back to Germany, thus adding fuel to the conflict.

---

56 "İşte bunlardan bir tanesi de 5 yıl 10 aya mahkûm olmuş olan güya sözde gazetecidir. Sözde gazeteci bir boşluktan yararlanmış kaçmış Almanya'ya gelmiş sığınmıştır. Şu anda Almanya'dadır. Ve kendisi taltif edilmiştir. El üstünde tutulmuştur".
   Cumhurbaşkanı Erdoğan'dan Almanya'da flaş açıklamalar. In: Hürriyet, 29.09.2018.

57 "Hele hele işte bu devasa güçlü zannettiğimiz ülkeleri başında olanların değil medyalarının yönettiğini gördüm. Çünkü yaptığım görüşmelerde; "medya şöyle diyor, medya böyle diyor", söyledikleri bu. Ben de kendilerine şunu söyledim: "Halkınız ne diyor bunu düşünmüyor musun? Bırakın medyayı" dedim". T.C. Cumhurbaşkanlığı. Yükseköğretim Akademik Yılı Açılış Töreninde Yaptıkları Konuşma, 2018.

Figure 14: Narrative Distribution within Political Dimension

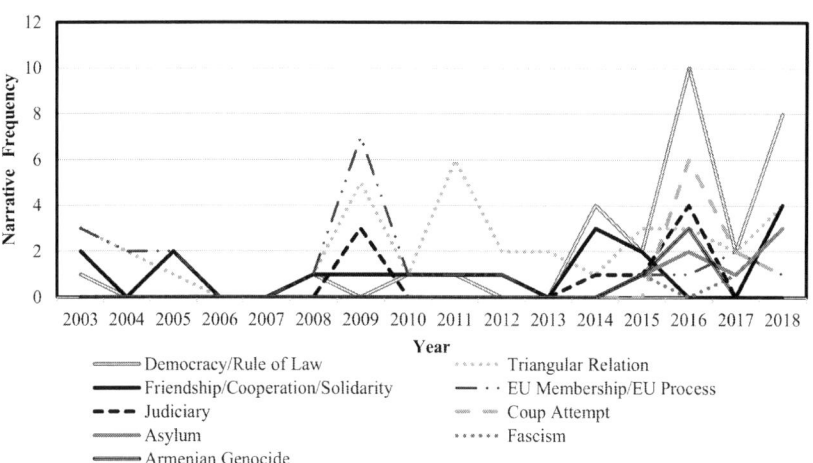

Source: own compilation.

The political dimension also includes the *triangular relation* between Turkey-Germany-EU and the debate of *Turkey's membership to the EU* (see Figure 14). It is remarkable to note that the *triangular relation* is referred to continually throughout the relevant years between 2003 and 2018. In this sense, Erdoğan also regards Germany as one of the most important actors to be persuaded on the road to *full membership*. Particularly, his objection to the *'privileged partnership'* suggested by Chancellor Angela Merkel and Turkey's emphasis on *full membership* in 2008 and 2009 have a remarkable place in the *triangular relationship*. An example of Erdoğan's stance on the *'privileged partnership'* approach is an interview with Turkish news channel, NTV, where he criticised the idea saying: "There is no such thing in the [EU] acquis communautaire, but Merkel insists upon a "privileged partnership" . Whatever it is".[58] Addressing the Turkish Parliament in 2018, he expressed his disappointment on the stagnating membership process and suggested unequal treatment of Turkey by the EU: "Of course, we could not remain silent in the face of injustices and double standards applied to our country in the process of full membership of the European

---

58 "Avrupa Birliği müktesebatı içinde böyle bir şey yok ama Merkel tutturmuş "imtiyazlı ortaklık". Nasıl bir şeyse". Erdoğan'ın konuşmasının tam metni. In: NTV, 11.06.2009, https://www.ntv.com.tr/turkiye/erdoganin-konusmasinin-tam -metni,aLzuEGq-8k6LVNb_uQWamg [12.07.2021].

Union. Some European countries turned their animosity against Turkey into a domestic policy issue which deepened and expanded certain problems".[59] Despite Erdoğan's continual emphasis on positive narratives such as *friendship, cooperation and solidarity*, he periodically resorts to conflictual statements demonstrating Turkey's resentment due to injustices and double standards caused by the European side.

4.3. The Economic Dimension

Economic relations and partnership are historically among the most prominent aspects of bilateral relations between Turkey and Germany. Thus, this section analyses those speeches that have been categorised under the *economic dimension*, which comprises certain sub-dimensions such as: *economic cooperation, investment, tourism, economic assistance, refugee aid, German companies, growth rate* and *economic crisis*. Erdoğan's economic references peaked in 2011 and 2018 (see Figure 15).

Figure 15: Narrative Distribution of Economic Dimension over Years

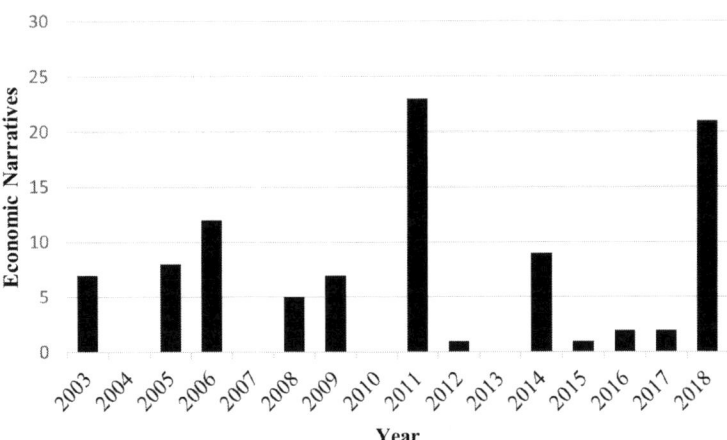

Source: own compilation.

---

59 "Avrupa Birliği tam üyelik sürecinde ülkemize yapılan haksızlıklar ve uygulanan çifte standart karşısında elbette sessiz kalamazdık. Kimi Avrupa ülkelerinin Türkiye karşıtlığını bir iç politika malzemesi haline dönüştürmesi, sıkıntıların derinleşmesine ve yaygınlaşmasına sebep oldu". T.C. Cumhurbaşkanlığı. TBMM 27. Dönem 2. Yasama Yılı Açış Konuşması, 2018.

These two years respectively mark the period of post-2008 global economic crisis and the relative recession of Turkey's economy in 2018. During the first years of the AKP administration at the beginning of the 2000s, Turkey endeavoured to accelerate neoliberal institutionalisation building on the 'double anchors' of the International Monetary Fund (IMF) and the EU.[60] Indeed, inflation proved to be continually negative and GDP growth was very stable, which contributed to 'AKP's electoral success' in the post-2001 era.[61] This period of relative stability and growth came to an end, though, after the 2008 global economic crisis when the Turkish economy experienced an economic recession. Although Turkey was "slightly touched"[62] by the 2008 economic crisis, the same cannot be said for the post-2016 era. With increasing capital outflows and political uncertainty, Turkey's economy experienced serious recession in the third quarter of 2016 for the first time since the global financial crisis in 2008/09.[63] The impact of this on the economy was further exacerbated by the August 2018 currency crisis.[64] As argued below, such shifts in Turkey's economy created the already existing need for capital and had an essential impact on the *economic dimension* of Erdoğan's messages.

The sub-dimensions of *investment* and *economic cooperation* are of particular importance in explaining the peaks of economy-related narratives in 2011 and 2018. Erdoğan encourages and promotes German investment initiatives in Turkey, especially during the years associated with economic recession in the post-2008 period and in 2018. He often refers directly (and sometimes indirectly) to German companies and in doing so he conveys mainly two narratives: he praises the economic partnership between Germany and Turkey based on mutual benefits, as understood from his following speech:

---

60 Cf. Bedirhanoğlu, Pınar/ Yalman, L. Galip. State, class and the discourse: reflections on the neoliberal transformation in Turkey. In: Alfredo Saad-Filho, and Galip L. Yalman. Economic transitions to neoliberalism in middle-income countries: policy dilemmas, economic crises, and forms of resistance. London, 2009.

61 Cf. Öniş, Ziya. The Triumph of Conservative Globalism: The Political Economy of the AKP Era. In: *Turkish Studies*, 2012, 13(2). p. 138.

62 "Kriz teğet geçti dedim, etkilemedi demedim". In: CNN Türk, 03.04.2009, https://www.cnnturk.com/video/2009/04/03/programlar/5n1k/index.html [12.07.2021].

63 Cf. Akçay, Ümit. Türkiye'de neoliberal popülizm, otoriterleşme ve kriz. In: *Toplum ve Bilim*, 2019, 147. pp. 64–65.

64 Cf. Bedirhanoğlu, Pınar. Social constitution of the AKP's strong state through financialisation: state in crisis, or crisis state? In: Pınar Bedirhanoğlu, Çağlar Dölek, Funda Hülagü, Özlem Kaygusuz (Eds.). Turkey's new state in the making: transformations in legality, economy, and coercion. London, 2020.

"More than 4,000 German companies are active in our country. Germany is the country with the most companies in Turkey. In one sense, leading German companies operating in Turkey profit by various price advantages and increase their profitability benefiting from incentives, and besides, they also contribute to the production, technology and export levels of Turkish industry".[65]

He also highlights the longstanding history of the economic partnership by stating for instance "German companies have played an active role in the development initiatives of late Ottoman period and have undertaken the management of economic activities in different fields".[66] This indicates that he has a consistent element in his narratives on *economic cooperation* and *investment*.

The sub-dimension of *tourism* and German tourists represent a similarly consistent and important element in Erdoğan's economy-related narratives. *Tourism* is extremely significant for Turkish economic development in that foreign currency inflows fuel investment and employment opportunities. In a 2006 speech, he stated: "Germany is the country that sends the highest number of tourists to Turkey, followed by Russia. My heart's desire is that Russia does not catch Germany. I want this difference to continuously increase".[67] In 2017, Erdoğan encouraged German Turks to organise their weddings and celebrations in Turkey saying: "Our foreign guests that will come to Turkey for such reasons will find an opportunity to personally see, recognise and experience the beauties of Turkey, and I

---

65 "Ülkemizde 4 binden fazla Alman firması faaliyet gösteriyor. Sayı bakımından Türkiye'de en çok şirketi bulunan ülke Almanya. Türkiye'de faaliyet gösteren önde gelen Alman firmaları, bir yandan Türkiye'deki çeşitli fiyat avantajları ve teşviklerden yararlanarak karlılıklarını artırırlarken, öte yandan, Türk sanayisinin üretim, teknoloji ve ihracat seviyesinin geliştirilmesine de katkı sağlıyorlar". Cf. "NATO'nun ne işi var Libya'da?". In: Sabah, 28.02.2011, https://www.sabah.com.t r/gundem/2011/02/28/natonun_ne_isi_var_libyada [12.07.2021].

66 "Alman firmaları, Osmanlı'nın son dönemlerinde hayata geçirilen kalkınma hamlelerinde etkin rol oynamış, farklı alanlarda yürütülen ekonomik faaliyetlerin işletmesini üstlenmişlerdir." Cumhurbaşkanı Erdoğan'dan Almanya'da flaş açıklamalar. In: Hürriyet, 29.09.2018.

67 "Almanya, Türkiye'ye en fazla turist gönderen ülkedir. Rusya şimdi arkadan geliyor. Gönlüm şunu arz ediyor; Rusya turizmde Almanya'yı yakalamasın istiyorum. Bu farkın artarak devam etmesini istiyorum". Erdoğan Alman turist istedi. In: Internethaber, 06.10.2006, https://www.internethaber.com/erdogan-alman-turist-i stedi-46121h.htm [12.07.2021].

believe that they will re-visit Turkey every year".[68] Again, the message is welcoming and does not address political leadership but people directly in attracting tourists to Turkey.

Economic activity in EU-Turkey relations is not restricted to investments and trade partnerships. Through the 3+3 billion Euro 'Facility for Refugees in Turkey' (short: Refugee Facility), the EU funds infrastructure development and direct financial support for refugees living in Turkey.[69] Hence, the issues of *economic assistance* as well as *humanitarian and refugee aid* were considered as sub-dimensions of the economic dimension. However, our findings show that these sub-dimensions are seldomly treated in purely economic terms, but are connected to the relationship's political or geopolitical dimensions. Erdoğan utilises funding from the Refugee Facility as an instrument embedded in his political and geopolitical narratives. Indeed, a row over the pace of fund disbursements characterised implementation of this Facility.[70] Funds are framed as an unpaid bill and unfulfilled political responsibility by the EU and thus connected to the *political dimension* and *geopolitical dimensions* – areas where the EU supposedly mistreats Turkey. For instance, in a 2016 speech Erdoğan says of the *refugee aid:*

> "I do not understand the attitude of demanding projects for the contribution they speak of. Merkel actually visited Nizip.[71] What we, Turkey, have done is very visible. What project are you asking for? What you call projects is what we have already accomplished. No one should try to deceive us by saying things like projects".[72]

---

68 "Böyle vesilelerle ülkemize gelecek yabancı misafirlerimizin Türkiye'nin güzelliklerini bizzat görme, tanıma, yaşama imkânı bulduklarında ziyaretlerini her yıl tekrarlayacaklarına inanıyorum". T.C. Cumhurbaşkanlığı. Turizm Sektör Temsilcileri ile Buluşmasında Yaptıkları Konuşma, 2017.

69 Cf. European Commission. The EU Facility for Refugees in Turkey, 2021, https://ec.europa.eu/neighbourhood-enlargement/news_corner/migration_en [12.07.2021].

70 Cf. Gotev, Georgi. EU and Turkey agree on €3 billion refugee deal. In: Euractiv.com, 30.11.2015; Guarascio, Francesco, Gümrükçü, Tuvan. EU, Turkey in stand-off over funds to tackle new migrant crisis. In: Reuters, 06.03.2020, https://www.reuters.com/article/us-syria-security-turkey-eu-idUSKBN20T1RH [21.07.2021].

71 Nizip is a district and city of Gaziantep Province of south-eastern Turkey. It is a strategically important place at the Syrian border.

72 The focus of the visit was the use of EU funds for concrete projects developed for refugees in Turkey. This is a controversial issue, as the funding is being used only in the form of project funding rather than a general budget allocated

Hence, it is plausible that aspects of the economic dimension, such as *economic assistance*, are becoming increasingly conflictual and embedded within some of his political and geopolitical narratives, whereas his narrative of the economic dimension of the relationship in other areas promotes an active economic partnership and a cooperative attitude, as shown above in examples of the sub-dimensions *investment, economic cooperation* and *tourism*.

4.4. The Societal Dimension

The *societal dimension* entails a variety of sub-dimensions which were selected in line with the most important societal developments affecting the triangular relationship between EU, Germany and Turkey. These include the following sub-dimensions: *German Turks, religion (Islam), education, racism, Turkish Associations in Germany, culture* and *language (German)*. As with other thematic dimensions, the *societal dimension* entails both cooperative and conflictual narratives most of which are related to social, political and economic issues faced by *German Turks*.

As presented earlier, Erdoğan frequently draws his audience's attention to alleged differences and dualities between Turkey and the EU and Germany. This corresponds with narratives that occur under the *societal dimension* of his statements. Herein, the emphasis on *societal integration* of Turks in Germany or Germans of Turkish origin (*German Turks*) as well as their economic and political relations and ties within the German society are central to Erdoğan's narrative, being by far the mostly referred to sub-dimension under the *societal dimension*, as shown in Figure 16. Under the sub-dimension of *'German Turks'*, which entails references to *assimilation*[73]/*integration* and *Gastarbeiter*,[74] there is a relative consistency

---

for the use of officials. "Sözünü ettikleri katkı için Türkiye'den proje isteme eğilimlerine de anlam veremiyorum. Mesela Merkel, Nizip'i gezip gördü aslında. Türkiye olarak bizim yaptıklarımız ortada. Bizden neyin projesini istiyorsunuz? Sizin proje dediklerinizi biz çoktan hayata geçirmişiz. Proje vesaire diyerek hiç kimse bizi aldatmaya kalkmasın". Erdoğan'dan anayasa çıkışı: İslam vurgusuna ihtiyaç yok. In: Hürriyet, 28.04.2016, https://www.hurriyet.com.tr/gundem/laiklik -ladinilik-olursa-itiraz-gelir-40095714 [12.07.2021].

73 Erdoğan'dan Köln'de Adeta Seçim Öncesi Propagandası. In: Bianet, 11.02.2008, https://m.bianet.org/biamag/siyaset/104793-erdogan-dan-koln-de-adeta-secim-once si-propagandasi [12.07.2021].

74 A German notion used to identify foreign labour force that came to Germany from the late 1950s to the 1970s.

in the distribution by years (see the black line in Figure 16). Erdoğan keeps this dimension on top of his agenda, frequently repeating it with a consistent emphasis and message over the years.

Figure 16: Narrative Distribution within Societal Dimension

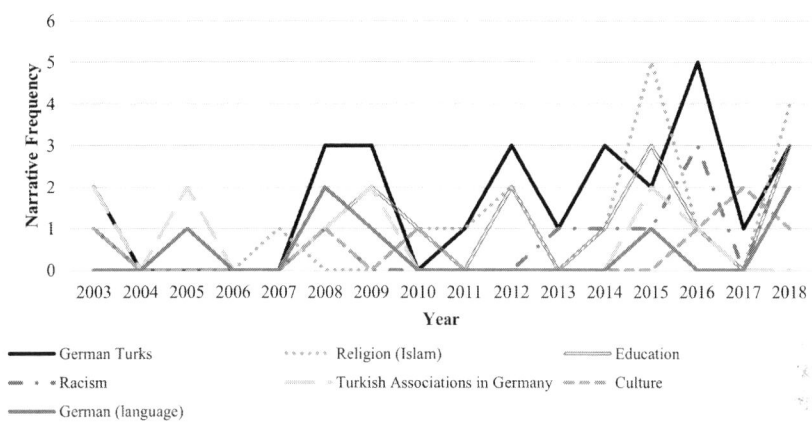

Source: own compilation.

The two sub-dimensions of *education* and *religion* are equally important in his narrative. On education, Erdoğan affirmatively emphasises the importance of language learning (German) for *German Turks* as well as opening high schools offering Turkish education. *Religion* is also mentioned equally frequently, despite its sensitivity, underlined by critical or accusatory statements on the matter. Erdoğan mostly talks about *discrimination* against Muslims as a religious group in Europe. Criticising campaigns and signboards of the Federal Ministry of Interior in 2012 associating a headscarved woman with religious fundamentalism, for instance, he urged Germany to cancel out such campaigns stating: "I'm calling out to Germany. What is being done to our sisters wearing headscarves, putting them on billboards as a means of exclusion, cannot be considered as freedom of belief dear Merkel! You have to take action!"[75]

---

75 "Almanya'ya sesleniyorum. Orada başörtülü kızlarımıza yapılan, dışlama sebebi olarak billboardlara yerleştirmek inanç özgürlüğü olarak değerlendirilemez ey Merkel. Onun için adımlarını atmak zorundasınız." Erdoğan'dan AK Parti kongresinde tarihi konuşma. In: Hürriyet, 30.09.2012, https://www.hurriyet.com.tr/g undem/erdogandan-ak-parti-kongresinde-tarihi-konusma-21589232 [12.07.2021].

Another finding under the *societal dimension* points towards a narrative revision in terms of the citizenship status of *German Turks*. While Erdoğan firmly encourages *German Turks* to apply for *German citizenship* in the pre-2010 period, this emphasis is revised thereafter. He starts drawing more attention to the importance of *dual citizenship* for *German Turks*. In a Berlin press conference speech with Merkel, he declares his revised stance by claiming: "We find it more prudent to open the path of dual citizenship for our citizens here so that they become German citizens".[76] This may be linked with the increasingly stagnating accession process after 2007 and *Turkey's membership* goal slowly fading away. Another related finding concerning the sub-dimension of *integration* is that Erdoğan generally refers to this together with *assimilation*. In a 2008 Köln address to around 15,000 German Turks, he stated: "Nobody can expect you to be assimilated. For assimilation is a crime against humanity. We need to know that".[77] This speech is particularly significant in having attracted negative press in Germany for the Turkish president and was perceived as open confrontation. However, in the same speech Erdoğan also points towards the importance of *integration* saying: "In today's Germany, in Europe, in today's world, you can no longer and you should not see yourself as the "other" or temporary".[78] In other words, he consistently encourages *German Turks* to integrate with German society whereas he also warns them against the danger of *assimilation* in his speeches.

Overall, *German Turks* have formed an important element under the *societal dimension* for Erdoğan which he referred to consistently between 2003 and 2018. During the initial years of the AKP, he emphasised their societal and economic *integration* pointing towards the importance of *language learning* and *education*. However, over time conflictual statements about issues including *racism* and *discrimination* appeared more frequently in Erdoğan's speeches which may reflect his personal sensitivities. With the backsliding of bilateral relations between Germany and Turkey post-2013,

---

76 "Biz buradaki vatandaşlarımızın, soydaşlarımızın Alman vatandaşlığına alınması noktasında çifte vatandaşlık yolunun açılmasını çok daha isabetli buluyoruz." Erdoğan: Açlık grevi tamamen şov. In: Hürriyet, 01.11.2012, https://www.hurriyet .com.tr/gundem/erdogan-aclik-grevi-tamamen-sov-21820930 [12.07.2021].

77 "Kimse sizden asimilasyon konusunda hoşgörü beklemez. Zira asimilasyon bir insanlık suçudur. Bunu böyle bilmemiz lazım". Erdoğan: "Asimilasyon İnsanlık Suçudur", In: Haber7,12.02.2008, https://www.haber7.com/siyaset/haber/299710-e rdogan-asimilasyon-insanlik-sucu [12.07.2021].

78 "Bugünün Almanya'sında, Avrupa'sında, bugünün dünyasında artık kendinizi öteki olarak, geçici olarak göremezsiniz, görmemelisiniz". Erdoğan: "Asimilasyon İnsanlık Suçudur". In: Haber7,12.02.2008.

his *societal dimension* narratives assumed a harsher tone, notably his call out to *German Turks* not to vote for CDU/CSU, SPD and the Green Party in 2017.[79] As elsewhere, Erdoğan's *societal dimension* narrative reveals contradictory signs of conflict and cooperation.

4.5. The Cross-Cutting Dimension

The *cross-cutting dimension* entails several sub-dimensions including *governmental issues, economy, education, press, informatics & technology, transportation, health* and *social life*. Indeed, comparison with other countries is a common element in Erdoğan's speeches. In a variety of issues cutting across different dimensions, he frequently compares Turkey with other countries, and this is mostly true for Germany. While Erdoğan uses comparison as a method to counter criticisms concerning government policies from time to time, this style is also used to praise Turkey's successes in different fields.

Our analysis demonstrates that Erdoğan often takes Germany as a reference point for several thematic sub-dimensions such as *education, transportation, health* and *governmental issues*. However, he generally perceives and uses this reference point in a competitive manner. As mentioned earlier, Germany is referred to not as a model or an example for Turkey to follow or to imitate, but as a reference point to beat or to draw lessons from. For instance, in the societal dimension, we identified the sub-dimensions of *young population* and *"at least three children"* policy,[80] that shall encourage young people to have three or more children to counteract Germany's aging population. In 2012, Erdoğan stated that "if you did not have three children, we would become as today's Germany in 2037. I do not want to become as they are. I want our population to be young. We would be successful if an educated, young and dynamic population existed".[81]

---

79 Cf. Erdoğan'dan Almanya'daki Türklere: O partilere oy vermeyin. In: Evrensel, 2017.

80 Cf. Erdoğan Insists on Demanding Three Children. In: Al Monitor, 13.08.2013, https://www.al-monitor.com/originals/2013/08/erdogan-asks-turks-to-have-three-children.html [12.07.2021].

81 "Çünkü 3 çocuk doğurmadığımız takdirde 2037'de Almanya'nın bugün geldiği duruma geleceğiz. Ben bu duruma gelmek istemiyorum. Nüfusumuzun genç kalmasını istiyorum. Eğitimli genç dinamik bir nüfus olursa başarılı oluruz". Başbakan Erdoğan: Üç Çocuk Doğurmazsak... In: Beyaz Gazete, 31.10.2012,

Yet, Erdoğan occasionally refers to Germany as a success story that Turkey should aim to catch up with. For instance, he stresses and compares the number of *universities* and university students in Turkey with those in Germany even though he admits that Turkey needs a breakthrough in terms of *education* quality. Addressing Justice and Development Party (AKP) members in 2018, he puts forward the following:

> "When I was talking to the Chancellor during my trip to Germany, I asked her, *"What is the number of students in your universities?"* Germany's population is around 82 million and ours 81 million. She told me that they had 3 million university students including those at various institutes. Here, we have 7 million 600 thousand university students. We may not be at their level in terms of the quality of education right now; but after 5 or 10 years, we will reach and exceed that level if God's willing".[82]

Again, Erdoğan refers to Germany in a competitive manner stating Turkey's desire to surpass the quality of German universities even though Germany's success is acknowledged.

The President is apt to make historical references and comparisons between Germany and Turkey occurring in his narrative mostly in terms of *governmental issues* for the sake of justifying current Turkish domestic politics (see Figure 17). For instance, as a response to the criticisms against the expulsion of thousands of civil servants with alleged connections to the failed coup attempt in 2016, he stated in 2017: "Now some people say; *"Aren't these people victimised?"* What victim? Do you know how many people were expelled from the state after the reunification of East Germany and West Germany? 600 thousand people were expelled".[83] A similar comparison was used to counter criticisms concerning low levels

---

https://beyazgazete.com/haber/2012/10/31/basbakan-erdogan-uc-cocuk-dogur mazsak-1481012.html [12.07.2021].

82 "Almanya seyahatimde Şansölyeyle konuşurken kendisine sordum, "Üniversitelerinizdeki öğrenci sayısı nedir" diye. Almanya'nın nüfusu 82 milyon civarında, bizim de 81. Bana enstitüleriyle beraber 3 milyon üniversiteli öğrencilerinin olduğunu söyledi. İşte bizim bakın 7 milyon 600 bin üniversiteli öğrencimiz var. Nitelik olarak onların seviyesinde şu anda olmayabiliriz; ama 5 yıl, 10 yıl sonra Allah'ın izniyle biz o seviyeyi de yakalayacağız ve aşacağız". T.C. Cumhurbaşkanlığı. AK Parti Grup Toplantısında Yaptıkları Konuşma, 2018.

83 "Şimdi bazıları diyor ki; "Bu insanlar mağdur edilmiyor mu?" Ne mağduru? Doğu Almanya-Batı Almanya birleşmesinden sonra devletin yapılanmasında ne kadar kişi devletten çıkarıldı biliyor musunuz? 600 bin kişi çıkarıldı". T.C. Cumhurbaşkanlığı. 35. Muhtarlar Toplantısında Yaptıkları Konuşma, 2017.

of precautions in the 2014 mining disaster in the town of Soma leading to the death of 301 miners, where Erdoğan referred to similar disasters in 19th-century Britain so as to prove mining disasters "typical" and bypass criticisms.[84]

Figure 17: Narrative Distribution within Cross-Cutting Dimension

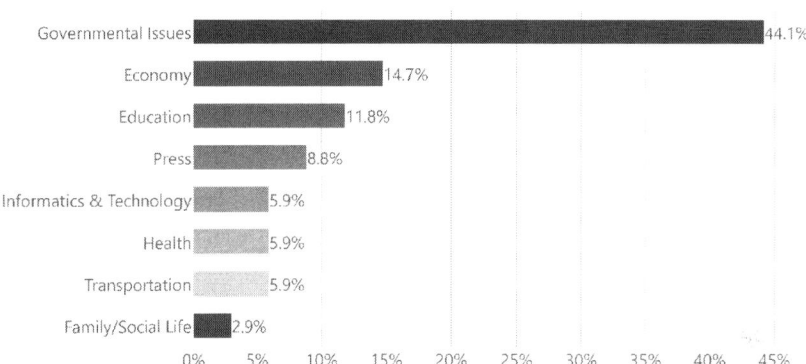

Source: own compilation.

In Erdoğan's narratives, Germany appears as a reference country which Turkey aims to draw lessons from in a variety of governmental and public policy issues even after the deterioration of bilateral relations. Particularly after the backsliding of EU-Turkey relations following Gezi Park protests in 2013, he capitalises on historical misdoings of his Western counterparts or Western countries to justify Turkish policies today. Hence, the under-lying allegation of Turkey's unfair treatment by the EU or Western countries is a frequent narrative of Turkey's relationship with the EU over recent years. However, these allegations from the Turkish side are voiced alongside positive and cooperative narratives regarding bilateral relations between the two countries.

---

84 Cf. Turkish PM cites 19th-century Britain to prove mine accidents are "typical". In: Hürriyet Daily News, 14.05.2014, https://www.hurriyetdailynews.com/tur kish-pm-cites-19th-century-britain-to-prove-mine-accidents-are-typical-66472 [12.07.2021].

5. Conclusion

As our findings indicate, there are no clear-cut boundaries between thematic dimensions[85] as detailed above in the *refugee deal* example. Our analysis shows that President Erdoğan's framing of bilateral relations has been multifaceted and dependent upon historical, contextual and conjunctural conditions. Research showed that his statements in different thematic dimensions are not always in harmony with each other, and at certain times even conflictual. To illustrate, Erdoğan's occasional accusatory narratives go hand in hand with his calls for cooperation and friendship under different dimensions. Consequently, our analysis indicates a conflictual cooperation scenario between Turkey and Germany based on either timewise or dimension-related inconsistencies in his narrative, which is inevitably reflected in EU-Turkey relations and Germany's role in these relations. Our findings do not reveal any turning points in Erdoğan's narratives resulting from his position as a Prime Minister or a President. Rather, turning points and changes in his narratives stem from domestic and international conjunctures.

Politically, the Gezi Park Protest in 2013 appears as a turning point in terms of Erdoğan's increasing use of an accusatory and conflictual narrative in response to growing Western concerns and criticisms about Turkey's democratic state of affairs. Whereas positive narratives such as *friendship, cooperation and solidarity* find an extensive place in Erdoğan's narratives until 2010, his accusatory narratives peak particularly after the failed coup attempt in 2016 when several topics including the *Syrian issue, refugee deal* and *terror/terrorism* become controversial issues within the *triangular relationship* between Turkey-Germany-EU.

Despite his accusatory narratives used regarding several political issues including the convicted journalist Can Dündar, Erdoğan puts vast emphasis on *economic cooperation* through initiatives such as encouraging *tourism* and *investment,* which he narrates within a friendship framework by implying a shared and common history. Economically, Germany is seen as a major economic partner which Turkey does not want to lose. Yet, within the societal dimension, issues concerning *German Turks* continue to feature heavily in Erdoğan's narratives, albeit with certain changes over time. Nevertheless, the Turkish president seems to aim at separating economic issues from politics because of the economic importance he assigns

---

85 Cf. Turhan, Ebru. The Asymmetrical Development of Political and Economic Relations between Turkey and the EU, 2015.

to Germany and EU. Historical references for the economic partnership between Germany and Turkey can be found in the same speeches where Erdoğan takes a critical stance against Germany's attitude and policies over *terror/terrorism* related issues.[86] Hence, it is plausible to argue that he uses different narratives at the same time to pursue several approaches in Turkey-Germany relations over diverse dimensions.

---

86 Cumhurbaşkanı Erdoğan'dan Almanya'da flaş açıklamalar. In: Hürriyet, 29.09.2018.

EU Leaders' Narratives on Turkey: From Membership Aspirant to a Transactional Partner and Problematic Neighbour

Moritz Rau, Denise Ersoy, Wolfgang Wessels

1. Introduction: Why Should We Study EU Leaders' Narratives on Turkey?

Relations between the European Union (EU) and Turkey have been highly topical in recent years. Growing hostilities, political turmoil and verbal skirmishes have kept this partnership in the limelight and aroused heated discussions in academic, political and public debate. Rather than being the exception, tensions and conflicts in EU-Turkey affairs have become the new normal. Turkey's backsliding democracy and shift towards a more assertive foreign policy in Syria, Libya and the Eastern Mediterranean have largely contributed to the EU's perception that "Turkey is increasingly moving away from the Union".[1] Between autumn 2016 and summer 2022, the European Parliament has adopted sixteen critical resolutions vis-à-vis Turkey.[2] In October 2019, the Foreign Affairs Council imposed a framework for restrictive measures to protest against Turkey's illegal offshore drilling activities in the Eastern Mediterranean. Yet, Turkey is still an accession candidate country and remains a "key partner for the EU"[3] in a number of policy areas – such as migration, security and trade. Facing such contradicting trends in EU-Turkey relations, policy and decision makers in Brussels need a pragmatic perspective so as to assess opportunities and constraints for joint actions with Ankara constructively.

---

1 Council of the European Union. Enlargement and Stabilisation and Association Process. Council conclusions. Brussels, 26.06.2018, https://www.consilium.europa.eu/media/35863/st10555-en18.pdf [23.09.2020].

2 Cf. European Parliament. EP resolutions. Brussels, 23.08.2022, https://www.europarl.europa.eu/delegations/en/d-tr/documents/ep-resolutions [23.08.2022].

3 European Union External Action. Role of Turkey in the Eastern Mediterranean: Remarks by the High Representative / Vice-President Josep Borrell at the EP plenary. Brussels, 15.09.2020, https://www.eeas.europa.eu/eeas/role-turkey-eastern-mediterranean-remarks-high-representative-vice-president-josep-borrell-ep_en [23.09.2020].

Aiming to shed light on the various forms and areas of interactions in EU-Turkey relations, this chapter studies European Council conclusions since the 1970s, focussing on narratives about Turkey generated by the EU Leaders' – the Heads of State or Government of the Member States. Our use of the term 'narrative' is understood as "interpretations by political actors of the evolution, drivers and actors, as well as the goal (or 'finalité') of EU-Turkey relations".[4] This analysis of narratives provides a framework for understanding the complex interplay between the accession process, areas of cooperation and tense conflicts that have shaped EU-Turkey relations over the past five decades. The aim is to clarify how EU Leaders' portray and communicate the EU's relationship with Turkey. This chapter takes the form of three parts. Following the introduction, there is a brief overview on the historical context of EU-Turkey relations. Then, the main part presents and discusses the empirical evidence of the European Council conclusions on Turkey. Finally, this chapter ends with a conclusion and a brief outlook on the future of EU-Turkey relations. Our analysis shows that after a period of convergence throughout the 1990s, which paved the way for Turkey's candidacy and in which the *membership narrative* predominated, there now exist two opposing narratives, one which centres on partnership whilst the other perceives Turkey as an increasingly problematic neighbour. This stems from strategic cooperation in selected policy fields such as migration and anti-terrorism on the one hand and growing divergences with regard to European fundamental values as well as foreign policy interests in the broader region (in particular: Syria, the Eastern Mediterranean and Libya) on the other. Hence, EU Leaders perceive Ankara as an important, but increasingly difficult partner.

2. The European Council – The European Union's Agenda Setter and Framer of EU Narratives on Turkey

EU narratives on Turkey have been shaped in various ways and by a number of different political actors within the Union. Previous research has examined public debates in the European Parliament and regular reports on Turkey by the European Commission.[5] However, little attention has so far

---

4 Özbey, Ebru Ece et.al. Identity Representations in the Narratives on the EU-Turkey Relations. FEUTURE Online Paper No. 32. Cologne, March 2019, p. 4.

5 Cf. Hauge, Hanna-Lisa et. al. Narratives of a Contested Relationship: Unravelling the Debates in EU-Turkey Relations. In: Saatçioğlu, Beken/ Tekin, Funda (Eds). Turkey and the European Union. Key Dynamics and Future Scenarios. Turkey and European Union Studies. Vol 3. Baden-Baden, 2021, pp. 31–56.

been paid to the European Council's role in framing EU narratives on Turkey.[6] The European Council is a leading institution in the Union's political architecture.[7] It comprises the Heads of State or Government of EU Member States, the President of the Commission and the President of the European Council. The High Representative of the Union for Foreign Affairs and Security Policy "shall take part in the work".[8] It is the EU's club of the highest political leaders and is understood as the EU's "collective head of state".[9] The European Council provides "the Union with the necessary impetus for its development" and defines "general political directions and political priorities".[10] In political practice, it has developed a state-like agenda by focussing on several issues in the EU's policy making.[11] As the EU's political platform of agenda-setting, the European Council has also emerged as the EU's leading international voice and crisis manager. It is a high-level meeting place for EU Leaders, in which the Union's positions, interests and key policy concerns are negotiated, balanced and presented; this is where Heads of States or Government can find compromise on divergent interests.

The treaty foresees four regularly scheduled meetings of the European Council per year. However, the actual number including informal and extraordinary – emergency – meetings has increased over recent decades. On 29 November 2015 and on 18 March 2016, for example, the European Council gathered for two extraordinary EU-Turkey summits and identified emergency actions to cope with the migration crisis. Through the European Council's conclusions, which are published after each summit, the Heads of States or Government set the EU's policy agenda and define "issues of concern and actions to take".[12] The conclusions result from careful preparations over several administrative and political levels which aim at reaching consensus among Member States' political leaders and have a strong impact on the way other EU institutions prepare, implement and monitor ongoing policies. Since the tone of these documents is highly diplomatic with

---

6   Ebru Turhan/ Wolfgang Wessels. The European Council as a Key Driver of EU–Turkey Relations: Central Functions, Internal Dynamics, and Evolving Preferences. In: Wulf Reiners/ Ebru Turhan (Eds): EU-Turkey Relations. Theories, Institutions, and Policies, Cham 2021, pp. 185–217.

7   Cf. Wessels, Wolfgang. The European Council. London, 2015.

8   Article 15(2), TEU.

9   Schoutheete, Philipp. The European Council and the Community Method. Policy Paper No. 56, July 2012, p. 36.

10   Treaty on European Union. Article 15(1).

11   Cf. Wessels, European Council, 2015, p. 8.

12   European Council. European Council conclusions. Brussels, 23.08.2022, https://www.consilium.europa.eu/en/european-council/conclusions/ [23.08.2022].

carefully chosen wording, their conclusions provide evidence for the EU Leaders' agenda on Turkey, both in terms of key concerns and political actions, albeit their analysis often requires background and historical context information.

2.1. Turkey in the EU's Spotlight: Relationship Milestones

The history of EU-Turkey relations has been dominated by a number of ups and downs, contradicting trends and distinct dynamics of divergence and convergence over the last seven decades. Academic debate labels these different trends in EU-Turkey relations as the partnership's 'ebbs and flows'.[13] Different paths in the history of EU-Turkey relations evoke an ambiguity towards Turkey's role in EU affairs. Previous research has identified the relationship's key milestones:[14]

Figure 18: Milestones in EU-Turkeys Relations

Year	Milestone
1963	Ankara Agreement: Association Agreement between Turkey and EEC
1974	Turkish Intervention in Cyprus
1980	Military Coup in Turkey
1987	Turkey's Membership Application to the EU (rejection in 1989)
1996	EU-Turkey Customs Union
1997	Luxembourg Summit
1999	Helsinki Summit
2004	Failure of the Annan Plan in Cyprus & EU's Big Bang Enlargement
2005	Start of Turkey's Accession Negotiations
Since 2015	Turkey & EU Common Actions on Migration
2016	July Failed Coup Attempt in Turkey
2018	Introduction of the Presidential System in Turkey
Since 2018	Increasing Tensions over Turkey's power projection in the Eastern Mediterranean; Turkey's military activities in North East Syria and Libya

Source: based on Özbey et al., Identity representations in the Narratives on the EU-Turkey Relations, 2019.

---

13 Cf. Aydın-Düzgit, Senem/ Tocci, Natalie. Turkey and the European Union. London, 2015, p. 9.
14 Cf. Özbey et al., Identity representations in the Narratives on the EU-Turkey Relations, 2019.

Both, the signing of the Ankara agreement in 1963 and Turkey's official application for membership in 1987, are often presented as initial reference points, linking Turkey to the European integration project.[15] Having spent more than 20 years at the EU's doorstep, Turkey's accession process with the EU has been the longest so far and is still lacking a realistic accession perspective. The history of Turkey's EU accession process has witnessed alternating phases of political progress and setbacks. In 1989, the EU rejected Turkey's membership application for the first time. Seven years later, Brussels and Ankara agreed to upgrade their economic relationship and completed the Customs Union, thereby achieving the aim of the 1963 Ankara Agreement. However, this was followed by another disappointment for Ankara: the EU's Heads of State or Government objected to granting Turkey the status of official EU candidate country at their 1997 summit in Luxembourg. Yet, only two years later in 1999 at the European Council summit in Helsinki this decision was fundamentally revised and Turkey finally obtained candidate status. Shortly after the EU's so-called big bang enlargement in 2004/2007 when ten central and eastern European countries plus Malta and Cyprus acceded to the EU, Turkey's accession negotiations started in 2005. But negotiations have so far met with little prospect of accession eventually being realised. By 2020, 16 out of 35 chapters had been opened, but only 1 provisionally closed.[16] In view of political developments in recent years, negotiations have been at a dead-end for some time. On 24 November 2016, the European Parliament adopted a non-binding resolution to temporarily freeze the EU's accession negotiations with Turkey. Two years later in June 2018, the EU's General Affairs Council added "that Turkey has been moving further away from the European Union. Turkey's accession negotiations have, therefore, effectively come to a standstill and no further chapters can be considered for opening or closing and no further work towards modernisation of the EU-Turkey Customs Union is foreseen".[17] Even though negotiations remain in a consolidated stalemate, neither the EU nor Turkey are politically willing to signal their official termination. Accordingly, Turkey's EU accession process, albeit lacking in enthusiasm and a real accession perspective for

---

15 Cf. Hillenbrand, Olaf. Europa ABC. In: Werner Weidenfeld, Wolfgang Wessels (Eds.). Europa von A bis Z. Vol. 12. Baden Baden, 2011, p. 453.

16 Cf. Council of the European Union. European Enlargement Turkey. Brussels, 23.08.2022, https://www.consilium.europa.eu/en/policies/enlargement/turkey/ [23.08.2022].

17 Council of the European Union, Enlargement and Stabilisation and Association Process, 2018.

the time being, is still in place and as such a framework for EU-Turkey relations. In recent years, the EU's focus vis-à-vis Turkey has shifted from the accession process and domestic politics to foreign policy. In particular, Turkey's past and potential unilateral offshore drilling activities in maritime areas claimed by Greece and the Republic of Cyprus have added another layer of tension to the already contested EU-Turkey relationship.

2.2. *Empirical Evidence: European Council Conclusions on Turkey*

This chapter builds on qualitative data analysis, based on all European Council conclusions between 1978 and 2021 dealing with Turkey.[18] Ultimately, there are 64 conclusions that include the term 'Turkey', which were coded and evaluated using the data analysis software MAXQDA. For the analysis, three generic categories of narratives were segmented (*membership, transactional partnership and conflict*), each of which contains a number of sub-codes. The membership category includes all text passages that deal with Turkey as a candidate state in a broader way, therefore codes such as 'adoption of acquis', 'political criteria' or 'candidate state' were used. Focussing on the issue of compliance to the Copenhagen Criteria the membership category also refers to the political and the economic dimension of the partnership. The normative category (political criteria) contains sub-codes such as 'human rights', 'fundamental freedoms' or 'rule of law' and the 'attempted coup in Turkey'. The cooperation category concerns all possible forms of cooperation. This means that the codes refer to both policy-related cooperation, such as 'migration' or 'the fight against terrorism', and institutional cooperation, such as 'Customs Union' or 'Association Agreement'. The conflict category reflects the EU's criticism towards Turkey identified by codes such as 'strongly condemns', 'calls upon Turkey to' or 'expects Turkey to'. The coding followed a procedural approach, meaning the creation of the code system was designed as a continuous process and constantly adjusted during the coding process.

---

18 The selected period of time covers all references to Turkey in the conclusions by the European Council. Please note: The European Council has been established on 10 December 1974.

Looking first at Figure 19 below, two striking dynamics are revealed:

Figure 19: European Council Conclusions on Turkey 1978–2021

Source: own compilation.

Firstly, Turkey received practically no attention from the European Council in the 1970s and 1980s. A rare exception appeared in March 1982, with European Council comments on the 1980 military coup. Secondly, Turkey has increasingly been mentioned since the 1990s, once the EU started to discuss the country's political and economic ability to become an EU Candidate country. In recent years – especially since 2015 – Turkey has certainly been prominent on the EU Leaders' agenda. But contrary to the 1990s and the early 2000s, interest in Turkey has not been provoked by the accession process, but rather by other topical issues such as migration and the EU Leaders' unease vis-à-vis the direction of Turkey's foreign policy.

2.3. Narrative of Membership: Turkey as a Candidate for EU Accession

The European Council did not comment on Turkey's attempt to join the EU until early in the 1990s. Even though Turkey officially applied for membership in 1987, which was subsequently rejected in 1989, this was a decision taken by the European Commission rather than the Council. At the time major obstacles to progress were quoted as being domestic politics, the economic situation, persistent conflicts with Greece and Cyprus as well as threats to minority rights.[19]

The European Council then started to deal with Turkey early in the 1990s. After the end of the Cold War, in light of the EU's enlargement strategy towards Central and Eastern European states as well as the Balkan Wars, the European Council tried to find ways to deal with Turkey's new geopolitical role in the EU's neighbourhood. Consequently, demands for Turkey's EU membership began to gain more weight with EU policymakers.

Figure 20: *Share of 'Accession Topic' in the European Council Conclusions on Turkey 1978–2021*

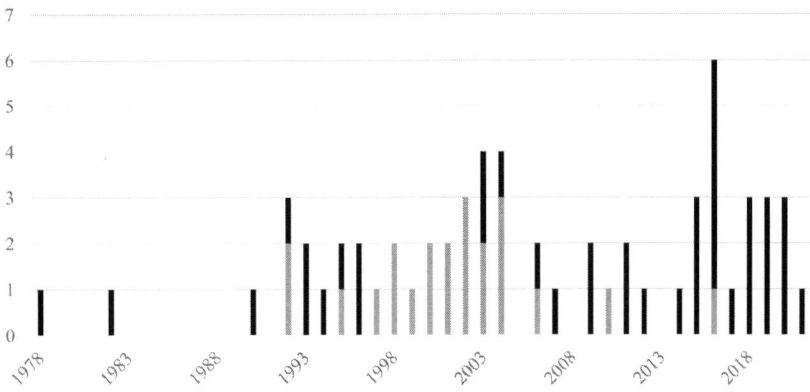

■ European Council Conclusions in total ■ European Council Conclusion on the "Accession topic"

Source: own compilation.

During the 1990s and the early 2000s, EU Leaders' agenda on Turkey was dominated by two themes, namely *politics* and *economics.* Paradoxically, both appeared either as driving forces or as obstacles for Turkey's EU accession process. In December 1995, the European Council commented on finalisation of the EU-Turkey Customs Union linking it to "the consolidation and strengthening of a political, economic and security rela-

---

19 Cf. University of Luxembourg (CVCE). Commission Opinion on Turkey's request for accession to the Community. Luxembourg, 20.12.1989, https://www.cvce.eu/content/publication/2005/2/4/4cc1acf8-06b2-40c5-bb1e-bb3d4860e7c1/publishable_en.pdf [02.11.2019].

tionship crucial to the stability of that regio".[20] In view of the political and economic situations in Turkey, the European Council further added that, "it notes with regret that certain issues remain to be resolved in the relationship", but "emphasises the need for the observance of the highest standards of human rights" in Turkey.[21] According to these statements, intensified economic collaboration with Turkey was presented as a means of maintaining and reinforcing regional stability. The Council was in no doubt that the Customs Union established a new dimension of trade relations between the EU and Turkey. Yet, it also reflected EU Leaders' preference at the time for upgrading economic relations, rather than beginning accession negotiations. This approach changed between 1997 and 1999. Within this short time-span of two years, European Council thinking went through a significant turnaround in regard to Turkey. Whereas the Luxembourg Summit in 1997 rejected Ankara's membership bid, in 1999 the Helsinki Summit accepted Turkey as an official accession candidate to the EU. In 1997, the Heads of State or Government stressed that, "Turkey will be judged on the same criteria as the other applicant states".[22] With this statement the European Council argued that Turkey would join the EU, if it sufficiently meets the Copenhagen Criteria. Furthermore, the Council stated at that time that the "political and economic conditions allowing accession negotiations are not satisfied". In addition, EU Leaders demanded "the establishment of satisfactory and stable relations between Greece and Turkey in particular by legal process, including the International Court of Justice; and support for negotiations under the aegis of the UN on a political settlement in Cyprus on the basis of the relevant UN Security Council Resolutions"[23] Looking at this aspect more closely, in 1997 Turkey and Greece appeared to be on the edge of war with one another over a conflict regarding the purchase of S-300 air defence missiles. Political tensions lasted until 1998, at which point they were resolved through a massive diplomatic intervention by the US.[24] One year later, in 1999 following the Helsinki Summit the European Council approved Turkey as

---

20 European Council. Presidency Conclusions. Madrid European Council. 15 and 16 December 1995. Madrid, 16.12.1995, https://www.consilium.europa.eu/media/21 179/madrid-european-council.pdf [08.11.2019].

21 Ibid.

22 European Council. Presidency Conclusions. Luxembourg European Council. 12 and 13 December 1997. Luxembourg, 13.12.1997, https://www.consilium.europa. eu/media/21114/luxembourg-european-council.pdf [08.11.2019].

23 Ibid.

24 Cf. Hale, William. Turkish Foreign Policy, p. 181.

a candidate state.[25] Instead of denouncing economic and political criteria as creating an obstacle for Turkey to obtain candidate status, as it was done before, on this occasion it was argued that candidate status will further support Turkey in its reform process. Academic research provides three explanations for this rapid turnaround. Firstly, between 1997 and 1999 both Germany and France experienced changes of government, which gave rise to a more Turkey friendly policy approach.[26] Secondly, on 17 August 1999 Turkey was heavily affected by a severe earthquake near Istanbul. This led to an immediate change in the atmosphere of Turkey-Greece relations and evoked waves of sympathy and empathy within the societies.[27] Thirdly, Greece changed its stance on Turkey's accession, preferring to use it more as a bargaining tool. In return for accepting Turkey as a candidate country, Athens received a guarantee that the Republic of Cyprus would become an EU member, even if the island's reunification process would fail.[28]

After a number of political reforms including official suspension of the death penalty in Turkey, the European Council decided in December 2004 to "open accession negotiations with Turkey without delay".[29] In the respective statement, the Heads of State or Government praise Turkey for a "far-reaching reform process" and expressed its "confidence that Turkey will sustain that process of reform".[30] Furthermore, the European Council set out the framework for the negotiations. It is stated that, "the shared objective of the negotiations is accession", but the "negotiations are an open-ended process, the outcome of which cannot be guaranteed beforehand".[31] Moreover, it is argued that in "case of a serious and persistent breach in a candidate state of the principles of liberty, democracy, respect for human rights and fundamental freedoms and the rule of law on which the Union is founded, the Commission will, on its own initiative or on the request of one third of the Member States, recommend the suspension

---

25 European Council. Presidency Conclusions. Helsinki European Council. 10 and 11 December 1999. Helsinki, 11.12.1999, https://www.consilium.europa.eu/media /21046/helsinki-european-council-presidency-conclusions.pdf [08.11.2019].
26 Cf. Soler I Lecha, Eduard/ Tekin, Funda/ Sökmen, Melike Janine. It Takes Two to Tango: Political Changes in Europe and their Impact on Turkey´s EU Bid. FEUTURE Online Paper No. 17. Cologne, April 2018.
27 Cf. Hale, Turkish Foreign Policy, p. 181.
28 Ibid, p. 180.
29 European Council. Presidency Conclusions. Brussels European Council. 16 and 17 December 2004. Brussels, 17.12.2004, https://data.consilium.europa.eu/doc/do cument/ST-16238-2004-INIT/en/pdf [08.11.2019].
30 Ibid.
31 Ibid.

of negotiations and propose the conditions for eventual resumption".[32] In light of this announcement, the current impasse of Turkey's EU accession process is in full compliance with accession procedure rules.

Overall, the respect for human rights, rule of law and fundamental freedoms in Turkey have for several generations of EU Leaders been pivotal concerns regarding the country's ability to become an EU member state. In all statements on progress towards opening accession negotiations and additional comments on this process, the Heads of State or Government have demanded implementation of these political norms, the first Copenhagen criteria, as a precondition for opening negotiations (conditionality) and for any further development of relations. This also applies to modernising the Customs Union which should be 'rules based'. Overall, the EU Leaders' conclusions on Turkey from the 80s to the early 2000s confirm a narrative which states that the Union extends well beyond an economic grouping with a single market into a community of values. More precisely these are seen as normative values, which it seeks to advance towards states within the region, in this case Turkey. Comparing the European Council's references to the Copenhagen criteria, it appears that economic criteria are considerably less frequently mentioned than this normative political dimension, while assessing Turkey's eligibility to become an EU member state.

2.4. Narrative of a Transactional Partnership: Forms and Areas of Cooperation

More recently the EU Leaders have attached greater importance to Turkey, but the *membership* narrative is increasingly off the agenda. This dynamic can be accounted for in two ways. Firstly, it reflects growing 'enlargement fatigue' in the EU and mounting internal challenges for the community, which in turn lead to a decreased willingness by EU institutions and Member States to integrate new members into the Union. Secondly, it results from the overall course of events in EU-Turkey relations. Instead of a *membership narrative*, EU Leaders refer to Turkey as an important partner in particular policy areas such as migration, the fight against terrorism and economic cooperation.

---

32 Ibid.

Figure 21: Share of 'Cooperation Topic' in European Council Conclusions on Turkey 1978–2021

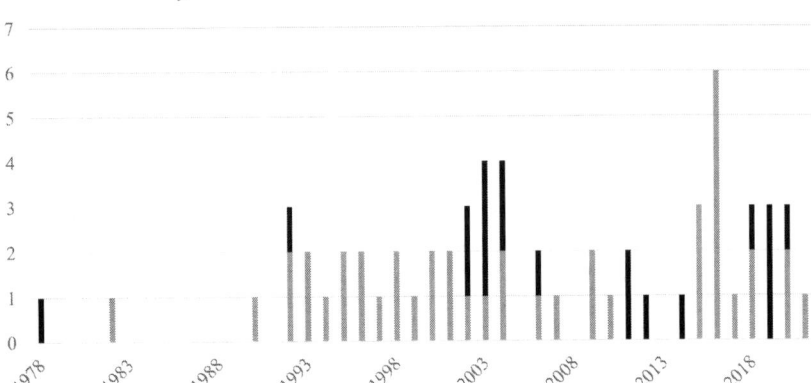

■ European Council Conclusions in total ■ European Council Conclusion on the "Cooperation Topic"

Source: own compilation.

In view of new and alternative forms of cooperation, 2015 and 2016 were pivotal years for EU-Turkey relations. During 2015, there was an overwhelming number of people, around 1.5 million, seeking to enter Europe through Turkish territory. According to FRONTEX (European Border and Coast Guard Agency), almost 900,000 people reached EU territory via the Eastern Mediterranean route throughout this period.[33] Responding to this political situation, Turkey appeared as a key geopolitical partner for the EU's migration regime in prioritising externalisation of the migration issue. The common agenda between Turkey and the EU at that stage of the relationship is illustrated by declaration of the EU-Turkey joint action plan on 15 October 2015, in which it is stated that "challenges are common and responses need to be coordinated".[34] This action plan aimed to implement a number of collaborative actions to "supplement Turkey's efforts in managing the situation of massive influx of persons in need of temporary protection".[35] Within this context, on 29 November the EU and Turkey identified 11 points of common action, following which the EU provided humanitarian aid and financial support

---

33 Cf. Wollscheid, Marcel. Frontex chief: 'Turkey has delivered' on refugee deal. In: Euractiv, 30.05.2016.

34 European Commission. EU-Turkey Joint Action Plan. Brussels, 15.10.2015, https://europa.eu/rapid/press-release_MEMO-15-5860_en.htm [31.10.2019].

35 Ibid.

to Turkey. Moreover, the EU and Turkey aimed not only to improve energy and economic relations, but also to facilitate enhanced collaboration in geostrategic related issues. For that purpose, the EU-Turkey statement announced the introduction of High-Level Dialogues covering political, economic and energy issues. Moreover, it was intended that negotiations would be opened for upgrading the Customs Union and visa liberalisation for Turkish citizens in the Schengen area.[36] On 18 March 2016, the EU and Turkey further intensified their efforts to address the migration crisis by agreeing on terms to mobilise additional funds to facilitate the handling of refugees in Turkey.[37] Since then, the European Council has frequently demanded implementation of the EU-Turkey joint action plan agreements. There is one recurrent narrative behind these migration-related statements: Turkey is regarded as a key partner in dealing with challenges of vital interest for both sides. Recurrent references to the implementation of this 'joint action plan' imply that Turkey's actions are being carefully monitored in this context. Turkey is seen from a geopolitical perspective as a buffer zone for the EU. However, political changes have effectively blocked significant progress with joint action plan in regard to migration. Among other factors, political conditionality has put a brake on upgrading the Customs Union and Visa liberalisation process.

Since summer 2020, EU leaders have mainly sought to strengthen the partnership with Turkey to resolve the conflict in the eastern Mediterranean and thus to promote regional stability in the EU's immediate neighbourhood.[38] According to the conclusions by the European Council, Turkey is offered a positive agenda in return for mediation efforts and steps towards de-escalation in the Eastern Mediterranean. The envisaged positive agenda between the EU and Turkey, in addition to strengthening economic relations, aims at intensifying cooperation in the health sector as well as with regard to climate change and contacts between people and mobility.

---

36 Cf. European Council. Meeting of heads of state or government with Turkey. EU-Turkey statement, 29 November 2015. Press release. Brussels, 29.11.2015, https://www.consilium.europa.eu/en/press/press-releases/2015/11/29/eu-turkey-meeting-st atement/ [05.01.2021].

37 Cf. European Council. EU-Turkey statement, 18 March 2016. Press release. Brussels, 18.03.2016, https://www.consilium.europa.eu/en/press/press-releases/2016/03/18/eu-turkey-statement/ [05.01.2021].

38 Cf. European Council. Erklärung der Mitglieder des Europäischen Rates. SN 18/21. Brussels, 25.03.2021, https://www.consilium.europa.eu/media/49005/250321-vtc-euco-statement-de.pdf [11.08.2021].

Overall, the *transactional partnership narrative* is based on the notion of geostrategic challenges in a shared neighbourhood that require joint actions to be taken. EU-Turkey efforts to deal with the migration crisis exemplify this narrative. In the future, it can be expected that, in addition to traditional security policy interests, topics such as public health and climate change will increasingly be on the agenda of cooperation between the EU and Turkey. Moreover, cooperation is (and will) not (be) based on common values and a mutual alignment of the political agenda, but rather on transactionalism and package deals.

2.5. Narrative of Conflict: Turkey as a Problematic Neighbour

The image of Turkey as a *strategic partner* is increasingly combined with a narrative of conflict that portrays Turkey as a *problematic neighbour*. This combination is very well illustrated when EU institutions state that "Turkey is increasingly moving away from the Union" on one hand, but "is a key partner" on the other hand.[39] Hence, EU-Turkey relations are classified by the simultaneous paradoxical experience of disputes and cooperation, in other words a 'conflictual partnership'. Referring to these conflictual elements, the European Council is increasingly dismayed with the general course of Turkey's domestic politics and the calibration of Turkish foreign policy towards Syria, Libya, Cyprus and the Eastern Mediterranean (Figure 22).

Regarding Turkey's domestic policies, it was after the failed coup attempt during July 2016 that EU Leaders raised their concerns about the state of democracy, rule of law and press freedom in Turkey. On 18 July 2016, the conclusions stated that, "The EU underlines the need to respect democracy, human rights and fundamental freedoms and the right of everyone to a fair trial in full compliance with the European Convention for the Protection of Human Rights and Fundamental Freedoms, including Protocol 13 on the abolition of the death penalty".[40] This quote refers to the debate about a possible referendum on reintroduction of the death

---

39 Council of the European Union, Enlargement and Stabilisation and Association Process, 2018.
40 Council of the European Union. Council Conclusions on Turkey. Press release. Brussels, 18.07.2016, https://www.consilium.europa.eu/en/press/press-releases/2016/07/18/fac-turkey-conclusions/ [08.11.2019].

penalty in Turkey, a topic that was raised after the coup.[41] It was also added that, "The EU reiterates that it expects Turkey to respect the highest standards when it comes to democracy, rule of law, respect of fundamental freedoms, including freedom of expression".[42]

Figure 22: Conflict Topics in European Council Conclusions on Turkey 1978–2021

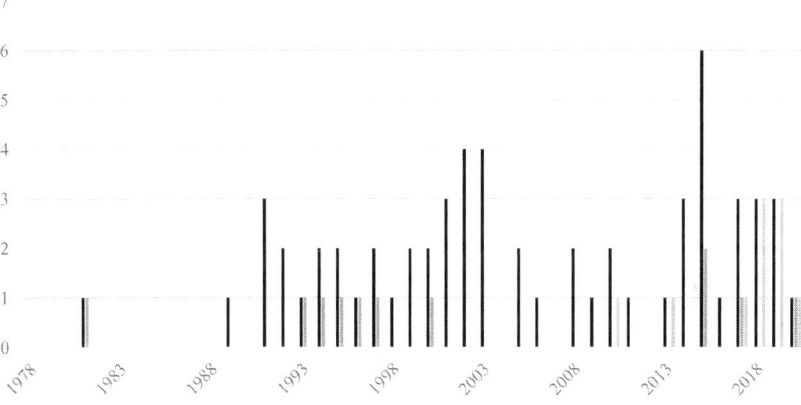

■ European Council Conclusions on Turkey ■ Normative Conflict Topics ■ Foreign Policy Conflict Topics

Source: own compilation.

The EU's foreign policy related criticism towards Turkey is a more current phenomenon. On 9 October 2019 Federica Mogherini, at that time High Representative, called "upon Turkey to cease the unilateral military action" and went on to say that, "renewed armed hostilities in the north-east will further undermine the stability of the whole region, exacerbate civilian suffering and provoke further displacements".[43] In addition, she stated that

---

41 Cf. European Parliament. Turkish referendum on the reintroduction of the death penalty. Parliamentary Question. E-003342/2017. Brussels, 15.05.2017, https://ww w.europarl.europa.eu/doceo/document/E-8-2017-003342_EN.html [08.11.2019].

42 European Council. European Council Meeting (15 October 2015). Conclusions. Brussels, 16.10.2015, https://data.consilium.europa.eu/doc/document/ST-26-2015-I NIT/en/pdf [08.11.2019].

43 Council of the European Union. Declaration by the High Representative on behalf of the EU on recent developments in north-east Syria. Press release. Brussels, 09.10.2019, https://www.consilium.europa.eu/en/press/press-releases/2019/10/09/d eclaration-by-the-high-representative-on-behalf-of-the-eu-on-recent-developments-i n-north-east-syria/ [08.11.2019].

Turkey's actions in Northern Syria "threatens the progress achieved by the Global Coalition to defeat Da'esh". With these statements the High Representative perceives Turkey's actions in North East Syria as a source of instability for the region. In addition, she questions Turkey's role in fighting terrorism and rather sees the country's actions as creating a potential threat towards the EU's prioritised goal in Syria, namely to defeat ISIS. This becomes obvious, when it is stated that, "the EU condemns Turkey's unilateral military action in North East Syria which causes unacceptable human suffering, undermines the fight against Da'esh and threatens heavily European security".[44]

Another point of concern is the Eastern Mediterranean, in particular Ankara's disputes with Athens and Nicosia. The continental shelf, claimed by Turkey and the Turkish Cypriots, to a large extent overlaps with the Republic of Cyprus' exclusive economic zone as defined via bilateral agreements with Cyprus and Egypt in 2003 as well as Israel in 2010. With reference to Turkish offshore energy exploration activities, from October 2014 the European Council has on several occasions and with increasing alarm "expressed serious concern about the renewed tension in the Eastern Mediterranean and urged Turkey to show restraint and to respect Cyprus' sovereignty over its territorial sea" as well as "Cyprus' sovereign rights in its exclusive economic zone". In 2019 Turkey conducted drilling activities inside the exclusive economic zone of the Republic of Cyprus. This action represented an exclusive maritime right violation and a new dimension of confrontation between Turkey and a member state of the EU. Responding to this, the European Council condemned "Turkey's continued illegal actions in the Eastern Mediterranean" and put emphasis on "its full solidarity with Cyprus".[45] The European Council not only sent a verbal note of protest, but also invited "the Commission and the European Union External Action Service to submit options for appropriate measures without delay, including targeted measures" to protest Turkey's activities in the Eastern Mediterranean. On 15 July 2019, the EU Foreign Affairs Council reacted to the presence of Turkey's drilling ships in Cyprus's EEZ (Exclusive Economic Zone) by adopting measures on Turkey. They suspended negotiations for an Air Transport Agreement, they cancelled

---

44 Council of the European Union. North East Syria: Council adopts conclusions. Press release. Brussels, 14.10.2019. https://www.consilium.europa.eu/en/press/press-releases/2019/10/14/council-conclusions-on-north-east-syria/ [08.11.2019].

45 European Council. European Council meeting (22 March 2018). Brussels, 23.03.2018, https://www.consilium.europa.eu/media/33457/22-euco-final-conclusions-en.pdf [08.11.2019].

EU-Turkey high-level dialogues and declared a further cut in pre-accession assistance to Turkey in 2020.[46] In addition, the EU Foreign Affairs Council opened up opportunities for imposing restrictive measures on individuals and institutions participating in Turkish gas exploration in the Republic of Cyprus' EEZ. To date, the EU has fined two individuals with travel bans and asset freezes for their participation in Turkey's drilling activities off the coast of Cyprus. During summer 2020, Turkey's assertive foreign policy in the Eastern Mediterranean reached a new dimension. As the Turkish navy was in a stand-off with the Greek navy about contested maritime boundaries around the island of Kastelorizo and offshore Crete. Turkey questions Greece's exclusive economic zone as it is partly defined in bilateral agreements between Athens and Rome in 2020 and Athens and Cairo in 2020 and authorized seismic research surveys in disputed areas. This action is strongly opposed by the European Council, who "calls on Turkey to abstain from similar actions in the future, in breach of international law".[47] Further it "underlines that delimitation of the Continental Shelf and Exclusive Economic Zone should be addressed through dialogue and negotiation in good faith, in full respect of international law".[48] To prevent Turkey from continuing with their activities, the European Council threatened: "in case of renewed unilateral actions or provocations in breach of international law, the EU will use all the instruments and the options at its disposal, including in accordance with Article 29 TEU and Article 215 TFEU, in order to defend its interests and those of its Member States".[49] Moreover, the European Council holds out the prospect that "provided constructive efforts to stop illegal activities vis-à-vis Greece and Cyprus are sustained, the European Council has agreed to launch a positive political EU-Turkey agenda".[50] The concept of a positive political EU-Turkey agenda was used as an attempt to incentivise Turkey to abandon its activities in the Eastern Mediterranean, in exchange for an upgrade of the Customs Union, Visa facilities for Turkish citizens and further

---

46 Council of the European Union. Turkish drilling activities in the Eastern Mediterranean: Council adopts conclusions. Press release. Brussels, 15.07.2019, https://www.consilium.europa.eu/en/press/press-releases/2019/07/15/turkish-drilling-activities-in-the-eastern-mediterranean-council-adopts-conclusions/ [08.11.2019].

47 European Council. Special meeting of the European Council (1 and 2 October 2020). Conclusions. Brussels, 02.10.2020, https://www.consilium.europa.eu/media/45910/021020-euco-final-conclusions.pdf [23.10.2020].

48 Ibid.

49 Ibid.

50 Ibid.

financial assistance to manage the refugee situation.[51] In December 2020, two months later, the European Council evaluated Turkey's willingness to engage within the framework of a positive agenda. It is stated that "regrettably, Turkey has engaged in unilateral actions and provocations and escalated its rhetoric against the EU, EU Member States and European leaders".[52]Nonetheless, the members of the European Council "reaffirm the EU's strategic interest in the development of a cooperative and mutually beneficial relationship with Turkey" and that the offer of a "positive EU Turkey agenda remains on the table".[53] This approach can largely be explained by different views in European capitals about how to deal with Turkey. On the one hand countries such as Austria, France, Greece and the Republic of Cyprus demand harsher sanctions. On the other hand, countries such as Germany, Italy and Spain put emphasis on the political costs of a tougher conflict with Turkey and therefore prefer restraint from harder reactions.[54]

Overall, the *problematic neighbour narrative* has become increasingly dominant in the European Leaders' agenda vis-à-vis Turkey with its climax in 2020. This mainly results from Turkey's increasing power projection in the Eastern Mediterranean that spans from offshore drilling activities inside maritime areas that are claimed by Greece and the Republic of Cyprus through the unilateral partial re-opening of Varosha, the Cypriot ghost town, to military involvement in the Libyan Civil War. The EU's renewed interest in establishing a positive agenda emphasises the changed framework of EU-Turkey relations: in the past the EU aimed to implement a positive agenda in EU-Turkey relations in order to initiate progress in Turkey's EU accession process; now the positive agenda is designed to address Turkey's foreign policy direction and incentivise Ankara to seek a peaceful resolution of conflicts with EU Member States (Greece and Cyprus).

---

51 Cf. Seufert, Günter. Ankara traut der EU keine Sanktionen zu. In: SWP Aktuell. Nr. 95. Berlin, Dezember 2020.

52 European Council. European Council meeting (10 and 11 December 2020). Conclusions. Brussels, 11.12.2020, https://www.consilium.europa.eu/media/47296/101 1-12-20-euco-conclusions-en.pdf [05.01.2021].

53 Ibid.

54 Cf. Seufert. Ankara traut der EU keine Sanktionen zu, 2020.

3. Conclusion and Outlook

The aim of this chapter has been to examine EU Leaders' narratives on Turkey. In broad terms, the Council contextualises the EU-Turkey relationship within the realm of three narratives: potential member, transactional partner and problematic neighbour. At the outset, the domestic reform processes and the assessment of Turkey's accession eligibility on the basis of the Copenhagen criteria were central to the conclusions. By now, a mixture of pragmatism and detachment from Turkey's domestic and foreign policy policies dominates the statements of the heads of state and government. Time and again, the strategic importance of cooperation is emphasised, while simultaneously a range of differences are highlighted and an increasing distancing is evident. The tool of the 'positive agenda' illustrates the changing political parameters of EU-Turkey relations in recent years. Initially, it offered a starting point to revitalise the stalled accession process. Later, it was supposed to facilitate comprehensive cooperation on migration. Most recently, the 'positive agenda' was used as an incentive to mitigate the escalation between Turkey and the EU Member States Greece and Cyprus. A fundamental attitude, however, which is reflected in the conclusions of the European Council throughout the years, has not changed until today: regional stability in South-Eastern Europe, the Eastern Mediterranean and the Middle East can only be achieved in a cooperative and not in an oppositional relationship with Turkey. Therefore, although the accession negotiations are suspended and the stalemate appears consolidated by now, neither the EU nor Turkey are sending signals indicating official termination of the process. A reopening of negotiations under new political conditions, nevertheless, also seems very unlikely at the moment. It remains to be seen if this state of uncertainty will change in the future as a result of shifts in political parameters. The current status quo increasingly reflects a dilemma: Brussels depends on Turkey's cooperation in migration management and the fight against international terrorist groups, yet lacks political leverage to confront Turkey's backsliding democracy and progressively more assertive foreign policy that increasingly appears to differ from the EU's external interests. This lack of political leverage vis-à-vis Turkey materialises in the observation that the European Council is stressing the same criticism again and again over a longer period of time without considerable policy modifications by Turkey. Unlike the 1990s situation, Turkey's membership process does not serve as a backbone for structuring the relationship and for encouraging Turkey to converge its policies with those of the EU. Prospectively, EU-Turkey relations will probably remain to be shaped by political realism and pragmatism that do not result in major changes. The EU will need to find incentives to engage Turkey in meaningful cooperation and will also have to demonstrate political costs, if Turkey continues with repressive domestic policies and confrontational actions towards individual EU Member States, in particular Greece and Cyprus.

Turkish Public Perceptions of Germany: Most Popular among the Unpopular

Özgehan Şenyuva, Esra Çengel

1. Introduction

Turkish-German relations are a popular study subject, with extensive literature covering historical, political, social and economic dimensions includeing a number of interdisciplinary approaches.[1] The historical aspect of these studies focuses mainly on relations during the Ottoman period and two world wars, as well as Cold War era alliances against the communist threat.[2] Studies focusing on Turkish-German relations are much more extensive than most of those analysing Turkey's relations with other states both in terms of numbers as well as the scope and depth of issues covered, competing only with those on Turkish-Greek and Turkish-American relations. Yet, despite this wide range, one issue remains understudied: Turkish public opinion towards Germany. As outlined elsewhere in this volume,[3] narratives shape perceptions of reality and might in turn influence actions. In another contribution, the Turkish President's narration of

---

1 Cf. Nuroğlu, Elif/ Bayrak Meydanoğlu, Ela Sibel/ Bayraklı, Enes. Turkish German affairs from an interdisciplinary perspective. Frankfurt am Main, 2015.
2 Cf. Güçlü, Yücel. Turkish-German relations on the eve of world war two. In: *Turkish Studies*, 2000, 47, (2), pp. 73–94.; Bayraktar, Hatice/ Çalik, Ramazan. One Step Forward and Two Steps Back: The Slow Process of Re-establishing Diplomatic Relations between Germany and Turkey after the First World War. In: *Middle Eastern Studies*, 2011, 1, (2), pp. 315–327; Ozkan, Behlül. Cold war era relations between West Germany and Turkish political Islam: from an anti-communist alliance to a domestic security issue. In: *Southeast European and Black Sea Studies*, 2019, 19, (1), pp. 31–54; Schönlau, Anke/ Schröder, Mirja. A Charged Friendship: German Narratives of EU-Turkey Relations in the Pre-accession Phase, 1959–1999. In this volume, pp. 57-77.
3 Cf. Tekin, Funda/ Schönlau, Anke. The EU-German-Turkish Triangle. A Conceptual Framework for Narratives, Perceptions and Discourse of a Unique Relationship. In this volume, pp. 9-30; Özbey, Ebru Ece/ Hauge, Hanna-Lisa/ Eralp, Atila. Identity Representations in Narratives on EU-Turkey Relations. In this volume, pp. 31-55.

EU-German-Turkish relations has been analysed.[4] To complement those contributions, this chapter considers the public perception of Germany in Turkey.

More recent studies have also engaged in the political and military aspects of bilateral relations with the 'Syria question' as well as the 'refugee crisis' of 2015, considered among the most challenging issues for Turkish-German relations.[5] They assume that shifting dynamics on bilateral relations would reflect on the future of the so-called 'refugee deal' (the EU-Turkey Statement on migration).[6] Additionally, it is assumed that the volatility of relations would prevent a rapprochement period between the two sides in the near future.[7] It is a significant yet unanswered question as to how these developments are perceived by the public in Turkey and what reaction will be provoked. Over recent years, especially under the Justice and Development Party (AKP) government, foreign policy, specifically relations with other European states, has become much intertwined with domestic policy and consequently public opinion towards foreign policy is increasingly considered as a crucial factor in electoral strategies.[8]

Such an analysis is not possible without comparing historical and present Turkish public perceptions of Germany. Extensive studies on public opinion focus mainly on German perceptions of Turkey, rather than the reverse. In general, German public opinion towards Turkey is characterised as 'Turkish-sceptic'.[9] Literature on the social aspect of bilateral relations concentrates predominantly on this Turkish-scepticism within

---

4 Cf. Bedir, Nurdan Selay/ Gedikli, Ardahan Özkan/ Şenyuva, Özgehan. So Close Yet So Far: Turkey's Relations with Germany in Recep Tayyip Erdoğan's Narratives (2003–2018). In this volume, pp.111-139.

5 Cf. Turhan, Ebru. The Implications of the Refugee Crisis for Turkish-German Relations: An Analysis of the Critical Ebbs and Flows in the Bilateral Dialogue. In: *Öneri*, 2018, 13, (49), pp. 187–210.; Trunov, Philipp. German-Turkish Relations during the Modern Period: Military-Political Aspects. In: *Vostok. Afro-Aziatskie Obshchestva: Istoriia i Sovremennost*, 2019, 94, (5), pp. 94–105; Hintz, Lisel. Rethinking Turkey's 'Rapprochements': Trouble with Germany and Beyond. In: *Survival*, 2019, 61, (3), pp. 165–186.

6 Cf. Turhan, The Implications of the Refugee Crisis for Turkish-German Relations, 2018.

7 Cf. Hintz, Rethinking Turkey's 'Rapprochements', 2019.

8 Cf. For a discussion on AKP foreign policy see: Canan-Sokullu, Ebru. "Transformation in Foreign and Security Policy in the AKP Era: Realpolitik Codes versus Instrumental Soft-Power". In: Ebru Canan Sokullu (Ed.). Turkey in Transition: Politics, Society and Foreign Policy. Berlin, 2020, pp. 175–192.

9 Cf. Turhan, Ebru. Germany´s Domesticated European Policy: Implications for the EU and Turkey. In: Ebru Turhan (Ed.). German-Turkish Relations Revisited. The

German public opinion as well as integration problems encountered by Turkish immigrants and their descendants in Germany.[10] Some of these studies underline the relevance of identity as one of the primary reasons for Turkish-scepticism among German people.[11] Others stress the German media's role in reproducing Turkish-scepticism.[12] Moreover, these studies argue that the accumulation of integration related issues of individuals with Turkish origins produce a negative impact on German society's perception of Turkish immigrants. There are also further studies on public opinion which investigate German citizens' attitudes towards Turkey in comparison with other EU Member States.[13] These studies underline rising Islamophobia and the economic crisis as being primarily responsible for anti-Turkey sentiment among people living in Germany and the EU. For instance, it is argued that Turkish electoral campaigns in German cities for the series of elections that took place in the period 2014–2018[14] and the 2017 constitutional referendum created negative feelings among German people, hence contributed to Turkish-scepticism.[15] Other studies, such as those in this volume, suggest that the Gezi protests and the Turkish state's reaction in 2013 had already marked a turning point in the German Parlia-

---

European Dimension, Domestic and Foreign Politics and Transnational Dynamics. Turkey and European Union Studies. Vol. 2. Baden-Baden, 2019, pp.143 – 163.

10   Cf. Yılmaz, Hakan. Turkish identity on the road to the EU: basic elements of French and German oppositional discourses. In: *Journal of Southern Europe and the Balkans*, 2007, 9, (3), pp. 293–305.; Mora, Necla. Turkey and Turks in the German media. In: *Journal of Human Sciences*, 2009, 6, (2), pp. 606–625.; Mueller, Claus. Integrating Turkish communities: a German dilemma. In: *Population Research and Policy Review*, 2007, 25, (5–6), pp. 419–441.; Ramm, Christoph. The Muslim Makers. In: *Interventions*, 2010, 12, (2), pp. 183–197.

11   Yılmaz, Hakan. Turkish identity on the road to the EU.; Kaya, Ayhan. German-Turkish Transnational Space: A Separate Space of Their Own. In: *German Studies Review*, 2007, 30, (3), pp. 483–502.

12   Mora, Turkey and Turks in the German media, 2009.

13   Gerhards, Jürgen/ Hans, Silke. Why not Turkey? Attitudes towards Turkish Membership in the EU among Citizens in 27 European Countries. In: *JCMS: Journal of Common Market Studies*, 2011, *49*, (4), pp. 741–766.; Öner, Selcen. Influential internal and external factors in German policy towards Turkey's EU membership: more than 'privileged partnership'; less than full membership? In: *Eastern Journal of European Studies*, 2014, *5*, (2), pp. 95–118.

14   Turkish citizens resident in Germany have voted in the following: 2014 and 2018 Presidential Elections; June and November 2015 and 2018 Turkish General (Parliamentary Elections) and 2017 Turkish Constitutional Referendum.

15   Kuru, Deniz. Turkish Electoral Campaigns in Germany and the Wider Western Europe as Transnational Practices. In: Ebru Turhan (Ed.). German-Turkish Relations Revisited. Baden Baden, 2019, pp.187 – 205.

ment's narration of Turkey.[16] Likewise, some argue that political developments in Turkey after the failed coup attempt of 15 July 2016 created a mistrust towards Turkey as a modern democratic state.[17]

This chapter will address a considerable gap in the literature on perceptions of Turkish public towards Germany by analysing a number of opinion polls that have not yet been contextualised so as to shed light on the following questions: (1) Looking at a recent 15 years period, have public perceptions of Germany displayed significant changes, considering the amount and weight attributed to Germany in the Turkish political agenda (see other chapters in this volume)? (2) Is Germany perceived as having a special position compared with other European states? (3) Finally, are perceptions of Germany reflected on the present political polarisation that dominates the Turkish political scene? In other words, does Germany represent a fault line between supporters of the governing bloc and the opposition?

The time frame for our analysis is from 2004 to 2019, which was chosen as a basis given the availability over time of Turkish public opinion data on Germany and Turkish foreign policy. It also covers the AKP's rule, which came into being with the 2002 general elections.

2. Methodology and Data Sources

In order to answer these questions, this chapter uses two data sources. Firstly, we scrutinised the opinion polls Transatlantic Trends Survey (TTS) by the German Marshal Fund (2004–2008) and the Public Perceptions on Turkish foreign policy survey conducted by the Kadir Has University (2016–2019),[18] that included questions regarding Germany, thereafter creating a secondary data set by way of building on these two survey data.

Secondly, in depth statistical analysis is based on data provided by Istanbul Economics Research, taken from two public opinion surveys, one con-

---

16 Weise, Helena/ Tekin, Funda. German Narratives, Strategies and Scenarios of EU-Turkey Relations 2002–2018: Towards a Unique Partnership – Yet to be defined. In this volume, pp. 79-109, p. 91.

17 Aydın, Yaşar. German-Turkish Relations at Continuous Crossroads – Political and Structural Factors. In: Ebru Turhan (Ed.). German-Turkish Relations Revisited. Turkey and European Union Studies. Vol. 2. Baden-Baden, 2019, pp.165 – 183.

18 Cf. Aydın, Mustafa et. al. Research on Public Perceptions on Turkish Foreign Policy. Center for Turkish Studies. Kadir Has University. Istanbul, 2019.

ducted in September 2018 with 2,500 respondents and the other in December 2018 with 1,500 respondents across Turkey using the Computer Aided Telephone Interview (CATI) surveying technique. Results are deemed representative at a national level with a 95 % confidence interval, with +/- 2.2 percentage points and 2.5 percentage points accuracy, respectively.

3. Analysis and Findings

Analysis of available data reveals that from 2004 to 2019, our chosen timeframe, Turkish public opinion carried a rather negative view of other countries in general. Germany was no exception.

Data from the TTS demonstrates this negative attitude very clearly (Figure 23).

Figure 23: Feelings Towards Countries Between 2004–2008[19] (0–100, mean scores)

	TTS 2004	TTS 2005	TTS 2006	TTS 2007	TTS 2008
The UK	n/a	29.91	25.42	n/a	n/a
France	34.02	29.44	24.86	n/a	14.29
Germany	**45.63**	**44.22**	**43.56**	**n/a**	**31.47**
Spain	n/a	35.41	30.70	n/a	17.52
USA	27.86	27.97	19.84	11.35	14.28
Russia	20.98	24.39	21.40	21.13	16.92
Israel	12.50	14.43	12.41	4.96	6.44
China	40.60	46.33	39.38	28.09	26.76

Source: Transatlantic Trends Survey Data Set, calculations by the authors.

Respondents were asked to rate their feelings towards different foreign countries on a thermometer scale (0=Very Cold, 100=Very Warm) and opted for colder rather than warmer views for the countries investigated, all of which received mean scores below 50. The United States of America (USA) mean score is amongst the lowest, reaching only 20.26 out of 100 across all years investigated.

Even though Germany registers below 50 points for the years investigated here, it is actually the most popular country in this study with on

---

19 In particular years, certain countries were not included by the survey research team.

average 'warmer' feelings when compared with others included.[20] The mean score for Germany is 41.22/100 across the years 2004–2006 and 2008, while other states at that time in the EU, France, the UK and Spain, are rated significantly lower.

3.1 Glass half full: Germany as a Partner

About a decade later, the same characteristics of public opinion in Turkey still prevail, as suggested by the findings of the 2017 Kadir Has survey on Turkish foreign policy. The generally negative attitude towards other countries remains, particularly towards the Western states. Nonetheless, Germany is again the most popular among the unpopular, as it were.

Following the crisis and heated rhetoric that dominated 2017 after the failed coup attempt of 15 July 2016 and the referendum on Turkey's political system in April 2017, public perceptions appear to have improved both in regard to Germany and other European states. The most recent findings of the Kadir Has Survey investigating this issue all indicate a bounce and increase in positive assessments.

As the Kadir Has University's 2019 survey illustrates, the percentage of individuals who think Turkey should cooperate with Germany in its foreign policy has jumped from 1.7 % in 2016 to 8.9 % in 2019 (Figure 24). This figure makes Germany not only the most popular European state, but also the most popular Western state. Only the European Union as an institution is slightly more popular with 10.4 %, implying an increase of approximately three percentage points. It is noteworthy that North Atlantic Treaty Organisation (NATO) countries are considered as favourable partners to cooperate with. Respective support having more than doubled from 7.1 % in 2017 to 15.7 % in 2019. Comparing support for cooperation with individual NATO member countries, Germany also scores comparatively well with a level of 8 % compared to 3.1 % or 2.3 % for the United Kingdom and France respectively.

---

20 Except for 2005, when China received a mean score of 46.33, two points above Germany; the reason for this exceptional spike is unclear and hence it must be subject to further investigation.

Figure 24: *Preference With Which Countries Turkey Should Cooperate in its*
Foreign Policy Between 2013–2019 (%)

	2013	2015	2016	2017	2018	2019
Azerbaijan	12.4	18.7	48.5	59	45.4	44.5
Turkic Republics	11.3	16.2	16.7	37.4	31.8	41.2
Muslim Countries	12.5	19.5	9.8	22.4	23.4	19.2
NATO Countries	-	-	-	7.1	8.1	15.7
Russian Federation	6.8	9.4	3	7.8	13.2	12.9
European Union	10.3	7	8.1	4.1	7.6	10.4
China	4.2	3.7	3.1	3.4	4.8	10.4
Germany	**7.2**	**4.3**	**1.7**	**2.2**	**2.7**	**8.9**
USA	14.2	12.6	7.2	2.5	1.7	8.4
Qatar	-	-	-	-	-	6.9
Neighbour Countries	-	-	-	-	-	6.6
Pakistan	0.8	1.3	1.3	4.7	4.6	5.3
Iran	5.7	5.4	1.3	1.7	1.9	5
Shanghai Cooperation Organization	-	-	-	-	-	4.8
United Kingdom	3.6	1.8	1	0.9	1.4	3.1
France	2.1	1.3	1.2	0.4	1.5	2.3
Israel	1.4	0.6	0.3	0.2	0.3	1.8
Turkey should implement its foreign policy alone	20.7	22	22.6	14.7	15	15.6

Source: Aydın, Mustafa et al. Research on Public Perceptions on Turkish Foreign
Policy, 2019.

The increased willingness to cooperate correlates with a growing perception of Germany as a friend. Participants of Kadir Has University's survey
were asked explicitly to name 'Turkey's friends'. As seen here in Figure 25,
almost 10 % of respondents consider Germany as a friend compared to
5.5 % for the UK and 4.9 % for France, making it once again the most popular EU country and Western state. Answers to this question also highlight
the Turkish public's negative opinions about foreign countries and sense
of isolation, generally unable to identify any friends of Turkey. However,
as an exception 65 % of the public do consider Azerbaijan to be Turkey's
friend, along with Qatar and Pakistan with 36.6 % and 34 % respectively,
followed by Iran and Russia. The positive evaluation of Russia is a new
phenomenon, as in the 2018 edition of this study only 4.1 % of the respondents considered Russia as a friend.

Figure 25: Results on the Question of Whether These Countries are Friends of Turkey (2019)

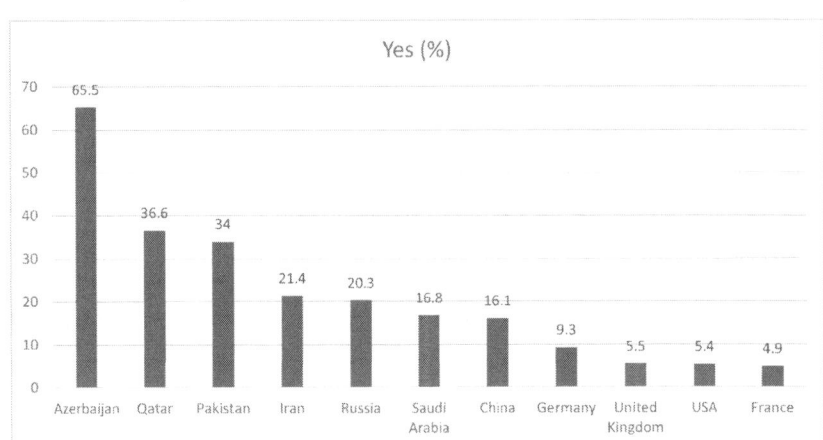

Source: Aydın, Mustafa et al. Research on Public Perceptions on Turkish Foreign Policy, 2019.

The numbers from different data sources point in similar directions, with Turkish public opinion regarding foreign policy displaying some scepticism towards other countries. Indeed, historically positive evaluations of other states remain low, particularly so for those in Europe and the USA. In general terms, perceptions of amity are also significantly low as far as these states are concerned. However, it is significant that Germany is clearly perceived differently. Turkish public opinion has more positive evaluations of Germany, with the country being regarded as a potential partner for cooperation, more so than other European states and the USA.

3.2 They are Out to Get Us: Threat Perceptions

Yet, threat perceptions among Turkish public opinion are very high. When asked whether the listed countries posed a threat to Turkey or not, most respondents indicated that they consider almost all foreign countries as potential threats and Germany is no exception (see Figure 26).

Almost 60 % of respondents stated that Germany poses a threat to Turkey, while 27 % disagreed and 15 % said that they did not know. It is striking that Germany is regarded as posing a larger threat than Greece, 58.8 % versus 53.5 %, respectively. Traditionally, Greece is considered as the historical other and a constant threat due to disagreements about the Aegean Sea.

Figure 26:   Results on the Question of Which Country or Countries Pose a Threat to Turkey? (2019)

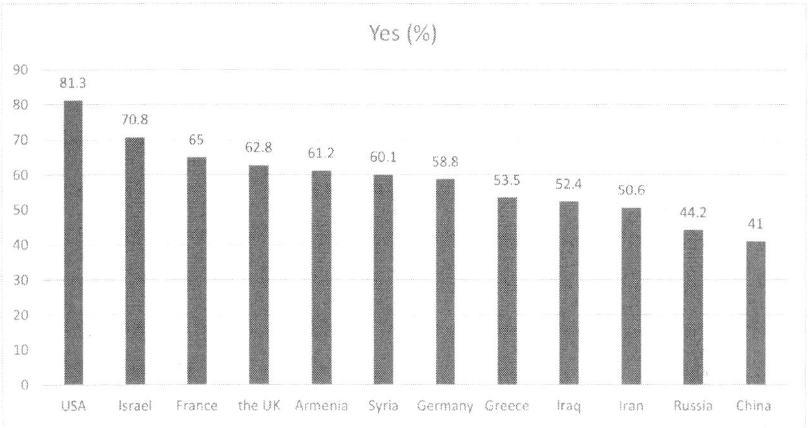

Source: Aydın, Mustafa et al. Research on Public Perceptions on Turkish Foreign Policy, 2019.

Data on threat perception was also collected in a public opinion survey in March/ April 2021, titled 'Turkish Perceptions of the European Union' conducted by The German Marshall Fund of the United States (GMF): It seems that the threat perception coming from Germany has decreased over time. When asked, 'Which country or international community is the biggest threat to the national interests of Turkey according to your opinion?' only 2.9 % have responded as Germany, making it the ninth country on the list, way under the USA (60.6 %); Israel (24 %); Russia (19 %) and Greece (15.3 %).[21] Hence, Germany is considered a threat by about 60 % (cf. Figure 27), but by far not the biggest or most important in comparison with other countries.

---

21 German Marshall Fund of the United States (GMF). Turkish Perceptions of the European Union. 2021, 29.04.2021, https://www.gmfus.org/publications/turkish-perceptions-european-union [24.05.2021]; German Marshall Fund of the United States (GMF). Turkish Perceptions of the European Union. 2022, 14.04.2022, https://www.gmfus.org/news/turkish-perceptions-european-union-2022 [21.06.2022]. The Survey is part of the Turkey, Europe, and Global Issues Program.

According to another survey focusing on public opinion and foreign policy conducted by Istanbul Economics Research in late 2018 and 2019, our initial two findings are confirmed. Firstly, in Turkish public opinion negative stances towards foreign countries are dominant and secondly Germany is still the most popular EU state (Figure 24). This is a recurrent finding over time, similar to those from the earlier surveys one decade before, as presented in Figure 23 and 24. Average scores (out of 10) are between 2.2 and 3.5 (1 = distant feelings and 10 = close feelings). Japan receives the most positive evaluation, with 1 out of 4 respondents awarding a score of 6 or higher, partly owing to the fact that many people lack a strong opinion of the country as it is not an everyday partner of Turkey. The USA receive the lowest evaluation, with 7 out of 10 people giving the lowest score of 1. Only 1 out of 10 gave a positive score of 6 or above for their feelings towards the USA. From a global perspective, Germany is the second most favourable country, with a mean score of 3.13 out of 10. Among EU countries,[22] the United Kingdom with an average score of 2.53 out of 10 is in second place. Considering the strong fallout with Germany in 2017 and the extensive negative rhetoric being applied at the time, Germany's more recent popularity is important to note.

---

22 Our analysis was conducted prior to the United Kingdom's exit from the European Union.

Figure 27: Turkish Public Perceptions of States in 2019. (1=distant feelings, 10=close feelings; mean scores)

	1	2	3	4	5	6	7	8	9	10	Total	Average (max=10)
Japan	44.4	6.8	7.1	6.4	10.8	7.4	4.6	5.1	2.4	5.0	100.0	3.48
Germany	**48.0**	**7.6**	**9.0**	**6.8**	**9.5**	**4.6**	**5.9**	**3.2**	**1.0**	**4.5**	**100.0**	**3.13**
China	47.6	10.3	8.8	5.4	13.5	4.0	3.9	3.3	-	3.2	100.0	2.93
Russia	54.2	9.0	8.9	6.3	11.0	3.8	2.8	2.0	0.5	1.5	100.0	2.57
United Kingdom	57.1	8.9	8.0	6.1	8.1	2.6	3.2	3.8	0.5	1.7	100.0	2.53
France	55.5	9.9	9.6	5.4	7.5	4.2	3.3	2.9	0.5	1.2	100.0	2.51
USA	70.3	6.2	4.8	3.0	5.4	2.2	2.0	1.8	0.8	3.5	100.0	2.20

Source: Istanbul Economics Research 2019 Foreign Policy Survey, calculations by the authors.

3.3 Leadership Matters: Foreign Leaders in the eyes of Turkish public.

The survey by Istanbul Economics Research includes separate items for assessing public opinion and foreign policy, with one question to do with perceptions of foreign leaders. The survey concludes that Turkish citizens perceive German Chancellor Angela Merkel as a successful leader. She is the second most popular world leader, immediately following Russian President Vladimir Putin. Putin spearheads this list as the leader considered most successful with a mean rating of 2.92 out of 5 points (1=not successful at all; 5=very successful, Figure 28).

Figure 28: Foreign Leaders according to the Turkish Public in 2019 (percent;1=not successful at all; 5=very successful)

	Not successful at all	Unsuccessful	Neither successful nor unsuccessful	Successful	Very successful	Total	Average (max=5)
Russia – Vladimir Putin	26.8	14.5	13.5	30.3	14.9	100.0	2.92
Germany – Angela Merkel	**30.5**	**22.2**	**18.4**	**20.8**	**8.0**	**100.0**	**2.54**
France – Emmanuel Macron	36.7	27.9	19.8	10.7	5.0	100.0	2.19
USA – Donald Trump	46.9	27.5	11.5	8.8	5.4	100.0	1.98

Source: Istanbul Economics Research 2019 Foreign Policy Survey – calculations by the authors.

Merkel has a mean approval score of 2.54 (out of 5). President Donald Trump is considered the least successful leader in Turkish eyes, with a success evaluation of 1.98 out of 5. President Putin's popularity is of great significance. Considering Turkey's polarised political scene between the government and opposition, it is important to see whether he is regarded as being successful across all parties or more positively evaluated by one particular group. The data reveals that individuals who voted for incumbent President Erdoğan in the presidential elections of 24 June 2018 had a significantly more positive evaluation of President Putin, compared with those who voted for another candidate. Among the Erdoğan voters, 41.5 % perceived President Putin as being successful and 19.2 % as very successful. Among those who did not vote for President Erdoğan, the figures are much lower, namely: 21.5 % successful and 11.8 % very successful. The average success score for President Putin is 3.34 (out of 5) for Erdoğan voters and 2.60 (out of 5) for those who did not vote for him (Figure 29).

Thus, we can clearly state that President Putin is considered to be the most successful foreign leader only by a certain group. These findings suggest that relations with Russia generally are part of party politics and part of the existing polarisation. A similar division on positive evaluations among Turkish voters is not valid for other leaders. For instance, the difference between President Erdoğan voters and non-voters on evaluations of President Trump, President Macron and Chancellor Merkel is insignificant and marginal (Figure 29).

Figure 29: World Leaders' Ratings by Presidential Vote Preferences in 2018 (Mean, max=5)

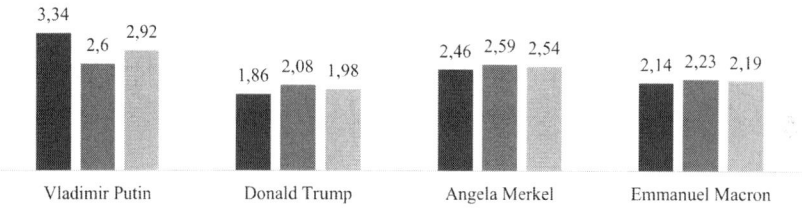

Source: Istanbul Economics Research 2019 Foreign Policy Survey, calculations by the authors.

This finding indicates that supporters of President Erdoğan are not only receptive to leadership cues, but also influenced by the close relationship between President Erdoğan and President Putin.[23]

Positive evaluations of Turkish public opinion towards Angela Merkel is a steady and stable one. In the 2001 GMF Survey, Chancellor Merkel is the third most positively evaluated foreign leader (13.3 % positive), following two Turkic leaders: President of Azerbaijan Ilham Aliyev (57.1 % positive) and the Prime Minister of Turkish Republic of Northern Cyprus Ersin Tatar (30.1 % positive).

---

23 For a detailed analysis on the evolution of Turkey-Russia relations and the impact of leadership, cf. Balta, Evren. From Geopolitical Competition to Strategic Partnership: Turkey and Russia after The Cold War. In: *Uluslararası İlişkiler Dergisi*, 2019, 16, (63), pp.69 – 86.

The evaluation of Germany shows less signs of correlation between party endorsement and leaders' approval. Hence, it is possible to posit that for Turkish people generally Germany is considered as special and moreover this view is shared across all political parties. By contrast, Russia is clearly evaluated more positively by those who feel closer to the government and President Erdoğan. Thus, it is possible to argue that Germany has the advantage of being able to reach all sections of society in conducting its public diplomacy towards Turkey. Furthermore, any initiative to advance relations between Turkey and Germany is very likely to receive bipartisan support.

3.4. Compartmentalisation of Relations: The Case of Education

As the results of analysing President Erdoğan's narratives on Germany in this volume demonstrate, the President has been careful to compartmentalise the relations with Germany. Hence, the message is mixed. On the one hand, while Germany is a potential threat to Turkey, jealous of its achievements and even occasionally supporting terrorist activities against the country, on the other hand it is also a preferred business and trade partner, with German business people and tourists being most welcome in Turkey.[24] This distinction of issues is also relevant in public opinion. People tend to differentiate and compartmentalise their perceptions towards states.

As the Istanbul Economics Research survey highlights, Turkish respondents perceive Western education as providing a path towards the most opportunities for their children. While 3 out of 10 Turkish citizens express a desire for their children to seek higher education abroad (subject to financial means), a mere 2.1% of those who indicated this preference chose Russia as their preferred destination. This is in clear contrast with the strongly positive feelings and desire for cooperation with Russia that exists in certain groups within Turkish society. It can thus be concluded that Russia is perceived as being a strong ally in the context of balancing Turkey's foreign relations. Nevertheless, from a higher educational standpoint even those who want to see improved relations between Turkey and Russia would still prefer to send their children to the leading destinations for realising self-fulfilment and prosperity, namely the United States, Ger-

---

24 Bedir/ Gedikli/ Şenyuva. Turkey's Relations with Germany in Recep Tayyip Erdoğan's Narratives (2003–2018), p. 128ff.

many and the United Kingdom. Moreover, this stance does not differ between voters of rival presidential candidates. Both those who voted for President Erdoğan and others who voted for his competitor Muharrem İnce in the presidential elections of 2018 list the same three destinations as their top targets for studies abroad.

In conclusion, although President Erdoğan's supporters view a political alliance with Russia and evaluate the Russian President Vladimir Putin significantly more positively than the rest of Turkish society, very few of them would choose Russia as their preferred destination for studies abroad.

This is a rather clear manifestation of the power that Germany has, along with the US and the UK, in terms of social relations and public perceptions in Turkey. Many studies on soft power include education as part of their evaluations, for which these results provide a very clear example. Hence, education appears as a very promising potential bridge to improve Turkish-German relations, which is popular and demanded by a large portion of Turkish society. Regardless of political relations between the two countries, for the Turkish people Germany is still a respected and popular destination for education. Further exploration of this potential is important in the strengthening of relations. A detailed analysis of higher education and further studies on the impact of cooperation in the field of education and learning mobility on bilateral relations needs to be supported and encouraged.

Figure 30: Choice of Destination for Higher Education by Presidential Vote (%)

	Recep Tayyip Erdoğan	Muharrem İnce	Meral Akşener	Selahattin Demirtaş	Overall
United States	30.4	21.2	22.2	28.6	26.9
Germany	**19.6**	**18.2**	-	**19.0**	**17.0**
United King-dom	19.6	21.2	5.6	4.8	17.0
Finland	2.2	7.6	16.7	9.5	7.9
France	2.2	1.5	16.7	4.8	3.7
Austria	2.2	1.5	16.7	-	3.6
Other	4.3	3.0	5.6	4.8	3.6
Switzerland	4.3	4.5	-	-	3.1
Norway	6.5	1.5	-	9.5	2.9
Belgium	2.2	3.0	-	4.8	2.8
Spain	-	1.5	-	4.8	2.2
Italy	4.3	1.5	-	-	2.2
Russia	-	1.5	5.6	9.5	2.1
Poland	-	4.5	-	-	1.8
Canada	2.2	1.5	5.6	-	1.6
Netherlands	-	3.0	-	-	1.0
Cyprus	-	3.0	-	-	1.0
China	-	-	5.6	-	0.8
Total	100.0	100.0	100.0	100.0	100.0

Source: Istanbul Economics Research 2019 Foreign Policy Survey, calculations by the authors.

In 2021, Germany remained the most popular EU destination of choice for higher education. 18.8 % of the respondents chose Germany, when asked 'In which European country would you prefer your child to get education?', placing it on top of the list.[25] The UK is second (14.4 %) and France is third, with only 4.9 % of the respondents preferring to send their child to France.

Germany is not only considered as a successful country with a successful leader in the eyes of the Turkish public. On a completely different perspective, the GMF 2021 survey also revealed emotional social connections exist

---

25 "Turkish Perceptions of the European Union" Report by The German Marshall Fund of the United States.

as well. When asked 'In terms of culture and lifestyle, to what extent do you consider people living in these countries close to yourself?' almost half of the respondents (46.4 %) deemed people of Germany *'close'*, placing it on top of the list, people of Bulgaria second with 33 %.

4. Discussion and Contextualisation

Turkish people's mistrust towards foreign states is nothing new. In this regard, all studies indicate that Turkish public opinion displays low levels of trust particularly in Western countries, albeit Turkey has been part of this grouping for over a century. Hakan Yılmaz utilises the term 'Sèvres Syndrome' and points to the early history of Turkish modernisation to explain euroscepticism and mistrust towards European states.[26] In his extensive analysis of euroscepticism in Turkey, he links the issue of West-scepticism to increasingly negative attitudes towards the EU, arguing that: "At the popular level, identity Euroscepticism revolves around four key issues: national sovereignty; morality; negative discrimination; and Europe's alleged hidden agenda to divide and rule Turkey (the so-called 'Sèvres Syndrome')".[27] Yılmaz continues,

> "The Sèvres Syndrome thus refers to a certain mode of perception and a resulting code of operation which are rooted in a traumatic past experience with the West and have not been revised since, no matter how the real relationship with the West has changed over the years. 'Memory' is not always what we 'remember' as autonomous subjects, but what we are 'reminded' of by those in positions of authority, using institutions that produce and disseminate ideology, such as schools, textbooks, museums, the media, cinema, literature, etc".[28]

'Anti-Westernism' is thus a historically deeply rooted sentiment, which goes well beyond traditional fault lines in Turkish politics. Turkey has

---

26 Yılmaz, Hakan. "Two Pillars of Nationalist Euroskepticism in Turkey: The Tanzimat and Sevres Syndromes". In: Ingmar Karlsson/ Annika Strom Melin (Eds.). Turkey, Sweden and the European Union: Experiences and Expectations. Stockholm, 2006, pp. 29–40.

27 Yılmaz, Hakan. Euroscepticism in Turkey: Parties, Elites, and Public Opinion. In: *South European Society and Politics*, 2011, 16, (1), pp. 185–208.

28 Yılmaz, Hakan, Euroscepticism in Turkey.

become a deeply polarised society, especially during the last decade.[29] Studies reveal that despite the deep polarisation, there are issues that remain as islands of agreements which reach across groups. Through their extensive polarisation analysis, Emre Erdoğan and Pınar Semerci demonstrate that this anti-Western attitude is one of the strongest negative islands of agreement that goes beyond party lines, education and socio-economic differences.[30]

A detailed analysis of euroscepticism in Turkey is beyond the scope of this chapter.[31] However, it is important to follow the proposition by Hakan Yılmaz on the issue of "reminding" by those in positions of authority.[32] Regarding Western Europe in general and Germany in particular, over the past five years the Turkish public has been increasingly reminded by leading government figures of the potential threat. In other words, European states, particularly Germany, have been presented as a potential threat and enemy of Turkey. Although low levels of sympathy for and perceptions of threat from foreign states have been a long-standing characteristic of Turkish people, extensive use of 'the enemy' narrative by politicians is rather new.[33]

In her analysis of the 2017 crisis between European states and Turkey, considering the latter's constitutional referendum campaigns in European states, Gözde Yılmaz argues that a post-truth strategy was actively adopted by the key AKP cadre, which relied on nationalist sentiments and the

---

29 Cf. Erdoğan, Emre/ Semerci, Pınar Uyan. Dimensions of Polarization in Turkey 2017. Istanbul Bilgi University, Center for Migration Research, 2017.

30 Erdoğan, Emre/ Semerci, Pınar Uyan. Fanusta diyaloglar: Türkiye'de kutuplaşmanın boyutları. In: *Istanbul Bilgi Üniversitesi Yayınları*, 2018.

31 If interested, for a detailed discussion and analysis on Euroscepticism in Turkey, in addition to the works by Hakan Yılmaz, see Yaka, Özge. Why Not EU? Dynamics of the Changing Turkish Attitudes towards EU Membership. *Journal of Contemporary European Studies*, 2016, 24, (1), pp. 149–170; Çarkoğlu, Ali/ Kentmen, Çiğdem. Diagnosing Trends and Determinants in Public Support for Turkey's EU membership. In: *South European Society and Politics*, 2011, 16, (3), pp. 365–379; Uguz, Hülya Eski/ Saygili, Rukiye. Euro-Scepticism in Turkey of AKP Period in the Context of Temporary Tensions and Permanent Interests. In: *Inquiry*, 2017, 2, (1); Dikici Bilgin, Hasret. Westernist sceptics and anti-western reformers in the Turkish party system. In: *Journal of Balkan and Near Eastern Studies*, 2017, 19, (2), pp. 191–208.

32 Yılmaz, Hakan. Two Pillars of Nationalist Euroskepticism in Turkey, p. 4.

33 Özbey, Ebru Ece et.al. Narratives of a Contested Relationship: Unravelling the Debates in the EU and Turkey. In: Beken Saatçioğlu, Funda Tekin (Eds.): Turkey and the European Union: Key Dynamics and Future Scenarios. Turkey and European Union Studies. Vol. 3. Baden-Baden, 2021.

underlying Sèvres Syndrome.[34] The portrayal of Germany and the Netherlands as states that are jealous of the "New Turkey" that is strong and influential was constructed and repeated by different actors on numerous platforms.[35] As Yılmaz argues, this post-truth portrayal of Germany constructed from half-truths and misinformation definitely took its toll on Turkish public opinion towards Germany. Yet, it is important to underline that despite the crisis as well as negative agenda setting and framing in 2017, attitudes towards Germany remain rather stable and are certainly not to be regarded as extremely negative.

5. Conclusion

Germany continues to be regarded as a popular country in Turkey. Most Turkish people at all different levels in society experience some level of exposure to news related with Germany through different channels: relatives and neighbours who are or have been part of the Turkish diaspora in Germany; millions of German tourists that visit Turkey; and music by Germans of Turkish origin (especially rap and hip hop).[36] Germany is also a popular country in the news, especially over the last five years, being considered as: the EU's main engine; one of the principal actors shaping Turkey's bid for EU membership; the main actor behind the 2016 EU-Turkey statement on migration; leading economic investor in Turkey and a key buyer of Turkish products. President Erdoğan speaks quite often about Germany and even uses it for comparison purposes to assess Turkey's achievements.[37] Despite adverse framing as well as increasingly negative and conflictual statements over recent years, so far as Turkish public opinion is concerned Germany's approval ratings remain stable. Indeed, Turks in general share a favourable view that Turkey should

---

34 Yılmaz, Gözde. Post-truth politics in the 2017 Euro-Turkish crisis. In: *Journal of Contemporary European Studies*, 2019, 27, (2), pp. 237–246.

35 For another detailed analysis and examples of the narrative on the powerful "New Turkey" and the envious European states (in particular Germany) resorting into dirty politics to stop its ascent, see Üstün, Çiğdem. The Rise and Fall of Europeanization, Bern, Switzerland, 2017, especially chapter II of this book, *Turkey – EU relations hit by populist rhetoric* (with Özgehan Şenyuva).

36 For a detailed historical analysis of rap and hip hop music establishing a bridge between Turkey and Germany see Güney, Serhat. Zor isimli çocuklar: bir gurbet hikâyesi. In: *İstanbul Bilgi Üniversitesi Yayınları*, 2015.

37 Bedir/ Gedikli/ Şenyuva. Turkey's Relations with Germany in Recep Tayyip Erdoğan's Narratives (2003–2018), p. 135.

continue to cooperate and work with Germany. It is very important to recognize that the perceptions of Germany are not reflected on the present political polarisation that dominates the Turkish political scene. In other words, Germany does not represent a fault line between the supporters of the governing bloc and the opposition and the evaluations towards Germany are bipartisan in nature. Thus, Germany in general and relations (economic, cultural, social and political) with Germany is not a divisive issue and such policies are very likely to receive public support.

However, such popularity comes as a mixed blessing. Turkish public opinion towards Germany is complex and conflictual, namely the favourite Western European state with a successful leader, but lacks translation into a stable and positive evaluation. People's generally negative attitudes towards the West include Germany. Over the years Turkish evaluation has been rather volatile, to the extent that Germany is also considered as a potential threat to Turkey and hence for some any cooperation should be avoided. Having said that, it is important to recognise that the Turkish public displays suspicions and a lack of trust towards almost all foreign states.

Thus, it would be fair to argue that Germany needs to invest more in public diplomacy so as to increase its level of trust and thereby improve Turkish public opinion in this regard. On a more positive note, Germany has built extensive credit in the eyes of Turkish people over a long period of time, despite constantly being on the political agenda and at times framed in a very negative narrative by Turkey's leadership. Germany's position is resilient and hence there is vast potential for building a positive agenda both through traditional diplomacy as well as public and citizen diplomacy. Considering the cultural affinity that is evident in the recent survey, the potential of public and citizen diplomacy is very significant. Education, as demonstrated in this chapter, is one such field that carries such a potential which could therefore be further exploited.

Agreeing to Disagree and the Way Forward: Conclusions Drawn From the Triangular Perspective on EU-Turkey Relations

Anke Schönlau, Funda Tekin

1. Introduction: Narrating a Roller Coaster Relationship

Cooperation is a theme which constantly returns in the sometimes difficult triangular relations between the European Union (EU), Germany and Turkey. Geography, geopolitical challenges and long-standing people-to-people contacts are very much here to stay. Moreover, all three parts of the triangle will not cease to cooperate on matters of mutual significance and interest. Our edited volume seeks to disentangle this complex relationship by focussing on narratives within the EU, Germany and Turkey on EU-Turkey relations. Narratives create political action but will also lead to political inaction and deadlock if no common aims or *finalité* can be identified. When looking to interpret political developments, narratives have so far been largely overlooked as an explanatory research tool, which could specifically assist in understanding to what extent a new institutional frame might help to break-up the conflictual spiral that has been determining EU-Turkey relations in recent years.

Turkey's relations with the EU and Germany often resemble a roller coaster ride with no end in sight and where rapprochement can alternate with conflict within months. In the past decade alone, we can observe a quite telling pattern: The European Commission's attempt to revive EU-Turkey relations by introducing a 'Positive Agenda' on cooperation in distinct fields during 2012[1] dissolved into thin air only one year later as the 2013 Gezi Park protests in Istanbul disclosed how state and police forces turned against the country's civil society. This is said to have marked a turning point in EU-Turkey relations.[2] In 2015, the influx of migrants

---

[1] Cf. European Commission. Positive EU-Turkey agenda launched in Ankara. Memo/12/359. Brussels, 17.05.2012.

[2] Cf. Weise, Helena/ Tekin, Funda. From EU-Accession to Unique Partnership – Narratives, Strategies and Scenarios of EU-Turkey Relations in the German Parliament 2002–2018. In this volume, p. 179-109, p.91.

from Syria into the EU and Germany gave rise to German-led negotiations, which eventually led to the March 2016 EU-Turkey statement on migration and constituted a sudden, short phase of cooperation.

However, immediately afterwards relations deteriorated once again following the failed coup attempt in Turkey of July 2016, which in Turkey's view produced a belated and inappropriate reaction from the EU. Shortly before, the German parliament with an almost unanimous vote officially recognised the 1915 mass deaths of Armenians during the Ottoman Empire as genocide. Relations weakened even more in 2017 due to a number of issues: a dispute about Turkish campaigning for the referendum on Turkey's presidential system in EU Member States; elections in Germany that further politicised relations with Turkey; and the fact that people of German nationality were arrested in Turkey following the failed coup attempt.[3]

In response to Turkey's continued backsliding in the rule of law and human rights issues, the EU's General Affairs Council decided in June 2018 that accession negotiations with Turkey were effectively frozen, with no chapters being considered for opening or closing. Finally, EU-Turkey relations reached rock-bottom in 2020 after months of Turkey's energy drilling and military conflicts off the coast of Cyprus and Libya in the Eastern Mediterranean Sea. Following the European Council's decision on targeted measures against Turkey, it offered "a positive political agenda [...] provided constructive efforts to stop illegal activities vis-à-vis Greece and Cyprus are sustained"[4] by Turkey. Since then, open conflict between the EU and Turkey has receded.

In the immediate aftermath of Russia invading Ukraine in February 2022, a series of high-level visits of German and EU officials to Turkey took place to discuss not only security cooperation, but also various other areas of concern.[5] At the same time, in late April 2022, a life sentence was hand-

---

3 Cf. Turhan, Ebru. Introduction. In: Ebru Turhan (Ed.). German-Turkish Relations Revisited. The European Dimension, Domestic and Foreign Politics and Transnational Dynamics. Turkey and European Union Studies Vol. 2. Baden-Baden, 2019, pp. 11–27, p. 12.

4 European Council. Conclusions. Special meeting of the European Council, 1 and 2 October 2020. EUCO 13/20. Brussels, 02.10.2020, p. 8.

5 Cf. European Commission. Executive Vice-President Timmermans in Turkey to strengthen cooperation on climate, 20.04.2022, https://ec.europa.eu/neighbourho od-enlargement/news/executive-vice-president-timmermans-turkey-strengthen-co operation-climate-2022-04-20_en [29.05.2022]; The Federal Government. Federal Chancellor Scholz visits Turkey, 14.03.2022, https://www.bundesregierung.de/breg -en/news/scholz-in-turkey-2015574 [29.05.2022].

ed down to prominent businessman, philanthropist and activist Osman Kavala, who had been convicted of having attempted to overthrow the government during the Gezi Park protests. This caused a further impairing of Turkey's relations with both the EU and the Council of Europe, the latter having earlier agreed on starting infringement proceedings against Turkey for not obeying the European Court of Human Rights' judgements that had clearly demanded Osman Kavala's release.[6] The clear and confrontational statements by the Turkish Minister of Foreign Affairs, Mevlüt Çavuşoğlu, and his German counterpart, Annalena Baerbock, during a joint press conference in Istanbul in July 2022, highlighted two issues: there are still various conflictual issues that strain both German-Turkish and EU-Turkey relations. Both sides are currently not willing to conceal their opposing positions.[7] All of these events are politically outstanding in themselves. While they have effectively sent EU-Turkey relations on a roller coaster ride, for the moment at least a train crash has been avoided.[8]

All contributions to our volume share the aim of contextualising this present state of affairs by entangling the complex, multi-layered EU-Turkish relationship through the analysis and deconstruction of respective narratives in the EU, Turkey and Germany. Broadly speaking, we understand narratives as the 'stories people tell' that mostly include a 'moral of the story' in terms of a normative statement on how the framework and intensity of EU-Turkey relations should be designed.[9] Why does this matter? Narratives play an important role for political behaviour in helping to

---

6   Cf. Council of Europe. Committee of Ministers refers Kavala v. Turkey case to the European Court of Human Rights, 03.02.2022, https://www.coe.int/en/web/porta l/-/committee-of-ministers-refers-kavala-v-turkey-case-to-the-european-court-of-hu man-rights [29.05.2022]; Human Rights Watch. Turkey: Council of Europe Votes for Infringement Process. Sanction Sought for Ankara's Refusal to Release Rights Defender Osman Kavala, 02.02.2022, https://www.hrw.org/news/2022/02/02/turkey -council-europe-votes-infringement-process [29.05.2022].

7   Cf. Reuters. Turkish, German ministers argue over policies in tense news conference, 29.07.2022, https://www.reuters.com/world/turkish-german-ministers-argue-o ver-policies-tense-news-conference-2022-07-29/ [(29.07.2022].

8   Cf. Tekin, F./ Wessels, W. Untangling German-Turkish Relations: Thinking Ahead. In: Ebru Turhan (Ed.). German-Turkish Relations Revisited. The European Dimension, Domestic and Foreign Politics and Transnational Dynamics. Turkey and European Union Studies. Vol. 2. Baden-Baden, 2019, pp. 269–279, p. 270.

9   Cf. Tekin, Funda/ Schönlau, Anke. The EU-German-Turkish Triangle. A Conceptual Framework for Narratives, Perceptions and Discourse of a Unique Relationship. In this volume, p.9-30, p. 61.

make sense of one's past and future.[10] A common understanding or at least comprehension of one's counterpart's perceptions and ideas provide the foundation for discussing, negotiating and envisioning a path towards the achievement of a future scenario. This means that diverging or even contested interests and priorities do not necessarily have to result in a conflictual relationship so long as they are embedded in the same story or share the same 'moral of the story'.

In this chapter we aim to answer the general research question of what impact narratives have on the relationship between the EU, Turkey and Germany by presenting the main findings of this volume's narrative analysis in a comparative, temporal and thematic approach. In the next section we revisit the chapters of this edited volume from the perspective of these analytical elements. In the third section we elaborate on whether or not those findings suggest a paradigm shift in EU-Turkey relations and outline a future scenario for the relationship. The final section provides an outlook on how our findings could possibly interplay between potential developments of differentiated integration in the EU.

2. Main Findings of the Narrative Analysis

The contributions to this volume analyse narratives on EU-Turkey relations from different angles and within different time periods up until the year 2019. Clearly, we could analyse the dialogue of many more actors, but nevertheless the combined results provide for a very good understanding of what themes have driven the relationship over the past few decades. We consider the stories that were told and which narratives shape our understanding of the way actors want us to perceive the relationship. This analysis also includes an assessment of Turkish public opinion, which facilitates our appreciation of how discourse about the relationship changes.

We structure the research findings in this volume by answering the question of whether and, if so, to what extent do EU, German and Turkish actors' narratives correlate or contrast in general terms, and, more specifically, with a view to the four thematic dimensions of politics, security, economy and identity. Within the political dimension, discussion focuses, often within the context of accession talks, on the state of the political system, particularly in light of: democracy, the rule of law, human rights,

---

10 Cf. Jones, Michael/ McBeth, Mark. A Narrative Policy Framework: Clear Enough to be Wrong? in: *The Policy Studies Journal*, Vol. 38, No. 2, pp. 329–353, p. 330.

as well as respect for and protection of minorities. Geostrategic arguments deal with Turkey's geopolitical significance in Europe and especially its role in Europe's security architecture, such as the country's vital role in NATO due to its geographic characteristics. The economic dimension subsumes all references made to bilateral and multilateral trade or relevance as mutual trading partners. Under the societal or identity-related dimension, we identify references to religion, cultural identification and ascriptions determining norms, values and behaviour of individuals as well as groups along with societal categories applied by the narrators, for instance 'us' vs. 'them'.[11] This style of analysis helps to identify recurring topics and define lines of argument that sometimes develop over wide timespans. We, therefore, additionally assess whether and if so to what extent such narratives change over time.

Having briefly introduced our conceptual frame, we now set off to merge individual analyses with common findings. We discover that narratives or stories in the EU, Germany and Turkey did not share a 'moral of the story' concerning the common *finalité* of relations in almost all cases over the past 60 years. Exceptions are the early 1960s and the end of the 1990s/early 2000s, when Turkey finally became a candidate country. Sometimes, different plots on each side about the very same issue lead to a different 'moral to the story' and proposed policy solutions. We identify three main turning points (two relating to Germany and the EU and one to Turkey), resulting in two paradigm shifts on the European side, but none on the Turkish side.

2.1 Narratives on EU-Turkey Relations: Three Main Storylines

Considering the multitude of narratives on EU-Turkey relations that the authors to this edited volume identified in the EU, Turkey and Germany, the picture seems at first sight to be rather complex. Figure 31 collects 24 narratives concerning different objects of analysis featured in the individual chapters.

---

11 Cf. Schönlau, Anke/ Schröder, Mirja. A Charged Friendship: German Narratives of EU-Turkey Relations in the Pre-accession Phase, 1959–1999. In this volume, pp. 57-77, p. 61.

Figure 31: Simplified Collection of Narratives on EU-Turkey Relations and their Moral of the Story

Actor	Time	Narrative	Moral of the story
Turkey	1959-1990	Westernisation	Accession
	since 1960s	Economic Cooperation	Accession
	1980-2000	Europeanisation	Accession
	since 1989	Eurasianisation	Accession
	2000/2002	Turkey as 'the Heir'	Accession
	since 2000s	Turkey as a 'Great Power'	Accession
	2013	Victim of Double-Standards	Accession
EU	1960-1980	Membership	Accession
	since 1960s	Strategic Partner	Cooperation
	since 1980s	Distant Neighbour	Cooperation
	1980s/1997/2005	Special Case/Candidate	Cooperation
	1997-2004	Membership	Accession
	1992-today	Transactional Partnership	Cooperation
	since 2015	Problematic Neighbour	Cooperation
Germany	1960s	Turkey as Partner of the West	Cooperation
	1970s	Complicated Military Ally	Cooperation
	1980s	Important Partner	Cooperation
	1980s	Political Concern	Cooperation
	1990s	European with Exceptions	Cooperation
	1990s	Geostrategic Partner	Accession
	2000s	Not European	Cooperation but no accession
	2000s, 2015	Geostrategic Asset	Cooperation
	2000s	EU Accession	Accession
	since 2013	Politically Unpredictable Country	Cooperation but no accession

Source: Own compilation based on the chapters present in this edited volume.

Upon closer observation those narratives in essence tell three different kinds of stories. Firstly, they explore the issue of how far Turkey and the EU converge in terms of identity or rather consider the question of whether and if so to what extent does Turkey belong to Europe/the EU. Respective narratives since the 1950s up to the 1990s on the Turkish side deal with Turkey's *Westernisation* or *Europeanisation*, considering Turkey as a "crucial part of the West" or owning a "rightful" place among European countries"[12] respectively. Narratives in the EU and Germany are by far more sceptical and build on the narrative of Turkey being "European with exceptions"[13] in the 1990s or simply describing Turkey as "not (belonging) to the European cultural circle"[14] in the early 2000s. Turkey's corresponding narrative dealing with this supposed clash between European and Turkish identity is the one on *Turkey as 'the Heir'*.[15] The storyline suggests, that "Turkey is European *because* of its past (… and that) European actors bring up so-called identity-related differences, strategically using Turkey's past and thereby masking their own underlying reluctance for further integration".[16]

Secondly, narratives assess Turkey's actorness. Turkish narratives since 1989 tell the story of Turkey becoming a regional power (*Eurasianisation* narrative) or a "great power"[17] considering Turkey's alternatives to the EU. In Germany, the narrative of Turkey's *Geostrategic asset*[18] was dominant between 2000 and 2013. The Gezi Park protests produced the German narrative on Turkey being a *Politically Unpredictable Country*.[19]

Thirdly, most narratives deal with questions about the EU-Turkey relationship's quality. While in Turkey one single mono-thematic narrative could be identified, which is simply concerning *Membership*,[20] narratives in Germany and the EU vary considerably. There is also a *Membership*/EU accession narrative but stories focus more on Turkey as a "special

---

12 Özbey, Ebru Ece/ Hauge, Hanna-Lisa/ Eralp, Atila. Identity Representations in Narratives on EU-Turkey Relations. In this volume, pp. 31-55, p. 42.

13 Schönlau/ Schröder, A Charged Friendship, 2022, p. 72.

14 Deutscher Bundestag. Michael Glos. Plenary Protocol 15/4. Berlin, 29.10.2002, p. 88, cited in Weise/Tekin, From EU-Accession to Unique Partnership, 2022.

15 Cf. Özbey /Hauge /Eralp. Identity Representations in Narratives on EU-Turkey Relations, 2022.

16 Ibid., p. 45.

17 Ibid., p. 40.

18 Weise/ Tekin. From EU-Accession to Unique Partnership, 2022, p. 105.

19 Ibid., p. 170ff.

20 Cf. Özbey/ Hauge/ Eralp. Identity Representations in Narratives on EU-Turkey Relations, 2022.

candidate",[21] "(important) strategic partner",[22] "partner of the west",[23] "geostrategic partner"[24] and "distant"[25] or even "problematic neighbour".[26] This corresponds with narratives of a relationship with a *Complicated Military Ally*[27] or *Transactional Partnership*.[28]

Our analysis has also highlighted the differences of storylines in the EU, Germany and Turkey respectively. Turkish narration reflects to a large extent on the country's position within the European and regional architecture, both geostrategic and politically. Turkish narratives are often explicitly about what Turkey is like and what role it holds (or should hold) in the world. Although Turkish narratives to a large extent define Turkey as part of Europe, the implicit question is how Turkey defines itself against (the idea of) Europe. This is not the case for the EU or Germany, where narratives on Turkey are mostly unidirectional and less self-reflective as they state something about Turkey, not about the EU. Although there are in general European narratives about Europe and the EU, such as the 'community of values' narrative,[29] this is not tied to EU-Turkey relations. Given that the EU is a decades-old bloc and Turkey is the country that wants to accede, this is certainly not surprising. However, this lack of self-reflection in the European and German narratives on EU-Turkey relations denies the fact that "it takes two to tango"[30] in this relationship. This means that even though developments in Turkey and Turkey's compliance with the accession criteria and actions in accordance with good neighbourly relations are crucial for the state of play in EU-Turkey relations, this represents only one side of the coin. Enlargement or even Turkey fatigue and absorption

---

21 Özbey/ Hauge/ Eralp. Identity Representations in Narratives on EU-Turkey Relations, 2022, p. 41.
22 Ibid., p. 40.
23 Schönlau/ Schröder, A Charged Friendship, 2022, p. 62.
24 Ibid., p. 75.
25 Özbey/ Hauge/ Eralp. Identity Representations in Narratives on EU-Turkey Relations, 2022, p. 49.
26 Rau/ Ersoy/ Wessels. EU Leaders' Narratives on Turkey, 2022, p. 154.
27 Schönlau/ Schröder. A Charged Friendship, 2022, p. 66.
28 Rau/ Ersoy/ Wessels. EU Leaders' Narratives on Turkey, 2022, p. 151.
29 Müller, Manuel. Individuelle und kollektive Selbstbestimmung jenseits des Nationalstaats: das kosmopolitisch-demokratische Narrativ der europäischen Integration. In: *integration*, 2021, Vol. 44, No. 4, pp. 251–265.
30 Cf. Soler i Lecha, Eduard/ Tekin, Funda/ Sökmen, Melike Janine. It Takes Two to Tango: Political changes in Europe and their Impact on Turkey's EU bid. FEUTURE Online Paper No. 17. Cologne, April 2018.

capacity as well as crises and trends of differentiated integration in the EU are just as important when it comes to assessing the relationship.

Each narrative has its own 'moral of the story'. In broad terms one key element is the question of whether EU accession/membership is the destined *finalité* of the relationship or alternative forms of institutional relations between the EU and Turkey need to be considered. Turkey's accession to the EU remains a "strategic priority".[31] A single exception is constituted in the Euro Crisis, when Turkey claimed to be considering alternatives to accession in light of the weak economic and political state of the EU.[32] In conclusion and as already stated, in Turkey there is only one 'moral of the story' and that is membership. In the EU and Germany, though, plots of narratives have repeatedly considered alternative options. The plot of narratives which claim that Turkey is not European or sufficiently European relates to the concept of privileged partnership in the early 2000s. In this case, both the plots of narratives and their 'moral of the story' diverge between the EU and Germany on the one side and Turkey on the other. This is bound to cause conflict in the relationship.

2.2 *The Difficulties of Breaking the Vicious Circle of Mutual Accusations*

Concerning the question whether and if so to what extent EU, German and Turkish narratives contrast in general terms, we can draw two main conclusions from our analysis.

Firstly, narratives grow increasingly rich in contrast over time, but interestingly correlate the more contrast can be identified. By the end of 2019, we see the German side relating to Turkey as an *Politically Unpredictable Country*[33] when it comes to the EU's main accession criteria democracy and the rule of law. Turkey, in return, identifies European partners as not trustworthy for criticising Turkish domestic policy-making.[34] Where

---

31 Ministry of Foreign Affairs. Türkiye's Enterprising and Humanitarian Foreign Policy. A Synopsis, https://www.mfa.gov.tr/synopsis-of-the-turkish-foreign-policy.en.mfa [04.07.2022].

32 Cf. Özel, Soli. Despite the eurozone crisis, and the ambivalent attitudes of the Turkish public, Turkey still stands to benefit from EU accession. In: LSE Blog, 29.10.2012 [04.07.2022].

33 Cf. Tekin, Funda/ Schönlau, Anke. The EU-German-Turkish Triangle, 2022.

34 Özbey/ Hauge/ Eralp. Identity Representations in Narratives on EU-Turkey Relations, 2022.

Turkey lifts itself up as *Great Power*[35] in its regional environment including European littoral states to the Mediterranean and the Black Sea, the EU sees in Turkey a "problematic neighbour"[36] behaving aggressively towards its (European) neighbours. These contrasting yet strongly correlating narratives provide an explanation for the vicious spiral of mutual accusations that the EU and Turkey as well as Germany and Turkey have been entrapped by for the past decade.

Secondly, narratives of different EU institutions differ widely, referring to different plots and therefore a different 'moral of the story'. Following their own institutional logic, self-perception and competences, they employ diverging narratives on EU-Turkey relations that impede establishing a common narrative that is easily comprehensible outside the EU institutions and translated into a comprehensive policy set or strategy towards Turkey. The European Council, representing the Member States who have their very own bilateral ties with Turkey, agreed in the past years on statements representing the lowest-common denominator among Member States' preferences. This narrowed the statements down to focus on criticising Turkey's relations with its neighbours and consequently defining cooperation as the determining form of EU-Turkey relations. The European Council's stance on Turkey is predominantly geostrategically induced. The European Parliament's emphasis is on the rule of law and human rights, but it is not able to lock or unlock any institutional path under the current institutional set-up. The European Commission's take is rather technical, although nuanced in regard to the rule of law in Turkey, since it is one of the parameters observed within the accession process.[37] However, these findings on the EU institutions' communication are not new to Turkey. Over time, Turkey has learned to play ball with the differing signals and follows its own (foreign) policy approach that is not related to EU foreign policy aims. Economic cooperation, embedded in a larger (geo-)political context, can be used for strategic escalation ("no one should try to deceive us"[38]) of rhetoric, or in a very cooperative way when it comes to bi- or

---

35 Ibid., p 46.
36 Cf. Rau/ Ersoy/ Wessels. EU Leaders' Narratives on Turkey, 2022.
37 Cf. Toygür, Ilke/ Tekin, Funda/ Soler i Lecha, Eduard/ Danforth, Nicholas. Turkey's foreign policy and its consequences for the EU. In-depth Analysis, Requested by AFET Committee, European Parliament, EP/EXPO/AFET/FWC/2019–01/Lot1/2/C/03.
38 Bedir, Nurdan/ Gedikli, Ardahan/ Şenyuva, Özgehan. So Close Yet So Far: Turkey's Relations with Germany in Recep Tayyip Erdoğan's Narratives (2003–2018). In this volume, pp. 111-139, p. 131.

multilateral trade, as in "German companies operating in Turkey profit by various price advantages (...) (and) also contribute to the production, technology and export levels of Turkish industry".[39] The Turkish president's promotion of cooperation and escalation at the same time, as identified by *Gedikli, Bedir and Şenyuva*, is a strategy for a transactional relationship, but not for sustainable rules-based cooperation and vision.

2.3 *Thematic Trends and Narrated Turning Points in EU-Turkey Relations*

Looking at the development of narratives across time, Turkey, the EU and Germany have come to agree to disagree. Shifts at national, regional or global levels, such as the consequences of the end of the Cold War and of the bi-polar structure of the international system are relevant factors in respective analyses. While there is mostly convergence during the 20th century, building on geostrategic interests, narratives become more diverse and more distinct from the 1990s onwards. Narratives have a 'plot', the actual theme that the narrator talks about. Analysing and comparing these thematic dimensions that drive[40] EU-Turkey relations helps to contextualise the narratives and then identify critical turning points in the narration. In EU-Turkey relations, narratives mostly take place within four thematic dimensions – geostrategic, political, economic, societal/identity – and one 'cross-cutting' dimension which is unique to the narration of Turkey's president Erdoğan.

The geostrategic dimension is a true evergreen and one of two most influential dimensions in narratives on EU-Turkey relations. Turkey's perception as a "cornerstone within our system of defence"[41] in Germany in the 1960s was matched by NATO's perceived role in the "reinforcement of [Turkey's] national security".[42] The first slight changes in this dimension appear in the 1970s and the emerging Cyprus conflict ("Support

---

39 Cf. Bedir, Nurdan/ Gedikli, Ardahan/ Şenyuva, Özgehan. So Close Yet So Far: Turkey's Relations with Germany in Recep Tayyip Erdoğan's Narratives (2003–2018). In this volume, pp. 111-139, p. 130.

40 Cf. Saatçioğlu, Beken/ Tekin, Funda/ Ekim, Sinan/ Tocci, Nathalie. The Future of EU-Turkey Relations: A Dynamic Association Framework amidst Conflictual Cooperation. FEUTURE Synthesis Paper.

41 Schönlau/ Schröder. A Charged Friendship, 2022, p. 64.

42 Özbey/ Hauge/ Eralp. Identity Representations in Narratives on EU-Turkey Relations, 2022, pp. 41.

for Greece is not meant to be against Turkey, an ally"[43]), but cooperation-prone narratives such as the *Strategic Partner* or *Important Partner*
narrative remain dominant in this dimension throughout the 1990s and
beginning of the 2000s. Conflictual narratives are commonly observed
in European Council Conclusions since Turkey started its energy explora-
tions and military exercises in the Eastern Mediterranean and pursued its
own strategy in Northern Syria that would "undermine the stability of the
whole region".[44] Narratives now address the same issue with a different
interpretation (i.e. Turkey's self-perception as the *Great Power* vs. the EU's
perception of Turkey as a *Problematic Neighbour*).

Though economic ties between Turkey and the EU have belonged to
the institutional basis of EU-Turkey relations since the Ankara Agreement
of 1963, the economic dimension appears relatively seldom throughout
the analyses. Hence, none of the narratives identified in Figure 31 (above)
is mainly driven by economics. During the 20th century, discussions in
Germany and the EU about Turkey's economy or financial assistance
are connected to the geostrategic dimension respectively understood as
a means of stabilising Turkey as a NATO member. In the 1990s, Turkey's
ability to fulfil the economic requirements of membership became more
prevalent. In Turkey, the economic dimension has indeed been frequently
mentioned since the 2000s, albeit used to pursue both cooperation and
conflict with its EU partners, as stated in the previous section.

The societal/identity dimension is perhaps the most difficult to grasp;
it appears from time to time in Germany and the EU during the 20th
century ("Turkey is a part of Europe"[45]). Interestingly, the dimension dis-
appears from the Chancellor's narratives in governmental declarations at
the time when Kohl's reservations against Turkey's cultural identity were
the main obstacle to Turkey's membership application. Rather, the stance
that Turkey is not fully European respectively *European with exceptions* was
disseminated by other ranks within his party.[46] In Turkey, contrastingly,
identity is ubiquitous but always intertwined with geostrategic or political arguments. The plot in this dimension changes over time, becoming
more conflictual and dominant since 2013: The earlier version related
that the EU will bring Turkey "to the level of contemporary civilisation

---

43 Schönlau/ Schröder. A Charged Friendship, 2022, p. 66.
44 Rau/ Ersoy/ Wessels. EU Leaders' Narratives on Turkey, 2022, pp. 155.
45 Özbey/ Hauge/ Eralp. Identity Representations in Narratives on EU-Turkey Rela-
    tions, 2022, p. 48.
46 Cf. Schönlau/ Schröder. A Charged Friendship, 2022, pp. 72ff.

it deserves"[47] in 2003 (politically induced); but by 2016 this had changed to, "Turkey is not a guest but the host in Europe"[48] (identity/geostrategic induced).

Finally, along the geostrategic dimensions, the political dimension has in recent years been the most relevant. Seldomly observed when the EU was still an economic, not a political union, it became more visible from the 1980s onwards. The narrative of *Political Concern* was introduced with the military coup in Turkey during 1980.[49] Since the Gezi Park protests in 2013, most discussions in the German Bundestag on Turkey where part of the political dimension on how to "adjust the political course towards Turkey".[50] In light of the attempted Coup d'etat in Turkey during 2016, the European Council even demanded Turkey's "full compliance with the European Convention for the Protection of Human Rights and Fundamental Freedoms, including Protocol 13 on the abolition of the death penalty".[51] From a Turkish perspective, as mentioned in the previous paragraph, the political dimension often became intertwined with the identity dimension, where the EU's political system was part of a vision of Turkey's future. Initiated by the Gezi Park protests, but stretching to 2015 and the so-called migration crisis in Europe, the political dimension becomes very relevant in Turkey, citing "injustices and double standards"[52] in the accession process and general treatment of Turkey. Still, the Turkish president also continued to speak about solidarity and cooperation, which leads *Gedikli, Bedir and Şenyuva* to the conclusion that he pursues several approaches at the same time to his EU and German partners.[53] Thus, there are certain thematic trends in the narration of EU-Turkey relations especially in Germany and the EU. The Turkish narrative, in this volume extensively displayed by the Turkish president's speeches, is more diverse both in terms of dimension as well as in quality: Erdoğan covers all dimensions from economics, political system, identity and geostrategic considera-

---

47 Özbey/Hauge/ Eralp. Identity Representations in Narratives on EU-Turkey Relations, 2022, p. 43.
48 Ibid., p. 45.
49 Cf. Schönlau/ Schröder. A Charged Friendship, 2022, p. 70.
50 Weise/ Tekin. German Narratives, Strategies and Scenarios of EU-Turkey Relations 2002–2018, 2022, p. 93.
51 Council of the EU. Council Conclusions on Turkey, 18.07.2016, https://www.consilium.europa.eu/en/press/press-releases/2016/07/18/fac-turkey-conclusions/ [08.01.2022].
52 Bedir/ Gedikli/ Şenyuva. So Close Yet So Far, 2022, p. 154.
53 Ibid., p. 138f.

tions frequently. He also uses cooperative and conflictual narrations of the relationship at the same time.

Having identified thematic trends over time, the contributions to this volume additionally identified several turning points in the narration on EU-Turkey relations. Furthermore, in light of the previous analysis, they are narrated differently in the EU, Germany and Turkey, because their narratives prevail and change for different reasons. In Germany and the EU, we observe two turning points.

Firstly, Turkey's acquiring of candidacy status in 1999 was strongly induced among other factors by a new government in Germany. This government coalition of the social democrats and the Greens offered a narrative of Turkey as an important geostrategic partner and concluded that it was in the EU's own interest to accept Turkey as a member.

Secondly, a significant turning point was formed by the Gezi Park protests of 2013, when under the impression of Turkey's repressive actions against civil society actors, the last advocates of Turkey's accession changed their narrative to Turkey being too unpredictable to qualify for EU membership. Quickly thereafter, at Union level the *Problematic Neighbour* narrative quickly spread. Since 2018, the accession process has been effectively frozen.

In Turkey, the turning point is less bound to one specific event, but rather a development from becoming more similar to Europe (*Westernisation, Europeanisation*, to some extend *Eurasianisation*) to a self-perception of important regional and geopolitical force/entity (*the 'Heir'* or the *'Great Power'*). During the Gezi Park protests in 2013 and thereafter, the Turkish narration of its relations with the EU became harsh, but it never stopped (officially) advocating for membership. Compared to the years of *Westernisation* and *Europeanisation*, the plot had changed: Turkey should not become EU member because of its Europeanness, but because of its geopolitical importance.

3. Scenarios – Is There a Paradigm Shift and Which Vision for the Future Does it Correspond to?

Three different scenarios for the (institutional) future of EU-Turkey relations guide our analysis. We asked whether or not we observe a fundamental change of story on EU-Turkey relations – and if so, what drives this change and to which future scenario can it be linked?

The first scenario suggests a revitalisation of EU-Turkey relations, including a return to a conventional accession paradigm in the EU, Germany and Turkey alike. This could be indicated by the re-emergence of narratives of Turkey's Europeanisation. In terms of theme, this would especially mean positive and shared narratives in the political dimension. Assessing the analysis presented in this edited volume, we cannot find any evidence for such a scenario or the possibility of a corresponding paradigm shift[54] that would render such a scenario likely in the foreseeable future. There is certainly no indication that there could be positive narrations on the developments in the political dimension over the foreseeable future. On the contrary, the joint press conference by the German and Turkish ministers of foreign affairs in July 2022 gave evidence of the vicious spiral of mutual accusations tightening: Çavuşoğlu accused Germany of siding with Greece and hence interfering in a bilateral conflict instead of taking a mediating role as Germany had done in the past. Baerbock was very clear on her demand that Turkey should refrain from further military operations in Syria and should free Osman Kavala from prison as requested by the Council of Europe.[55] With the Green party holding relevant ministries for EU-Turkey relations such as the Federal Foreign Office or the Federal Ministry of Economic Affairs and Climate Action as well as chairing the European Affairs Committee in parliament, a new more values-based narrative on EU-Turkey relations might emerge and be consolidated over the legislative term of the traffic-light coalition in Germany. This would mean that headwinds for Turkey and EU-Turkey relations might even intensify.[56]

It is quite telling that the EU-accession narrative disappeared in the EU and Germany after its brief revitalisation during the so-called migration crisis that the EU was facing at the end of 2015. Russia's invasion of Ukraine in February 2022 revitalised debates on the EU's enlargement as Ukraine, the Republic of Moldova and Georgia submitted their applications for EU accession. Interestingly enough, there is no mentioning of Turkey whatsoever in such debates. However, one can find evidence in the current debate on EU-Turkey relations of the expectation that the upcoming parliamentary and presidential elections in Turkey might represent a turning point in the country's democratisation. Opposition

---

54 'Paradigm shift' constitutes a fundamental change in the dominant narratives detailing how EU-Turkish relations are perceived and described by political actors, cf. Tekin/Schönlau. The EU-German-Turkish Triangle, 2022.

55 Reuters. Turkish, German ministers argue over policies in tense news conference, 29.07.2022, https://www.reuters.com/world/turkish-german-ministers-argue-over-policies-tense-news-conference-2022-07-29/ [29.07.2022].

56 Tekin, Funda. EU-Turkey Relations and General Elections in Germany – Headwinds for Turkey?, In: Brief Series, Berlin Bosporus Initiative, April 2021.

parties signed a memorandum of understanding that they would return the country to a parliamentary system if they won the elections. Yet, in spite of the economy being in a dire state and Erdoğan losing support among his constituencies, there is no guarantee that elections will bring about a political change that might eventually also trigger a change in narratives on EU-Turkey relations in Turkey, in the EU or in Germany. Additionally, the geostrategic narrative's 'moral of the story' from both EU and German perspectives is no longer promoting Turkey's possible EU membership. On the contrary, Turkey is increasingly narrated as the *Distant Neighbour* or even *Problematic Neighbour*. The war in Ukraine has put Turkey's geopolitical and geostrategic position back in the spotlight, but this has not triggered a turning point in the storyline. In Turkey, every narrative contains the element of *Membership*, even though it is questionable whether or not membership is now in the interests of the current Turkish government. This constellation of narratives renders the scenario of '(re)energised accession process' for EU-Turkey relations obsolete in short-, mid- and also long-term perspectives.

The second scenario of a 'Unique Partnership with privileges specific for Turkey', would be suggested by narratives in the EU, Germany and Turkey that focus on Turkey as a strategic or important partner. This scenario would entail a rules-based cooperation between the EU and Turkey, in specific defined areas, with some 'opt-ins' for Turkey. It would be unique to the extent that no other country shares the same format of relations with the EU. EU-Turkey relations are already institutionally unique because they are structured within the accession track, the association agreement that established a Customs Union in 1995 as well as some looser forms of cooperation within the framework of High-Level Dialogues concerning policy areas of mutual interest such as counter terrorism, energy or transport.

The boldest attempt in narrating this uniqueness of EU-Turkey relations is the concept of "privileged partnership" dubbed by the German Christian Democratic Union in the early 2000s.[57] This advance was, though, massively rejected by Turkey that claimed that EU-Turkey relations already resembled a privileged partnership and hence there was nothing to gain for Turkey by this concept and consequently Turkish leaders insisted on the accession perspective. The United Kingdom's (UK) decision to exit from the EU raised expectations among political stakeholders that this

---

57 Cf. Weise/ Tekin. German Narratives, Strategies and Scenarios of EU-Turkey Relations 2002–2018, 2022, p. 84.

'Brexit' could not only provide a blueprint for future EU-Turkey relations but could also provoke a paradigm shift in Turkey from insisting on EU membership to accepting some sort of privileged partnership. It was assumed that because the UK represented a large and powerful country which preferred to be associated to the EU rather than being a member, forms of EU-Turkey relations that were everything but membership could gain attraction for Turkey. Sigmar Gabriel, German minister of foreign affairs at the time, and Johannes Hahn, EU Commissioner for European Neighbourhood Policy and Enlargement Negotiations in the Juncker Commission, both promoted alternative formats for EU-Turkey relations in terms of "realistic strategic partnership".[58] As the Brexit-negotiations dragged on it turned out that both expectations had been false.

Generally, the narrative foundation of this scenario of a 'Unique Partnership' will become increasingly thinner if narratives in the individual thematic dimensions of the relationship become increasingly conflictual. If Turkey acts according to the narrative of Turkey as a *Great Power* and the EU and Germany focus on narratives of Turkey as a *Strategic Partner* at best or a politically unpredictable country that is increasingly turning away from European values, more positive and less contrasting narratives in the geopolitical or economic dimensions cannot provide sufficient counterarguments to balance the relationship within the delicate state of a Unique Partnership.

What we can identify instead is a scenario of 'conflictual cooperation',[59] which means that conflictual dynamics in certain dimensions such as politics and security go hand in hand with demands and interests for cooperation in others such as the economy, trade, migration and energy. This relates to the scenario of 'stagnating and increasingly conflictual relations with a difficult neighbour' in which the EU and Turkey cooperate within certain areas on a transactional basis, accompanied by conflictual narrations in the EU, Germany and Turkey and full disappearance of

---

58 Spiegel Online. Gabriel sieht Brexit als Vorbild für Türkei-Beziehungen, 26.12.2017, https://www.spiegel.de/politik/ausland/sigmar-gabriel-will-brexit-als-vorbild-fuer-eu-tuerkei-beziehungen-a-1185065.html [27.07.2022]; Daily Sabah. Despite Turkey's previous refusals, EU commissioner suggests 'strategic partnership', 07.11.2018, https://www.dailysabah.com/eu-affairs/2018/11/07/despite-turkeys-previous-refusals-eu-commissioner-suggests-strategic-partnership [27.07.2022].

59 Tekin, Funda. The Future of EU-Turkey Relations: Exploring the Dynamics and Relevant Scenarios. In: Saatçioğlu, Beken/ Tekin, Funda (Eds.): Turkey and the European Union. Key Dynamics and Future Scenarios. Turkey and European Union Studies. Vol. 3. Baden-Baden, 2021, p. 11.

the accession narrative. Referring to what we analysed in the previous scenario, this is the most likely scenario for EU-Turkey relations when looking at the narratives. Since 2013, narratives in the EU, Turkey and Germany have increasingly been shifting towards conflict. Whereas the Turkish side still underlines cooperation interest in the economic dimension, other actors have identified Turkey increasingly as unpredictable[60] or "hostile".[61] The few attempts of refreshed institutional cooperation, as explained under the 'Unique Partnership' scenario, have not translated into long-lasting changes of narratives.

Our narrative-analysis has shown that under the current circumstances, a stagnating and increasingly conflictual relationship remains the most likely scenario for the foreseeable future. Changing tracks to a more cooperative scenario, namely the Unique Partnership, would require substantial changes in the relationship, which are likely to be displayed by sustained new narratives. These could hint at special forms of partnerships with emphasis on areas of successful cooperation, possibly in trade or energy (in fact, there are numerous challenges to successful cooperation to be solved). Furthermore, we cannot expect the discontent between actors to disappear in full, even if the share of conflictual narratives would decrease.

Ultimately, we seek to find an answer to future cooperation potential in EU-Turkey relations, based on our narrative observations. Moreover, while we stated above that the EU and Turkey "agree to disagree", this disagreement cannot be solved before the EU itself finds a new approach to Turkey and accession, which would be a precondition for producing a new narrative.

4. Which Way Forward in EU-Turkey Relations and the Role of Germany

By aggregating the different analyses presented in this volume, we observe a number of interesting findings that explain why the triangular relationship is stuck in a spiral and what needs to happen to put relations on a new track. We argue that, if the EU wishes to leave this locked-in track, part of the solution must be to look for consensus among its own ranks to build a common path and discuss the future of its relations with Turkey. Beyond

---

60 Weise/ Tekin. German Narratives, Strategies and Scenarios of EU-Turkey Relations 2002–2018, 2022, p. 107ff.

61 Özbey/ Hauge/ Eralp. Identity Representations in Narratives on EU-Turkey Relations, 2022, p. 49.

questions on the fate of Turkey's democracy (though intertwined), the demand for 'good neighbourly relations' with Greece and Cyprus are at the core of the Union's continued conflicts with Turkey and drive the latest Council narratives. In this light, it will be difficult for Germany again to take "refuge in leadership"[62] when it comes to EU-Turkey relations. Nevertheless, the German government could capitalise on its outstanding relations with Turkey and aim to steer a discussion on the future of EU-Turkey relations.

Germany's role in this triangular relationship is special in the sense that Turkey's president, as *Gedikli, Bedir and Şenyuva* worked out, often addresses Germany when the actual addressee of a matter is (or should be) the EU and its institutions. After the German election in 2021, Turkey is now confronted with a new government, Germany's foreign ministry is now run by the Green party, whose emphasis (as written by *Weise and Tekin*) is focussed on the state of rule of law in Turkey, coupled with which a very critical stance on political developments. For a moment in spring 2022, in light of the Russian attack on Ukraine, the re-evaluation of relations with Russia and sudden revival of NATO, it appeared that geostrategic considerations might override the emphasis on the rule of law in Turkey for a while: Turkey organised dialogues between Russia and Ukraine; visits from Member State and EU officials mounted, including new High Level Dialogues; and an alternative meeting format was set up by the European Commission in light of the EU-Turkey refugee deal.[63]

Though the outlook for war in Ukraine in May 2022 shifted to prospects of a long-term war and therefore might have lasting impact on the geopolitical set-up in Germany and European security structures, Germany's Foreign Minister Baerbock has underlined concerns about the state of rule of law in Turkey, in particular Turkey's handling of judgements of the European Court of Human Rights, and criticised "abstract pre-emptive strikes"[64] of Turkey in Northern Syria for not being covered

---

62 Reiners, Wulf/ Tekin, Funda. Taking Refuge in Leadership? Facilitators and Constraints of Germany's Influence in EU Migration Policy and EU-Turkey Affairs during the Refugee Crisis (2015–2016). In: *German Politics*, Vol. 29, Issue 1, 2020, pp. 115–130.

63 Cf. European Commission. Executive Vice-President Timmermans in Turkey to strengthen cooperation on climate, 20.04.2022, https://ec.europa.eu/neighbourhood-enlargement/news/executive-vice-president-timmermans-turkey-strengthen-cooperation-climate-2022-04-20_en [29.05.2022].

64 Spiegel Online. „Warum kommen Sie immer wieder mit Osman Kavala?", 30.07.2022, https://www.spiegel.de/ausland/baerbock-und-cavusoglu-streiten-a

by international law. The host, Turkey's Foreign Minister Çavuşoğlu, as a rejoinder offered praise that during former chancellor Angela Merkel's leadership, Germany had been a "sincere mediator"[65] between Turkey and Greek interests. Hence, also under the new government, the roller coaster pattern in EU-Turkey relations described in the beginning will continue, with a general gap between structure and ambition.

Based on the findings above, EU-Turkey relations are currently stuck in what we initially referred to as conflictual cooperation: Cooperation is ad-hoc, transactional and takes place outside the institutional pathways initially created for candidate countries, with currently no possibility to turn back on this structured path. Even at times of an apparent positive atmosphere and more frequent bilateral visits, the relationship is highly prone to deviations into reciprocal accusations and conflicts. Such deviations may be induced by external shocks, specific policies of one of the parties or simply building on domestic policy calculation, namely in election campaigns. This is not specific to Turkish-German or EU-Turkey relations. Relations between individual EU Member States vary in their intensity, there being blocs, close partnerships and rather distanced relationships. The difference is the institutional structure and rules-based order in which member countries would always come back to the table and seek to find ways of cooperating.

In EU-Turkey relations, there is no longer such a common fall-back position or institutional structure. Accession negotiations remain on ice. High Level Dialogues take place when it is politically pleasing but have no structured and regular cycle (at least not in practice). This is reflected in the absence of an alternative format/designation in the narratives. When looking to other international cooperation formats such as NATO, the relationship has suffered a lot. A common understanding of the importance of geostrategic cooperation and mutual dependencies has not prevented open conflicts within the alliance.

As long as the EU and Turkey agree to disagree, conflictual cooperation will continue. Narratives on all sides provide different 'morals of the story', sometimes completely different interpretations, but they confirm that cooperation on matters of common interest is necessary and indeed vital. The

---

uf-der-pressekonferenz-warum-kommen-sie-immer-wieder-mit-osman-kavala-a-219
1a2dd-8faa-4029-865c-a28b2fdf3fa2 [(30.07.2022)].

65 Tagesspiegel. Türkischer Oppositionspolitiker lobt die „direkten Aussagen" der
    Außenministerin, 30.07.2022, https://www.tagesspiegel.de/nach-streit-zwischen-ba
    erbock-und-cavusoglu-tuerkischer-oppositionspolitiker-lobt-die-direkten-aussagen
    -der-aussenministerin/28561620.html [30.07.2022].

European Parliament will not change its stance towards Turkey, but the Council will cooperate as long as possible even with a distant – or hostile – neighbour.

There are various variables that might prevent the break-up of this vicious circle of mutual accusations within the narrative dimension of EU-Turkey relations. Hence, it will also be important to focus on setting up a sustainable institutional framework for this relationship. This has to imply considering forms of external differentiation.[66] Today, it is clear that Turkey does not belong to the EU's or Germany's narration of EU enlargement. The French President Emmanuel Macron launched a debate on additional frameworks for the EU's relations with third countries – the European Political Community. There are other concepts such as Andrew Duff's affiliate membership that contribute to this debate. Inspiration can also be drawn from Nathalie Tocci's 'principled pragmatism' as a way to acknowledge different practices and realities worldwide while making international law and its underlying norms "the benchmark of what is acceptable in a relationship and what is not".[67] Regardless of whether and how such concepts might be framed institutionally their narration will be just as important. As long as states that have been promised accession at some point perceive such concepts as alternative to the EU's enlargement instead of a stepping stone on the way into the EU, this debate will increase frustration among those states. Such fear of being stuck in the outer circle of the EU's concentric circles already caused the concept of the European Confederation promoted by Francois Mitterrand in the 1990s to disappear from debate rather quickly. The fear of a second-class membership will undermine any new concept of external differentiation if the EU cannot dilute the fear of being kept at its doorstep. Hence, any attractive concept of differentiated integration requires a thorough debate of how differentiated integration can bring the EU as a whole – including today's non-members – forward. EU-Turkey relations are currently absent from this debate. Our analysis concludes that conflictual cooperation will continue. Arriving at a different, perhaps Unique Partnership, will require different narratives.

---

66 Tekin, Funda. Differentiated Integration: An Alternative Conceptualization of EU–Turkey Relations. In: Wulf Reiners, Ebru Turhan (Eds.). EU-Turkey Relations. Theories, Institutions, and Policies, 2021, Cham, pp. 157–181.

67 Kaldor, Mary. Principled pragmatism: defending normative Europe. 12.12.2019, https://www.opendemocracy.net/en/can-europe-make-it/principled-pragmatism-defending-normative-europe/ [25.07.2022].

Acknowledgement

blickwechsel
Contemporary Turkey Studies Türkei
A Programme by Stiftung Mercator

The research project „TRIANGLE – Blickwechsel in EU/German-Turkish Relations Beyond Conflicts – Towards a Unique Partnership for a Contemporary Turkey?" was a cooperation between the Centre for Turkey and EU Studies (CETEUS) at University of Cologne and the Middle East Technical University (METU) in Ankara. The aim was to scrutinize the EU/German-Turkish relations. By adopting a distinct academic approach, the relations' institutional architecture as well as the dominant narratives were assessed. The aim of this comprehensive analysis was to identify possible turning points – a "Blickwechsel" – that might sustainably change the EU/German-Turkish relationship.

Between 01.01.2017 and 31.12.2020 the project was funded by the Blickwechsel Programme of the Stiftung Mercator. This programme explored different aspects of current Turkish society, economy, and politics. In five scientific projects researchers at German universities worked together with their Turkish cooperation partners.

"Blickwechsel" is a term that cannot be directly translated and which contains a double meaning: it stands both for eye-contact and for a change in perspective. The programme wanted to contribute to a dialogue across national borders, disciplines and the spheres of academic and non-academic public.

The exchange of knowledge and insights created a new perspective on Turkey and, at the same time, on Germany; it is only through the interplay of both perspectives that a comprehensive picture can be realised.

Within the programme, Stiftung Mercator funded the academic examination of Turkey in Germany and, simultaneously, interconnectedness of both countries in the areas of research and teaching.

Notes on Contributors

Esra Çengel is a Ph.D. candidate and a research assistant at the Department of International Relations at the Middle East Technical University (METU) and holds a master's degree from the METU Department of European Studies.

Atila Eralp is a Mercator-IPC Senior Fellow at the Istanbul Policy Center, Sabancı University and Emeritus Professor of International Relations at the Middle East Technical University (METU), Ankara.

Denise Ersoy is Project Manager for the Bergedorf Round Table at the department for International Affairs at Körber-Stiftung and former research assistant at the Centre for Turkey and European Union Studies (CETEUS) at the University of Cologne.

Ardahan Özkan Gedikli is a Doctoral Researcher at the German Institute for Global and Area Studies (GIGA) and previously held research assistant positions at both Koç University and Middle East Technical University.

Hanna-Lisa Hauge is an External Research Fellow at the Centre for Turkey and European Union Studies (CETEUS) at the University of Cologne.

Ebru Ece Özbey is a doctoral researcher at the International Max Planck Research School on the Social and Political Constitution of the Economy (IMPRS-SPCE).

Moritz Rau is a Researcher at the German Institute for International and Security Affairs and former research assistant at the Centre for Turkey and European Union Studies (CETEUS) at the University of Cologne.

Anke Schönlau is an External Research Fellow at the Centre for Turkey and European Union Studies (CETEUS) at the University of Cologne.

Mirja Schröder is a Senior Research Fellow at the Centre for Turkey and European Union Studies (CETEUS) at the University of Cologne.

Nurdan Selay Bedir is a Research Assistant and PhD candidate at the Department of Political Sciences and Public Administration at Middle East Technical University (METU).

Özgehan Şenyuva is an Associate Professor at the Department of International Relations at the Middle East Technical University.

Funda Tekin is Director of the Institut für Europäische Politik (IEP) in Berlin and a Senior Research Fellow at the Centre for Turkey and European Union Studies (CETEUS) at the University of Cologne, Germany.

Helena Weise is a freelance journalist and former research assistant at the Centre for Turkey and European Union Studies (CETEUS) at the University of Cologne.

Wolfgang Wessels is Jean Monnet Professor ad personam and Director of the Centre for Turkey and European Union Studies (CETEUS) at the University of Cologne, Germany.

Series Editors

Funda Tekin is Director of the Institut für Europäische Politik (IEP) in Berlin and a Senior Research Fellow at the Centre for Turkey and European Union Studies (CETEUS) at the University of Cologne, Germany.

Ebru Turhan is Associate Professor at the Department of Political Science and International Relations at the Turkish-German-University in Istanbul, Turkey and Senior Research Fellow at the Institut für Europäische Politik in Berlin, Germany.

Wolfgang Wessels is Jean Monnet Professor ad personam and Director of the Centre for Turkey and European Union Studies (CETEUS) at the University of Cologne, Germany.

The Centre for Turkey and European Union Studies (CETEUS) was founded in 2016 at the University of Cologne. With its focus on research and teaching in EU and Turkey related affairs and on the institutional evolution of the EU, it continues the work of the Jean Monnet Chair for European Politics of Prof. Dr. Wolfgang Wessels.

CETEUS' research activities target the European integration process as well as EU-Turkey relations and links to contemporary Turkey studies. They are embedded in an EU-wide network and founded on close relations to leading universities in the EU, Turkey and the neighbourhood. Within its research projects the centre engages in promoting academic exchange with young researchers from Germany, the EU and Turkey aiming at integrating them into the European Research Area. CETEUS is also a founding member of the EU-Turkey Bridge – A Standing Group on EU-Turkey Relations chaired by Funda Tekin (IEP) and Senem Aydin-Düzgit (Istanbul Policy Center, Sabanci University).

www.ceteus.uni-koeln.de

Annex

Coding Scheme Example of Chapter 3: Anke Schönlau & Mirja Schröder: A Charged Friendship: German Narratives of EU-Turkey Relations in the Pre-accession Phase, 1959-1999, pp. 57-77. The list of codes and subcodes is not exhaustive.

Thematic Dimension	Code	Subcode
Political: Debates concerning material and non-material political institutions, as well as historical conflicts that are 'institutionalised' in the political system.	Internationale Zusammenarbeit	EPZ
	Flucht	Menschenwürde; Zuflucht; Schutz
	Rechtsextremismus	Demokratische Ordnung; Brandanschlag
Economic: Debates concerning economic cooperation as in bilateral and international trade, development finance and financial institutions.	Assoziation	Assoziierungsabkommen; Zollunion
	Wirtschaftshilfe	Hilfsaktion; Wirtschaftliche Entwicklung
Geopolitical: Debates concerning military involvement and strategy, as well as non-state-actor armed involvement.	Ost-West-Konflikt	NATO; Ostflanke; weltpolitisch
	Golfkrise	Embargo; Krisenherd
	Griechisch-türkischer Konflikt	Militärische Hilfe; Verteidigungshilfe; Stabilisierung
Societal/Identity: Debates concerning identity-fueling elements other than nationality, such as religion, values, sensed belonging.	Brücke	Brücke
	Gäste	Gastfreundschaft; Gastrecht
	Kultur	kulturelle Identität

Coding Scheme Example of Chapter 4: Helena Weise & Funda Tekin: German Narratives, Strategies and Scenarios of EU-Turkey Relations 2002–2018: Towards a Unique Partnership – Yet to be defined, pp. 79-109. The list of codes and subcodes is not exhaustive.

Thematic Dimension	Code	Subcode
Political: Debates concerning material and non-material political institutions, as well as historical conflicts that are 'institutionalised' in the political system.	Demokratie/Rechtsstaat/Menschen- und Minderheitenrechte	Pressefreiheit; Wissenschaft;
	EU-Mitgliedschaft	Kopenhagen-Kriterien; EU-Türkei Gipfel; Ankara Abkommen
	Flucht und Asyl	Flüchtlingsabkommen
Economic: Debates concerning economic cooperation as in bilateral and international trade, development finance and financial institutions.	Wirtschafts-/Entwicklungshilfen/ humanitäre Hilfen	Entwicklungshilfe; Entwicklungszusammenarbeit; Humanitäre Hilfe;
	Tourismus	
	Zollunion	
Geopolitical: Debates concerning military involvement and strategy, as well as non-state-actor armed involvement.	Sicherheit	NATO, Berlin-Plus-Abkommen
	Syrien	Afrin; Idlib; Islamischer Staat
	Ressourcen & Energie	Energiesicherheit
Societal/Identity: Debates concerning identity-fueling elements other than nationality, such as religion, values, sensed belonging.	Wertegemeinschaft	Europäische Werte
	Religion	Islam, christlich
	Identität	Özil/Gündogan

Coding Scheme Example of Chapter 5: Nurdan Selay Bedir, Ardahan Özkan Gedikli & Özgehan Senyuva: So Close Yet So Far: Turkey's Relations with Germany in Recep Tayyip Erdoğan's Narratives (2003–2018), pp. 111-139. The list of codes and subcodes is not exhaustive.

Thematic Dimension	Code	Subcode
Political: Speeches concerning political developments, processes, and institutions, as well as periodical crises and/or convergences	Darbe girişimi	OHAL; 15 Temmuz; Şehit/Gazi
	AB süreci	Tam üyelik; İmtiyazlı ortaklık; Gümrük birliği
	Demokrasi/Hukuk devleti/Azınlık hakları	Basın özgürlüğü; Gazete/eleştiri; Alman/Batı medyası
Economic: Speeches concerning economic cooperation in form of bilateral and international trade, as well as financial aid and institutions	Yatırım	Alman şirketleri; Uluslararası firmalar
	Finans sistemi	Küresel kriz; Borsa
	Ekonomik Yardım	Kalkınma Yardımı; İnsani Yardım/Mülteci yardımları
Geopolitical: Speeches concerning military involvement and security strategy and institutions, as well as civil conflicts	Terör	IŞİD, DAEŞ, PYD/YPG/YPJ/PKK, FETÖ
	Birleşmiş Milletler	Daimi üye
	Doğal kaynaklar	Enerji; Nükleer santral
Societal/Identity: Speeches concerning societal and identity-related elements such as religion, values, sensed belonging	Din (Islam)	İnanç hürriyeti; Başörtüsü
	Almanya'daki Türkler	Entegrasyon/Asimilasyon; Deniz Feneri
	Ortak değerler/Batı değerleri	Sevgi, barış ve kardeşlik; İslam medeniyeti
Cross-cutting: Speeches cutting across different thematic dimensions and including comparisons within the contexts of education, health, governmental issues, press, transportation	Sağlık	
	Eğitim	
	Bilişim/Teknoloji	

Index